THE TERRORIST

Also available from Brassey's

BITTMAN
The New Image-Makers
Soviet Propaganda & Disinformation Today

COLLINS
Green Berets, SEALS and Spetsnaz

GODSON
Comparing Foreign Intelligence

LAFFIN
War Annual 2

LEVENTHAL & ALEXANDER
Nuclear Terrorism
Defining the Threat

Defense Analysis
An International Journal

THE TERRORIST

Maxwell Taylor

BRASSEY'S DEFENCE PUBLISHERS
(a member of the Maxwell Pergamon
Publishing Corporation plc)

LONDON · OXFORD · WASHINGTON · NEW YORK
BEIJING · FRANKFURT · SÃO PAULO · SYDNEY · TOKYO · TORONTO

U.K. (Editorial)	Brassey's Defence Publishers Ltd., 24 Gray's Inn Road, London WC1X 8HR
(Orders)	Brassey's Defence Publishers Ltd., Headington Hill Hall, Oxford OX3 0BW, England
U.S.A. (Editorial)	Pergamon-Brassey's International Defense Publishers, 8000 Westpark Drive, Fourth Floor, McLean, Virginia 22102, U.S.A.
(Orders)	Pergamon Press, Inc., Maxwell House, Fairview Park, Elmsford, New York 10523, U.S.A.
PEOPLE'S REPUBLIC OF CHINA	Pergamon Press, Room 4037, Qianmen Hotel, Beijing, People's Republic of China
FEDERAL REPUBLIC OF GERMANY	Pergamon Press GmbH, Hammerweg 6, D-6242 Kronberg, Federal Republic of Germany
BRAZIL	Pergamon Editora Ltda, Rua Eça de Queiros, 346, CEP 04011, Paraiso, São Paulo, Brazil
AUSTRALIA	Pergamon-Brassey's Defence Publishers Pty Ltd., P.O. Box 544, Potts Point; N.S.W. 2011, Australia
JAPAN	Pergamon Press, 5th Floor, Matsuoka Central Building, 1-7-1 Nishishinjuku, Shinjuku-ku, Tokyo 160, Japan
CANADA	Pergamon Press Canada Ltd., Suite No. 271, 253 College Street, Toronto, Ontario, Canada M5T 1R5

First edition 1988

Library of Congress Cataloging in Publication Data
Taylor, Maxwell, 1945-
The terrorist / Maxwell Taylor.
p.   cm.
1. Terrorists—Psychology. 2. Terrorists. I. Title.
HV6431.T42 1988   87-34154

British Library Cataloguing in Pubblication Data
Taylor, Maxwell
The terrorist.
1. Terrorism
I. Title
322.4'2   HV6431

ISBN 0 08 033603 5

Printed in Great Britain by A. Wheaton & Co. Ltd., Exeter

About the Author

Professor Maxwell Taylor has held the Chair of Applied Psychology at University College, Cork, since 1983.

Born in 1945, he holds a First Class Honours Degree in Psychology and was awarded his Ph.D. by the University of Liverpool in 1971.

He has held academic posts at the University of Liverpool, University College of North Wales, Concordia University, Montreal, and Ulster Polytechnic, where he was Director of Studies and Head of the School of Psychology from 1977 to 1983.

His many previous publications include a wide range of contributions on the application of psychology to the work of the police and security services with particular reference to terrorism — a subject which he has also studied in several European countries.

Acknowledgements

This book owes a great deal to the experience, time and effort of many people. Whilst it may be invidious to single out individuals, I must acknowledge the debt I owe to Bill Wilson, whose friendship and advice has been an invaluable support in the writing of this book, as in other ventures. Acknowledgement to authors for the use of scholarly material is included in the text and footnotes. My thanks are due to Helen Ryan who critically read earlier drafts.

Permission by the University of Wisconsin Press. Madison, Wisconsin, to reproduce the Organisation Table of ETA (militar) Directorate (Fig. 6.1) is gratefully acknowledged. Some of the material presented in this book was made possible by Contract Number DAJA45-84-M-0400 from the U.S. Army Research Institute for the Behavioral and Social Sciences through its European Coordination Office in London, England. The opinions expressed are those of the author and do not necessarily represent those of the U.S. Army.

Whilst not always helped by her presence, I am nevertheless grateful for Alice's contribution; I am very grateful for Ethel's.

Contents

9. Terrorist Behaviour

CHAPTER 1

Introduction

An explosion too loud for your eardrums to bear,
and young children squealing like pigs in the square,
and all faces chalk-white and streaked with bright
red,
and the glass and the dust and the terrible dead.

For an old lady's legs are ripped off, and the head
of a man's hanging open, and still he's not dead.
He is screaming for mercy, and his son stands and
stares
and stares, and then suddenly, quick, disappears.

And Christ, little Katherine Aiken is dead,
and Mrs McLaughlin is pierced through the head.
Meanwhile to Dungiven the killers have gone,
and they're finding it hard to get through on the
phone.

(From *Claudy*, by James Simmons[1])

The reality of terrorism is difficult for most people to imagine. We are used to seeing the bomb blasted ruins in Beirut or Northern Ireland. We hear of the numbers killed or injured, but we ourselves, or our families, are rarely the victims. We can take a voyeur's interest in the events, but very, very rarely are we more than distant spectators.

James Simmons is a Northern Irish poet who has lived through 'the Troubles' in Northern Ireland. The above extract from his poem approaches more closely than any flat news comment the reality of a terrorist bombing. It helps us to form the impression of a terrorist bombing attack in a way that pictures or abstract accounts can never convey. The setting for this poem is a small village in Northern Ireland, but the events described could have happened almost anywhere in the world. The attack is long forgotten, a minor incident amongst an array of similar incidents that have stretched across the past decade and a half of the history of Northern Ireland. While the horror of Claudy has been duplicated in most countries of the world at some time, unless a large number of people are

1

killed, it is a routine news story, forgotten and unremarked a day or two later. When we do remember, it is often in terms of the trial of a suspected terrorist. Rarely, if ever, do we remember the victim, the severely and permanently injured bystander, or the families drawn into tragedy by accidental presence. The poem also has another message for us about the terrorist acts. It captures the essential cynicism of the terrorist's attempt to avoid responsibility for death by issuing a warning, in this case not given, which serves for their part to excuse and absolve them from that burden — an act of double-thinking as frightening as the deed itself.

Bombings, shootings, kidnappings have almost become a way of life, a necessary feature of political protest in the latter part of the twentieth century. Paradoxically, through the extensive media resources available in modern society, we know more about the incidence of these events than has ever before been possible. Yet their emotional effects on us are probably less than they have ever been. Perhaps the only way to express the horror is through poetry, for pictures have become a debased currency. Disaffected groups of the right or left, nationalist groups, or the simply dissatisfied seem to have immediate recourse to violence as statements of their discontent, without particular concern as to the death or injury of innocents who happen to be present at the time of an explosion — incidental victims of some broader aspiration.

Every day we read in our newspapers and hear on television details of the latest terrorist outrage. The names of small places in Northern Ireland for example, like Crossmaglen and Andersonstown, are familiar to us not because of the qualities of the places themselves, but through accounts of death or destruction. The locations are often insignificant, in geographical, commercial or social terms; their significance for the world at large lies in their association with some violent terrorist incident or other. It would be difficult to underestimate the role of such incidents on our perception of the world, yet they are, in fact, relatively infrequent. Whilst we hear with temporary horror of the needless death of innocent victims, we know little about either the events or the nature of the people who commit these acts.

What is Terrorism?

There can be no doubt that terrorism is one of the most worrying features of contemporary life. There can be few regular air travellers who have not had occasion to worry about their own involvement in a hijacking. Yet recognition of its attributes presents major difficulties. As a term, terrorism seems to have a promiscuous use, characterised by a multitude of hypo-critical, hidden or implicit meanings. Very often, it is used as a term of abuse, or a term to distance the observer from the act — *other people* commit acts of terrorism, *our side* fights legitimately. The United States Ambassador to the United Nations in 1972, Charles Yost, expressed this quite bluntly:

'The fact is, of course, that there is a vast amount of hypocrisy on the subject of political terrorism. We all righteously condemn it—except where we ourselves or friends of ours are engaging in it. Then we ignore it, or gloss over it, or attach to it tags like "liberation" or "defence of the free world" or "national honour" to make it seem like something other than what it is'.[2]

In this book, the term terrorism is used from the perspective of a violent act aimed at influencing the political process, and the terrorist is the individual who commits that act. Whether the terrorist is inspired by ideological or religious motives, or some combination of both, or indeed whether he is driven by intense nationalistic fervor, his political aim is to change society through undermining authority, and ultimately inducing its overthrow. To achieve this, he will seek to both challenge the existing forces of law and public order, and demonstrate their fallibility. In doing this, his strategy may well be to try to create situations where the government, through its security services or legal system, will over-react and introduce repressive measures. This may well lead to what will be described in later chapters as the development of one form of 'State Terrorism', creating a spiral of high levels of tension, mistrust and unrest within society.

A typical example of the expression of such a spiral occurred in Northern Ireland when internment without trial was introduced, and subsequently abandoned. When public and international pressure forced the British Government to withdraw internment, it was replaced by the juryless 'Diplock' courts, a form of court procedure made necessary by the extensive intimidation of witnesses and jurors. As we will note later, the 'Diplock' courts are themselves seen as symbols of repression, and serve as a focus for further accusations of repression.

Whatever issue a particular terrorist campaign might be built around, a quality of terrorist action is that attainment of its ultimate end is frequently used as justification for the means employed to attain that end, however barbaric those means might prove to be. In trying to understand terrorist behaviour, we often have recourse to concepts like mental illness, or fanaticism, to help explain the terrorist's often barbaric or excessive actions. We will see in later chapters that terrorism and the terrorist may well be an inherent feature of society, and whilst some members of a terrorist group may well indeed be labelled as of unsound mind, this is by no means the general rule.

The approach taken will allow us to consider a multitude of situations without necessarily making judgements about the legitimacy or otherwise of the acts in question. Focusing on terrorist behaviour has the virtue of identifying a particular kind of act, a violent act, and using that as the principle feature for identification. It follows from this view that States for example can commit terrorist acts just as readily as a small secret society. By referring to a violent act, it includes not only the death of victims, but physical injury to them, *and* damage to property. The expression of violence in whatever form, as a means of influencing political decision making is the important attribute on which we must focus.

Such a perspective does not command universal support, however. To focus on the act, the very behaviour of terrorism, seems to ignore the context in which the behaviour occurs. Many would argue, in contrast, that it is the context of terrorism that is all important, for it allows us to identify the legitimacy of the political dimension of the act. For many, this is an equal or more important emphasis. In reviewing the way that we use the term, it is quite clear that the issue of the *legitimacy* of violence lies at the heart of the debate about the identification of terrorism, and it is claims to this attribute which complicate our analysis. Terrorism in the way in which we will examine it does not occur in isolation, and the political aspiration of terrorism allows us to distinguish it from, for example, violent crime; but to focus on the context of terrorism, and thereby the issue of legitimacy, reduces the precision allowed for by the use of violence as an essential attribute.

The approach taken here takes the uncompromising stand that legitimacy in the use of violence of the form we identify as terrorism cannot be conferred by the qualities of the political aspiration. This view will undoubtedly be rejected by the terrorist, and also by their politically committed supporters. Discussion of political legitimacy often obscures the moral issues of terrorism. They also, more pragmatically, obscure the descriptive analysis we need to undertake if we are to understand the psychology of the terrorist. Indeed, it can be argued that legitimacy is of little concern to a psychological or behavioural analysis. Whilst its discussion might be at the heart of the political or sociological debate about terrorism, claims to legitimacy are just one attribute, and perhaps a rather unimportant one at that, in psychological analyses.

When we look at actual acts of terrorism, we encounter further complexity. The events which we include as terrorist acts are very varied—they include incidents such as bombings, shootings and kidnappings. Sometimes, the violence of these acts is expressed at either a temporal or physical distance, where the terrorist has no particular contact with the victim. A bombing, for example, is usually carried out by planting a bomb which will explode at a later date, controlled either by a timer, or detonated by the terrorist at a distance by a command wire, or radio signal. An example of this kind of terrorist act occurred just before Christmas, 1986, in Northern Ireland. The Provisional IRA[3] placed and detonated an 800 pound bomb in a school bus outside a Police Station on Lisburn Road in Belfast. The bus was placed there just after midnight, and in a period of fifteen minutes, members of the security forces were able to evacuate the homes either side of the Station such that when the bomb exploded, although some 800 homes and shops were damaged, no one was seriously injured. In such explosions there is enormous potential for personal injury, as opposed to property damage. That so little personal injury was sustained is a tribute to the effectiveness of the security forces in evacuating the area, a fact presumably well known to the terrorists. Indeed, it would be reasonable to suppose that the efficiency of the security forces was itself a factor in the choice of this kind of target.

This was unquestionably a violent act, presumably aimed at causing as much property damage and disruption as possible at a sensitive time of the year. The bomb was detonated by a timing device, and the terrorists would be well away from the area when the bomb exploded. In a sense, this is terrorism at a distance; it is also terrorism with relatively little risk to the participants. This example contrasts, however, with some other forms of terrorism, such as kidnapping. An interesting example of this occurred in February, 1975, in West Germany. The terrorist group, The 2nd June Movement, abducted the Berlin Mayoral candidate, Peter Lorenz. He was abducted in an attempt to secure the release of six jailed terrorists and the suspension of sentences against demonstrators arrested after the death of Holger Meins, a German terrorist who died in prison. Lorenz was eventually released after the West German Government had allowed a humiliating series of broadcasts by the terrorists on German television, as well as their escape to South Yemen, as part of the deal negotiated with them for Lorenz's release. Lorenz's kidnapping resulted in governmental humiliation; while he himself remained relatively unscathed.

As an act of terrorism, this clearly addressed the political system, although the ultimate damage caused was to national pride rather than physical injury. Although it had the potential for violence, the focus of the violence was constrained (to Lorenz). It also had a clearly identifiable objective, which in this case was achieved. As a kidnapping, the above illustrates a successful outcome for the terrorists. It was from the terrorists' perspective a relatively high risk activity, and as such contrasts markedly with the earlier example. These two examples illustrate the difficulty of identifying terrorist acts. Both these incidents we would refer to as examples of terrorism, and they illustrate the range of activities which are embraced within the term.

These two examples also illustrate other aspects of terrorist behaviour. One had a highly focused outcome, the release of prisoners; the other had a much more general outcome, an increase in tension and creation of social disruption. They both belong, however, within a consistent strategy designed in some way to influence the political process, directly in the case of the German terrorists, indirectly in the case of the Irish terrorists. The political aspirations of both are expressed in some form of plan of campaign which gives meaning and direction to the terrorist acts. Thus, whilst to the observer, terrorism may appear to be little more than random violence, to the terrorist his actions are part of a strategy for political change.

As a means of exercising coercive pressure on governments and the political process, and as a way of propagating an idea or a cause, there can be no doubt that terrorism is very cheap and effective. In commercial terms, it might even be said to be highly cost effective! For the relatively small expense of a few chemicals, a bomb can be constructed which, on explosion in a crowded street, will generate publicity that if paid for as advertising would cost many millions of pounds. The hijacking of an aircraft can be guaranteed to allow media time for the presentation of the particular case by the spokesman of the group responsible for the hijack. Claims for responsibility of some brutal act by the Provisional IRA, for example, are invariably associated with comments demonstrating their particular views on the situation in Northern Ireland.

Even when terrorism is extended over long periods of time, the relative costs for the terrorists of sustaining their campaign are insignificant when compared to the cost to the authorities in responding to their actions. The cost of killing a single Malayan terrorist in the emergency in Malaya during the early 1950s was of the order of $200,000. During the Algerian War of Independence, the total cost of the Algerian FLN was of the order of $30 to $40 million per year; the French in attempting to counter this insurrection probably spent that amount within two weeks! Terrorism, and unofficial guerilla warfare, offers the opportunity to initiate combat with relatively little expense. It is hardly surprising, therefore, that as a means of attempting to produce political change, terrorism can seem very attractive to the minority group unable to attain political power through representative processes.

Who undertakes Terrorism?

If we are consistent in the use of our view of terrorism, we would have to say that both State and non-State organisations can be involved. The implications of this are that, in a sense, most countries in the world have the potential for undertaking terrorism whenever they become involved in violent acts aimed at influencing the political process (in suppressing a demonstration, for example). We do not usually think in these terms, of course, and we prefer to reserve the term terrorism for those States of which we disapprove. Leaving aside the involvement of States in terrorism (a point returned to later), we normally associate terrorism in some sense with illegal organisations. The political aspirations of terrorism emphasise organisational qualities, making the lone individual bomber, for example, difficult to classify as a terrorist. Terrorism outside of the State context is invariably, therefore, a group phenomenon.

It is often said that whilst terrorism is not a new phenomenon, the scale of contemporary terrorist violence is both qualitatively and quantitatively greater now than ever before. There is some truth in this view. Certainly, the kinds of violent acts which characterise contemporary terrorism differ from those of the nineteenth and early twentieth century. Before the First World War, a typical violent political act, which today we would probably term an act of terrorism, involved attempts on the lives of political leaders. Czar Alexander II was murdered in 1881, the Empress Elizabeth of Austria in 1891, Archduke Franz Ferdinand in 1914, etc.; the list is long and covers many countries. In contrast, contemporary terrorism rarely focuses on the political leadership directly, but finds expression against ordinary citizens of a country. This can be thought of as a transition from personal to impersonal terrorism[4] which cannot be wholly explained by better protection of Presidents, Prime Ministers, etc. The increase in the reported incidence of this form of terrorism since the First World War is, however, one of its most striking contemporary characteristics. Precise figures on the incidence of terrorist acts are largely meaningless, given the uncertainty over attributes; but it can be confidently asserted that there has been a many fold increase in the scale of terrorist activity.

Almost all countries in the world have, at some time or another in the recent past, shown evidence of some form of terrorist group. A recent listing of terrorist organisations by country[5] identifies 127 countries as having at least one terrorist group within them. These range from Afghanistan to Zimbabwe, and include all of the major industrial nations of the world. Within those countries, in excess of 1000 individual organisations have at some time since 1980 claimed responsibility for some act of terrorism — an astonishingly high number.

However, we should exercise some caution here. Many organisations which claim responsibility for a terrorist act are themselves a part of a larger group. A parent group may from time to time wish to distance itself from a particularly unsavoury act, or the demands of the moment might require it not to overtly become involved in violence. A *'nom de guerre'* may then be used to claim responsibility. Within Northern Ireland, one of the main protestant paramilitary groupings is the Ulster Defence Association (UDA)[6]. It is a legal organisation, and rarely if ever takes responsibility for any act of terrorist violence. The Ulster Volunteer Force (UVF) and the Ulster Freedom Fighters (UFF) are more likely to claim responsibility for protestant terrorist acts; yet the membership of both the UVF and the UFF may well be the same, and both are in loose association with the UDA.

Another example of the use of multiple names by a terrorist organisation can be seen in the Palestinian Abu Nidal group which has been responsible for a number of serious terrorist attacks against Israeli, Western and other Arab States. They appear to have operated under some ten different names, including the Palestinian National Liberation Movement (PNLM), Black September, The Revolutionary Organisation of Socialist Moslems, Al-Asifa (The Storm), Al-Iqab (The Punishment), etc. To confuse the matter further, some of the names used by the Abu Nidal group have also had earlier usage by other Palestinian organisations (Al-Asifa for example was also used by Fatah, a relatively early Palestinian Organisation). It is of course a part of the very nature of these organisations that it is difficult to gain information about them; their links between themselves and others are shrouded in secrecy.

A qualitative distinction must also be made when considering the kinds of organisations which claim responsibility for terrorist acts. We have already noted that terrorism is on the whole a relatively cheap endeavour. It does not require enormous resources to make a bomb, for example (although it may, if that bomb is in anyway sophisticated). Thus, small transient groups of disaffected people can easily become involved in terrorist violence. Such groups may not last long, nor will they necessarily achieve much. In contrast, some groups have existed for relatively long periods, and have become well established features of the political landscape. The Basque separatist group ETA[7] (*Euzkadi ta Askatasuna*) has been in existence since 1959 when it was founded by a group of young activists who saw terrorism as a way of advancing the cause of Basque Nationalism in Spain. Since that time, it has become a dominant regional force within the Basque country.

The policies and strategies of all terrorist groups from time to time receive internal challenges. On occasions, these challenges result in the development of splinter groups, maintaining the overall aims of the parent group, but perhaps seeking an escalation in violence or, alternatively, a movement towards political legitimacy. Sometimes, even well-established groups occasionally lack cohesion and present us with problems of identifying their aspirations when they fragment. ETA has been subject to divisions of this kind. ETA(M) *Euzkadi ta Askatasuna (Militar)*, split from the parent group in 1974, seeking an escalation of the military conflict with Spain. At the same time ETA(P-M)*Euzkadi ta Askatasuna (Politico-Militar)* was also founded, which sought a de-escalation of the military conflict and a shift in emphasis to overt political action. Very similar splits have occurred from time to time in the Republican movement in Northern Ireland. Reference to large numbers of different terrorist organisations must, therefore, be viewed with some scepticism, for they can hide very complicated commonalities and deceptions.

There are clearly a number of standpoints that can be adopted to make sense of terrorism. Focusing on the organisational aspects of terrorism is clearly important, but we should not lose sight of the fact that the terrorist group is made up of individuals. A focus on the group, and its interrelationship with the political process, is a necessary position from which to view the problem. We can however also ask meaningful questions at a more personal level. When faced with the horror of a terrorist bombing attack, for example, our immediate response is probably not to consider the overall strategy of the terrorists' aspirations, but to ask questions about the kind of individual who undertakes these acts. Issues of this kind are discussed at greater length in later chapters and, to a large extent, provide the focus for this book.

One of the strangest features in the study of terrorism is the extent to which we know relatively little about the terrorist. In part, this is because terrorists are few. Although a terrorist attack may gain great publicity, the number of people engaged at any one time in even a major terrorist group is relatively small. Furthermore, necessarily, their actions are shrouded in secrecy. We can only gain information about them when they have been caught or have given up terrorism. To study the active terrorist might be an attractive proposition for the researcher, but such an activity would give rise to such profound moral and legal issues, that it effectively excludes the possibility.

Nevertheless, we do have views about the nature of the terrorist. These views may well be more related to our prejudices rather than reality, but there are discernible consistencies in assumptions that we make. We often, for example, refer to the terrorist as someone who is mentally ill; alternatively, we sometimes refer to him as a fanatic. Indeed, these views are not necessarily mutually exclusive, and we can regard him as both these things. Chapters 3 and 4 discuss these issues in greater detail, and examine what we mean by these terms, and what bearing they might have on our understanding of terrorism.

The active terrorists who plant bombs, or ambush policemen, are certainly few in number. We need to note, however, that there are different kinds of terrorist group membership, and not all those involved in terrorism plant bombs. Similarly, we need to remember that there are different kinds of terrorist organisations, some of which may claim a relatively large *non-operational* membership. Indeed, even the smallest ideological group probably works within some kind of supportive social context. This context of membership may not itself plant bombs, but might offer information, a safe house, or help of other kinds. Nationalist groups, such as the Basque group ETA, or the Provisional Irish Republican Army particularly fall into this position. In such circumstances, who is the terrorist? The operational unit which ambushes an off-duty policeman? The activist who raises funds? In different ways, we will encounter ambiguities of this kind throughout our discussion of terrorism. Our attention here is primarily on the active terrorist, the individual who plants the bomb, or shoots the gun; but we should not forget the importance of the facilitating context through which he or she moves.

The Study of Terrorism

Terrorism is not something which occurs outside of a political context. The terrorist act is designed in some sense to create, or contribute to, a political outcome. As such, therefore, the act belongs in a complex system. The drama of terrorism can, however, help to obscure the reality of the process and aspirations of the terrorist movement. The rhetoric of terrorism often makes reference to humanitarian values and appeals to the reformist aspirations of the young and committed. By identifying and seeking to redress grievances, which from any objective position may often be well justified, the rhetoric of terrorism can be difficult to fault. But the relationship of terrorist theory to terrorist practice often leaves much to be desired. The liberal and revolutionary rhetoric of the Provisional IRA, for example, overlays a sectarianism and xenophobia in practice scarcely less terrifying than the acts they commit.

It is difficult to approach the study of terrorism as political violence from an objective standpoint. Terrorism has the capacity to polarise views. Within the academic community, for example, there has been a tendency towards what might be termed 'liberal' preoccupations with a romantic image of the terrorist as the freedom fighter, the lonely outpost of virtue in an otherwise illiberal and unfair world. The rhetoric and theory of terrorism, with its emphasis on the underdog and the redressing of social wrongs through necessary social action has an ambivalent appeal to the educated liberal westerner. The terrorist can easily become a Robin Hood figure, where political purity and a concern with post-colonial guilt can perhaps obscure the essential barbarity of the kinds of indiscriminate killing he or she perpetrates. In contrast, a preoccupation with the horror of terrorism can lead us to dismiss the terrorist as a madman, a bizarre and dangerous antisocial element which needs to be eliminated, rather than understood. Neither of these views facilitate rational understanding.

In thinking about terrorism, we must be careful not to fall into such traps which await the unwary. The liberal assumption of virtue in the terrorist must be resisted at all costs, for whatever cause the terrorist espouses, he merits the term by killing and injuring people, often in a cruel and incidental way. The routine apology offered by the Provisional IRA for the killing of the 'wrong' person, for example, can in no way condone the outrage of a murder. On the other hand, we must equally resist the temptation to be so absorbed in the horror and challenge of terrorism that we forget or ignore the circumstances that gave rise to it, and sustain it. The routine announcement of another Middle Eastern incident can obscure from public view the degradation experienced by many Palestinians living in inadequate refugee camps. In a sense, the reason for such conditions are of little importance when faced with their reality and existence. The rights or wrongs of the political assertions about Palestine then become rather irrelevant. Perhaps not all terrorism has its origins in social injustice, but certainly where it does, the existence of terrorists should not prevent us from addressing those social problems. In a paradoxical way, terrorism can actually enhance the social evils which give rise to it, by deflecting attention away from those evils on to the drama of the terrorist acts themselves. When this happens, the social group which the terrorist seeks to defend can be as much the victim of terrorism as the innocent bystander caught in the bomb blast.

Another trap which we must also be careful not to fall into is that of excessive secrecy which can so often be the response of Government and the Security Services to the problems of terrorism. Public debate about the problem, and public awareness of it is a necessary feature of the response of any democracy to terrorism. The role of the Police or Army expert may well be important in the operational management of a terrorist incident, but enormous dangers await an over concentration and seclusion of decision making, especially at a policy level. Terrorism affects members of the general public; it often seems to strike at our democratic assumptions. Yet all too often a Government's response to it is to diminish, rather than encourage, public discussion. Terrorism may well strike at the fundamental bases of democracy; but for democracy to remain strong it needs public awareness. Governments actually encourage and support the terrorist's intentions by limiting knowledge and discussion. When this happens, terrorist priorities alone are allowed to influence media coverage and thereby determine public knowledge and response. Prime Minister Margaret Thatcher has referred to the media as providing 'the oxygen of publicity' to terrorism. Unnecessary restriction on public debate may serve the same purpose.

Probably the most significant academic discipline which has contributed to the study of terrorism is Political Science[8]. Given the political agenda of most terrorist acts and organisations, this is not really surprising. Nor is it surprising that Sociological accounts often serve to supplement political analyses for, in a sense, terrorism is an important aspect of the social organisation of contemporary society. The dominance of these two disciplines is at its most apparent when considering definitional problems, and they have led much of the conceptual debate. In contrast, psychologically orientated contributions in this area have been relatively limited and, on the whole, have contributed less to both conceptual and practical accounts than other disciplines.

Quite clearly, however, individual discipline-based analyses of terrorism cannot stand in isolation. The complex nature of terrorism demands an interdisciplinary approach, and each discipline can offer to the problem its own perspectives. Later chapters in this book will attempt to adopt that approach and, whilst we will explore some of the psychological perspectives of terrorism, we will also consider the broader perspectives.

Although psychological analyses of terrorism are relatively limited, it might be argued that it is, in fact, in this area where most practical, as opposed to conceptual, knowledge might be gained. Psychology is concerned with behaviour, and particularly the factors that influence and control behaviour. Terrorism may be a social process, but it is also a behaviour and, as such, can be subjected to systematic analysis. By understanding more about the particular behaviours involved in terrorism, we offer the opportunity for operationally relevant analyses of the problem.

Looking Ahead

This book looks from a psychological perspective at some of the issues related to violent politically extreme behaviour. It takes as its focus the contemporary problem of terrorism, and through a discussion of its conceptual base, and a review of the psychological literature addressing the problem, it presents ways of thinking about the terrorist and his actions.

The approach taken is a personal one, in that it reflects the experience and interests of the author; it is not primarily addressed to the specialist psychological audience. As we will see, the 'psychology' of the terrorist may not be a particularly useful concept, and in any case, whilst psychology may not yet have fulfilled its promise in this area, it is not the psychologist who will have ultimately to deal with the terrorist and the threat he or she poses. This book, therefore, tries to place into a useful context psychological thinking about the terrorist. It takes as its starting point, an essentially behavioural and descriptive approach to psychology and views the area from that perspective.

In simple terms, a behavioural view emphasises the importance of the consequences of our behaviour in its development and expression. It seeks explanation in identifying the environmental events which both control and shape our behaviour. In this respect, therefore, it is essentially descriptive, focusing on the critical 'functional' properties of behaviour. In the context of analyses of the Terrorist, this approach emphasises the importance of the consequences of the terrorist act *to the terrorist* in helping us to understand its development. It sees acts of terrorism as 'behaviours' which occur because of their environmental (historical and contemporary) context and consequence. This approach contrasts with more common approaches to the analysis of the terrorist, which tend to assume that the psychological manifestations of terrorism are 'attributes' of the individual, which can be best understood from the perspective of understanding the individual, and his personal make up. This assumption (often not recognised as an assumption) tends to permeate the approach of other disciplines to this issue.

Addressing the problem in this way has certain implications in terms of the psychological concepts used to analyse terrorism and the terrorist. The emphasis on motivation as an attribute of the terrorist, for example, which has characterised much of the psychological literature on terrorism receives relatively little comment here. Motivational concepts assume inner causes to terrorist behaviour which, as we will see later, do not necessarily help our analysis of the terrorist. The essentially descriptive and analytical approach to motivation offered by Peters[9] captures in a specific sense the essential qualities of the general approach adopted. This will probably seem most unsatisfactory to the Sociologist or Political Scientist, schooled to be dismissive of descriptive (as opposed to theoretical) analyses. These notions are developed further in Chapters 8 and 9.

A brief note about the scope of the material to be presented is appropriate at this point. One of the intentions of this book is to try to develop some psychological understanding of the concept of terrorism. The scale of the problem inevitably means that geographical and conceptual areas chosen for discussion are limited. This book is not a survey of contemporary terrorists and their movements, nor a review of their ideological context. This means that areas of immediate concern to some readers will not be mentioned, or are dealt with briefly. The focus of those examples used, and the analysis presented, is Western European and American. There clearly are issues of terrorism related to Third World conditions which have received little, if any, mention here. It has to be accepted that because of the social and cultural differences in these areas, there may well be challenges to our Western view. Those challenges, if such they are, will not be particularly addressed here. Neither is this book a handbook of security procedures, or indeed a manual of terrorism. Its aims are much more modest and are confined to informing and analysing and, in doing so, thereby helping the reader to reflect on the nature of the terrorist. Many problems are more easily stated than solved and this applies as much to the analysis of terrorism as to other areas. This book does not attempt to solve the problems of terrorism; but if by raising issues it is possible to promote reflection, then a great deal will have been achieved.

We should also take note at the outset that the subject matter of this book, terrorism and the terrorist, is unquestionably complex and obscure. We have already noted that discussions of terrorism are fraught with double standards and cynical political judgements. The conceptual complexity and obscurity, however, lies in the main in the uncertainty surrounding its identification and attributes. The next two chapters, therefore, examine the nature and scope of terrorism. A more individual perspective is then introduced by considering the role of Mental Illness in the explanation of terrorism in Chapter 4, and Fanaticism as an explanation of terrorism in Chapter 5. Social and Psychological generalisations about terrorists are reviewed in Chapter 6, and individual accounts of particular terrorists are discussed in Chapter 7. Finally, in Chapters 8 and 9, alternative ways of thinking about terrorism are presented, in terms of psychological and behavioural analyses, emphasising the role of the context and consequences of terrorism in sustaining and developing terrorist behaviour.

CHAPTER 2

The Problem of the Identification of Terrorism

We have noted in Chapter 1 that there seems to be general agreement across a broad political spectrum that terrorism constitutes perhaps the greatest threat to the liberal democracies. Each new report of atrocity in Ulster, Lebanon or elsewhere in the world generates a sense of unease and concern that extends beyond the country where the event occurs to encompass us all. In one sense our fears are groundless for, as we will note later, we are unlikely personally to encounter a terrorist act. But the threat undoubtedly remains and its reality lies not perhaps in its effects on the individual but in the effects on the political process and government. Yet we have relatively little knowledge of the process of terrorism, its determinants or controllers. We show confusion in the way we use the term and there is little consensus as to its attributes. We are not even sure who the terrorist is—an abnormal person, a madman, a rational and honorable freedom fighter? Our fears grow, but the source of our fears remains shrouded in mystery. Sometimes we are even unsure and uncertain about what actually constitutes the problem.

Complexity of Analysis

Given that we are adopting in this book a broadly psychological approach to terrorism, a starting point is to explore the value of using a typical psychological method of analysis. Psychologists often seek to define 'operationally' the problems that they address[1]. Operational definitions are related to the identification, through description, observation, and measurement, of actions or activities. This is often a useful approach in circumstances where there is lack of conceptual clarity, because it helps us to focus on those attributes of a problem that are identifiable. Many psychological areas of interest present problems of identification and definition not unlike those with which we are dealing here. Whilst psychology might be defined as the systematic study of behaviour and mental life, many of the 'mental' qualities of life we cannot see directly — they occur 'in the head', and are therefore only available to observe *through* actions. We do not observe thinking, for example, but we can be told about thought. In order to undertake a psychological analysis of a phenomenon from this perspective, we need to be able to see it, describe it, identify its essential qualities and, preferably, explore its parameters experimentally.

The complexity of the concept of terrorism suggests that it might benefit from analysis in these terms. The reason for this lies in the nature of the terrorist acts themselves. Terrorism refers to behaviours that *as actions* are not necessarily unique to terrorism in themselves. Because they are not unique, we then have the problem of deciding exactly what behaviours we are to include within the notion of terrorism (as opposed to some other category of events). Operational approaches, with their emphasis on description, will be of value to our analysis.

Much of the next few chapters is concerned with the description and analysis of the problem of terrorism. In developing our analysis, we will see that we cannot assume terrorism to be a unique phenomena in its attributes. However, it may well be the case that *assumptions* which have been made about the uniqueness of terrorism have in fact contributed to our problems of analysis. Once we have established the nature of these assumptions, it may then be possible to re-examine more objective ways of analysing terrorism.

The complexity of deciding what we will call terrorist activity can be illustrated by an example from court proceedings in 1980 in the Republic of Ireland. On May 13th of that year a seventy-two year old man was sentenced to three years imprisonment in the Special Criminal Court in Dublin. He pleaded guilty to aiding and abetting an armed robbery at a bank in Tramore on the 7th August, 1979, in which a large sum of money was stolen and a customer of the bank was shot dead. The convicted man, Walter Morrissey, had fulfilled an arranged meeting with the bank robbers to pick up the guns and money from the robbery, and had hidden them in a sand heap at a partially built house owned by his son. The robbery appeared to have been conducted by the Provisional IRA in an attempt to raise funds. Morrissey had been approached by a man claiming to be from the Army Headquarters of the Provisional IRA who asked him to co-operate in the robbery. Morrissey was known to be a republican supporter, and presumably sympathised with the aims of the robbery. Can the person described by the judge as 'a foolish old man' also be described as a terrorist, and is the incident an example of a terrorist incident? Clearly, in one sense it was; in legal terms he had aided and abetted the robbery. On the other hand, if you were a republican sympathiser, would you regard the act as being so grave? Would his assistance be seen as part of his 'patriotic duty'? After all, the death of the bank customer was accidental!

This event illustrates many of the features that make analysis difficult; the crime had a political motive (provision of funds) which was met through an illegal act. Morrisey's part in the robbery, whilst secondary in character, was an undoubtedly necessary part of it. The crime was violent and, indeed, resulted in the death of an innocent bank customer. On the other hand, the robbery was not itself directed at a political target, but was executed to simply raise funds. Furthermore, what attributes of the act contribute to the term terrorism — the robbery, the death of an innocent bank customer, the intention behind the robbery, or the ultimate destination of the proceeds? There is clearly no simple solution to this issue; how the event is interpreted would for many people be somewhat arbitrary, and dependent to a considerable degree on the observer's own political perspective.

Another aspect of the problem may lie, however, in the very use of the term 'terrorist'. A rather sordid incident like this can become elevated out of the realms of crime to some higher and more acceptable level by the ascription of the term 'terrorist'. This in its turn can serve to confuse us further when we look at acts which are more clearly orientated politically. This incident obviously has links with terrorism — but is it a terrorist act? Part of the problem may lie with the assumption that the terrorist act (and the terrorist) is in some sense different from other acts (and persons). We are making value judgements as well as describing events.

The rest of this chapter discusses the nature of terrorism, and in doing so considers a number of circumstances where the assumption of qualities of 'uniqueness' and 'specialness' may complicate our analysis of terrorism. The search for such qualities is clearly related to the role of value judgements in the attribution of the term terrorism we have already noted above. It is very important to stress, however, that in examining the ascription of 'specialness' to terrorism, (and eventually arguing for a lack of special qualities as attributes of terrorism), there is no intention to reduce it to the mundane. Rather the intention is to clear the way for an alternative emphasis and way of thinking about terrorism within a broader psychological framework. Many aspects of contemporary life cause us concern: they benefit from systematic critical analysis rather than analyses based on assumptions. In the case of terrorism, it is of great importance that we retain a descriptive and behavioural base to our analysis. That terrorism represents a major challenge to the democratic states can hardly be doubted. The following considers whether that challenge can be best seen in terms of the uniqueness of terrorism, or as an array of problems and concerns, perhaps uniquely drawn together by terrorism, but not unique in themselves.

The Consequences of Terrorism in Psychological Terms

We will begin our analysis of terrorism by considering its consequences. This is a reasonable starting point, for we only become aware of terrorist activity when there is some kind of consequence to it. Very often the immediate (and probably definitive) consequence is a violent act of some form, which may be aimed at a variety of targets. However, an important quality of that act in the context in which we are discussing it, is that it rarely seems to be random.

There is relatively little literature analysing the 'victimolgy' of terrorism, but in a paper by Fattah[2] the nature and qualities of the terrorist victim are discussed. As in most crimes, the victim of terrorism is rarely random, in the sense that some measure of choice is exercised by the terrorist in the execution of his act. This therefore specifies certain kinds of victims. In Northern Ireland, where a comparison between political and non-political murders has been reported[3], for example, political murders rarely involve women and often have more than one victim. In contrast, non-political murders are rarely multiple, but victimise men and women equally. In general, it is clear that not all possible classes of individuals are represented amongst victims. Children, for example on the whole are infrequent victims. This is not to say, however, that some victims may not be incidental — unfortunates who happen to be in the wrong place at the wrong time. A critical issue here may be the *representativeness* of the victim, rather than any personal qualities or attributes.

The emphasis on planning and choice of victims has also been stressed by Pockrass[4], again with reference to political murder in Northern Ireland. Whilst Pockrass discusses the issue in relation to different kinds of motivation, the incidents he describes and categorises can be differentiated in terms of functions equally well. Although we lack analyses of this kind for other areas of terrorist activity, all this serves to emphasise the non-random qualities of terrorist violence. The victimology of terrorism is probably an important area for further investigation, and would be a fruitful vehicle for comparative studies. However, whatever the relationship between victim characteristics and circumstance may be, in most cases we can assert that a special quality of the terrorist victim is his or her helplessness, something which of course greatly adds to our horror. A further quality may well be the terrorist's indifference to the victim: but to understand the functions of a particular act properly, we may well need to see it from the terrorist's perspective and understand the determining qualities in his environment before we can make sense of it.

Again, however, we encounter difficulties, for the potential range of functions is considerable. Schmid[5], details some twenty interrelated purposes and functions attributed to terrorist acts, which identify audiences as diverse as the terrorist groups themselves, the public, political leaders, the security services and others. Such an array of potential audiences itself clearly complicates analysis. Although we tend to think of terrorism in terms of 'terrorising' or causing fear, placing the public in fear, in some sense, is only one possible function. Others might include the mobilisation of forces, the radicalisation of opinion amongst uncommitted groups, the maintenance of power, the creation of social disorder and loss of confidence, influencing government into making particular concessions, to gain publicity in situations outside the local context of the terrorist incident, and so on.

One perspective that can be taken in analysing the consequences of terrorism is to examine its effects from the point of view of the ordinary member of society. As the usually passive recipients or observers of terrorist activity, members of a society are unquestionably effected by terrorist action. The nature of that effect, however, may bear further analysis, and there is little consensus on this. Different authors have tended to emphasise different kinds of effect. For example, effects on public opinion have been emphasised by Bassiouni[6], the demoralisation of society by a number of authors[7].

The word 'terrorism' itself carries with it reference to terror, which in psychological terms may be characterised as an extreme, perhaps debilitating, emotional state. Some authors taking this notion, have developed it, and characterised the public effects of terrorism in the dramatic terms of terror (Crenshaw[8] for example). Thornton[9] similarly makes reference to extreme states as the consequence of terrorism and draws attention to three levels of response induced in the audience of terrorism — fright, anxiety and despair. Consistent with this view of the consequences of terrorism, Wilkinson[10] identifies as the central problem in defining terrorism the subjective nature of terror, presumably in the observer as a consequence of a terrorist act.

Whilst we might assume that a principal consequence of terrorism is to produce terror in some sense, there is, in fact, remarkably little systematic analysis on the effects on the individual in society of terrorism in this context. We have very little idea of what the effects of such 'terror' might consist, other than at a general, and essentially political, level[11]. Some analyses that are offered typically seek to describe pathogenic effects on particular populations, such as children growing up in Northern Ireland[12]. Others seem to make assumptions that the individual effects of an act of terror on a victim have, in some sense, a parallel effect on non-participants at a social level. Greisman's analysis of identification in the ascription of social meaning to terrorism[13] seems close to this kind of approach. Perhaps, however, a useful distinction might be drawn in psychological terms between the effects of terrorism on those involved directly in some sense, the effects of terrorism on the general public, and the effects on the political climate of a country. Such a distinction reflects the different kinds of audience of terrorism that we noted above.

The Hostage Victim

That those victimised by terrorism may well be subject to 'terror' (in a psychological sense) is probably the case. We know relatively little about this area, but in this context, the victim of the hostage situation has received most attention. Of all kinds of terrorist action, it results in the most clearly identifiable kind of victim. A special quality of the hostage situation relevant to a psychological analysis, is that, in the main, it requires a degree of interaction between the victim and the terrorist.

There is no doubt that, in psychological terms, being taken hostage has profoundly negative effects on the individual victims. We can identify four stages of response in victims of hostage situations[14]: shock when faced with the reality of forcible detention, and maybe abduction, perhaps associated with psychological arousal and hypersensitivity: denial of the event, perhaps as a means of adjusting to it: traumatic depression and recrimination, associated with feelings of helplessness: and resolution and integration as the individual adjusts to the reality of the situation.

An example of how these stages can occur can be seen in the experiences of Gerard Vaders, a hostage held for thirteen days during the Moluccan train siege in Holland in 1975[15]. The hostage incident began by the train being boarded by seven South Moluccan terrorists, who immediately took a number of hostages from the passengers, including Vaders. One hostage was immediately shot and two more were subsequently executed. Vaders appeared to show the stages of response described above, showing initial arousal during which period he was able to assess the threat, followed later by exhaustion and other symptoms. It is interesting to note that Vaders' professional occupation may well have played a part in his overall response to being a hostage. He was a newspaper editor, and this may actually have helped him to deal with the situation. The particular strategy he adopted to cope with being a hostage was to assume the role of the reporter, the observer, and this seems to have assisted him in dealing with the stresses of his ordeal. On his release, he was physically unharmed but appeared to suffer some psychological problems which, as time passed, became more evident in terms of the dynamics of his family, rather than himself.

We might note in parentheses that for the victim to distance himself from the event in some way may be an important element in coping with it. We know from the experiences of victims of other forms of imprisonment without warning or cause (victims in the concentration camps of Second World War for example) that looking at the situation as if you were an observer may well be important in dealing with the initial shock of imprisonment, and perhaps the stress of exposure to degrading or frightening conditions. Cohen [16], in his account of life in the concentration camps, describes the importance of 'estrangement from his surroundings' as an important factor in his capacity to adjust to that stress.

Similar consequences of being taken hostage have been identified amongst a group of prison officers held hostage in New Mexico in 1980 after a prison riot [17]. During the disturbances, thirty-three inmates were killed by violent prisoners, with a number of others seriously injured. Twelve prison officers in all were held hostage for thirty-six hours, of whom eight were uninjured, and four were badly beaten. During their ordeal, the psychological state of the prison officers was described as a combination of feelings of helplessness, fear, and sensory overload. Total helplessness, however, seems to be the predominant experience.

We can see from these accounts that there seems to be little doubt that this particular experience of terrorism (being held hostage) has considerable psychological consequences, which may persist [18]. Indeed, in psychological terms, we can very clearly say that being taken hostage has profound negative consequences, but we can also see that whilst the term 'terror' might describe some of those consequences, it does not fully convey the range of experience.

In psychological terms, the salient features of being taken hostage may well be the intense stress to which the individual is exposed. If this is so, then the response to being taken hostage may well be a particular example of what is known as the 'General Adaptation Syndrome' [19]. This syndrome is the consequence of exposure to intense anxiety and terror and has been characterised as having three stages: the alarm reaction, the stage of resistance and the stage of exhaustion. A soldier going into battle might show these stages as a period of intense alarm before battle, a period of extreme alertness and resistance to stress during the resistance stage, and a post-battle period of collapse and exhaustion. Before going into battle, the soldier will be apprehensive, perhaps not sleeping. During combat, he becomes involved in the action, probably showing relatively little overt stress, and perhaps finding himself capable of great alertness and strength. If the battle lasts for several days, he may well find himself capable of functioning with relatively little sleep or food. But such expenditure of energy is biologically expensive, and on withdrawal to the safety of his base, he shows signs of both physical and psychological exhaustion, manifest in psychological terms, perhaps, as apathy and lack of interest in his environment. The features described here are similar to the stages of development of the victim of the hostage situation and probably reflect common processes, expressed in terms appropriate to the situation in which they occur. Given that we are probably referring primarily to the biological consequences of stress, this seems a reasonable assumption.

Aside from the very evident stress of being taken hostage, one of the best known consequences of being held hostage is the so-called 'Stockholm Syndrome'—the development of a relationship, an 'affectionate bond', as the hostage situation develops, between the captor and captive[20]. This is also sometimes known as the Hostage Identification Syndrome (HIS)[21]. Not all hostages develop this, nor if it occurs are all its features necessarily present. However, it seems to occur with sufficient frequency for it to be regarded as an aspect of the hostage situation. Its development seems to be quite lawful, and can be facilitated by well understood features of inter-personal communication such as eye contact and verbal interaction, as well as other psychological pressures such as dependency on the captor for survival and so on. A critical feature in its development seems to be the extent of face-to-face contact between the hostage taker and the victim. Verbal communication of some form also seems to be a critical element necessary for the Stockholm Syndrome to develop. In aeroplane hijackings, where not all passengers have shared the language of the hijackers, for example, the syndrome may appear in those passengers that have the hijackers' language, and not appear in those that do not.

The Stockholm Syndrome takes its name from an incident that occurred in Stockholm, Sweden in August, 1973. A recently escaped prisoner, Jan-Erik Olsson, held up the Kreditbank in mid-Stockholm, took four hostages, and demanded the release of a friend of his from jail. The authorities quickly complied with this request, and the friend, Clark, joined Olsson in the bank with the hostages. The hostage situation lasted for six days and nights. Olsson and his friend demanded a large ransom payment, and indulged in protracted negotiations with the Swedish authorities (including the Prime Minister). Initially, the negotiations were conducted by Olsson, but after three days, the hostages began to intervene, placing further pressure on the authorities to give way to the demands.

The nature of that intervention by the hostages is of interest. It showed the development of a growing sympathy between the hostages and their captors. This can be seen in the conversation between the Swedish Prime Minister and Kristin Enmark, a twenty-one year old hostage. Indicating her disappointment with the slow progress of the negotiations, she said 'I think you are sitting there playing chequers with our lives. I fully trust Clark and the robber. I'm not desperate; they haven't done a thing to us. On the contrary, they have been very nice'. In a later interview, she said 'This may sound stupid, but I want to go with the two because I trust them'. In this context of forcible detention, these are quite extraordinary comments.

The negotiations continued, with some concessions made by the Swedish authorities, in return for being able to inspect the hostages. On inspection, they appeared relaxed and at ease. One of the captors even had his arm around two of the female hostages, and all appeared relaxed and friendly.

Eventually, the incident was terminated by aggressive police action (gassing the captors and victims alike). Olsson agreed to surrender, but when the hostages were asked to leave the bank first, they refused; both captives and captors left together to give some protection to Olsson and the other hostage taker. When all were outside, they embraced and kissed each other before the captors were arrested.

A strong bond of mutual friendship appeared to develop between the hostages and their captors, which survived, and even became strengthened by the stress to which they were put. Olsson recognised this, in the statement he made after the incident, when he said 'I was too soft, I should have shot one of the hostages'. He later confirmed a psychiatrist's suggestion that the girl hostages had become attracted to the captors; there was even some suggestion of sexual relations between them.

A critical general feature in the development of the Stockholm Syndrome is the mutual dependency of the captor and hostage in circumstances of extreme tension and stress. The hostage is, in a very obvious sense, dependent on the captor, and in his or her power; the hostage taker, however, is also in a sense dependent on the hostage, for it presumably is the presence of the hostage that inhibits the observing security services from all-out attack. This complex interrelationship seems to create between them a bond of some form, where initial acquiescence of the hostage turns to submission and, perhaps, even a kind of affection. Similarly, the captor is necessarily physically close to the hostage, and in a sense dependent on the hostage for achieving his ends. Both share danger (albeit created by the hostage incident), and that sharing, and the consequent development of group cohesion seems to change the relationship of dependency to one of, if not affection, at least tolerance. An extreme example of this, amounting to apparently total conversion to the kidnappers' cause, can be seen in the case of Pattie Hearst, who after, as far as can be ascertained, a reluctant kidnapping by the SLA (Symbionese Liberation Army)[22] in 1974, became a fully fledged member of the group, taking part in well documented terrorist actions, including bank robbery[23].

The Stockholm Syndrome seems to be a well-established phenomenon in hostage situations. It has also been noted in other contexts, which differ in circumstances from the kinds of hostage situations described above. For example, Sir Geoffrey Jackson, British Ambassador to Uruguay, was kidnapped in 1971 by the Tupamaros, and imprisoned for nine months. His account of his experiences[24] are very revealing, and show if not the development of affection, certainly the development of understanding and a form of closeness that would in some measure inhibit violence on the part of both captor and captive. We should note, however, that the Stockholm Syndrome is not an inevitable consequence of being taken a hostage, and did not seem to develop in the siege of the Iranian Embassy in London in May 1980, for example[25]. This may be because the hostage victims in this case were not passive and were as ideologically committed as their captors.

It might be thought that there are some superficial similarities between being held as a hostage, and being held captive as a prisoner of war, but we can draw distinctions between them. War is a much more embracing activity and individuals are usually involved as members of an organised army structure within a well established context. There seems to be no evidence for the development of the equivalent of the Stockholm Syndrome amongst prisoners of war. Frustration, helplessness and hopelessness are terms that have been used to describe the feelings of prisoners of war and, in the absence of adequate training and preparation to withstand this, detachment, emotionlessness and indifference seems to characterise their response. Indeed, the withdrawal and apathy can become so profound that the prisoners give up all effort to cope with their captivity. In these circumstances, the effects of captivity, as opposed to being held hostage, seem to be considerable and profoundly negative. American prisoners of war in Korea, for example, gave accounts of men simply curling up on their bunks and waiting to die, making no effort to feed or look after themselves. In psychological terms, therefore, this is clearly a different kind of situation from that described in the hostage takings.

The Public Response to Terrorism

Leaving to one side the problem of whether all hostage situations can be termed terrorist (their political dimension is the critical attribute), there can be no doubt that there are profound psychological consequences to being taken hostage. But can effects of this kind, perhaps described in terms of terror, be ascribed to the public in general *as the audience* of a hostage incident, or a terrorist act? We must seek an answer to this question, for whilst the focus of our discussion so far has been on the hostage victim, in terrorist terms, it is effects on that audience that are important. The victim in this respect may again be to a large extent incidental.

The answer to this question would seem to be 'no'. It is difficult to detect any of the apparent characteristics of victim development in the public response to situations like hostage-taking. Certainly, terror, as an extreme emotional state experienced by the victim, has no obvious psychological parallel for members of the public audience to the terrorist acts.

If terrorism does not produce states of 'mass terror' in its audience, it is not because such mass effects cannot occur. States of profound public response to dramatic and frightening events do occur. Perhaps the closest state to 'mass terror' we can identify in the sense referred to above is that which has been termed 'the Disaster Syndrome'[26]. But this seems to refer to a qualitatively different state of affairs to the effect following a terrorist incident, however dramatic, on its audience. The responses of victims of an earthquake, or other disaster, seem to be reasonably systematic, and are characterised by initial periods of intense activity, followed by apathy and

TT –C

exhaustion. This has very little in common with what might be termed 'terror' in our sense.

It is possible to identify states of what has been termed insurgency-induced 'terror' in populations, which has been created to assist the initiation of political change. Such states might be thought of as 'political' parallels to the extreme situations described above, and may have elements in common. Such states only seem to occur, however, in circumstances where close social control can be exercised over a population. The creation and effect of mass terror on the Chinese population during 1942–43 has been described in these terms[27]. In many ways, this stands aside from the accounts of terrorism we normally encounter, in that a well-organised revolutionary force (the Communist Party of China), which was in control of a part of the country, deliberately inflicted systematic terror on the population for the purpose of producing political compliance. Perhaps this might be seen as an example of something similar to 'State Terrorism'. Wang Ming[28] reports that officials in charge of the campaign '. . . used to summon the peasants of a village, to line them up and order them to confess to being "counterrevolutionaries", "enemy spies", or "national traitors". Those who "confessed" were allowed to go home; those who refused were subjected to processing—hung up by their arms, beaten and put under guard. Soon the vast majority of the local populace, irrespective of sex and age, had "owned up" to being "counterrevolutionaries" or "enemy spies" or "national traitors".' Post Vietnam war Cambodia may well have shared similar experiences.

Occupation by an invading army might also result in a similar form of mass terror. Meerloo[29] provides a moving account of the effects of German occupation of the Netherlands during the Second World War. His account, given added poignancy by being written whilst the war was still being fought, offers a view of living under 'terror' written by a committed participant. He was also in a rather unique position to observe the effects of enemy occupation on individuals in his work as a doctor who remained in practice. He notes that the initial result of defeat and occupation by the invading German armies was a complete disorganisation of both public and private life, which took several months to recover. In his view, the most profound initial effect was the loss of opportunity for contact with others, for '. . . one man cannot communicate with another without fear'. During the initial three months of the occupation, he suggests a '. . . kind of paralysis took possession of the people'. The parallels with the initial effects on the individual of being taken hostage are immediately apparent.

This paralysis did not last long, and after a period of attempting to control the population through propaganda, the German forces resorted to more and more explicit repressive and coercive tactics to obtain compliance and control dissent. The extent of repression practised by the German occupation forces in the Netherlands was considerable, and civilian casualties were on a much greater scale than anything produced by more recent terrorist action. Meerloo reports that some 2000 hostages were taken, 6000 people shot, more than 100,000 Jews were killed, and some 500,000 were taken to prison camps, where many died. The scale of repression left no one untouched, nor was it possible to avoid awareness of it. Yet the non-collaborating Dutch population continued to resist the German occupation. Meerloo draws attention to the importance of social gatherings of any sort in sustaining resistance, and especially to the role of the churches. More interestingly, relatively few of the resisting Dutch actually left the country. They remained, even in the face of great danger.

He also notes a resurgence in intellectual life—an '. . . intellectual revival'—which showed itself in both literature and art. 'A great deal of poetry is being written. Together with a deepened interest in religion there is an increased demand for books on philosophy'. Meerloo is not, however, without some insight into the processes that might underlie such a revival. He describes it as a flight from reality, but it remains important for all that, because it provided a context in which Dutch resistance could be expressed.

Experience in the Netherlands differs somewhat from the experiences in Communist China, in that the coercive tactics applied in the Netherlands, whilst effective in producing fear and disrupting society, failed to radically subjugate the population. Clearly there are important differences between the situations, however. The Dutch whilst occupied, remained at least on the periphery of a continuing war, with a government in exile able to broadcast to the Dutch population (the importance of this is something which cannot be overstressed). Nevertheless, both of these examples develop the notion of the effects of coercive violence on political change in society. In the case of the occupied Netherlands, even in extreme circumstances and extreme 'terror', political compliance did not result from explicit coercive campaigns directed against the civilian population. If we exclude areas like West Belfast, where the Provisional IRA are able to exercise coercive control over the community, and the Basque country, where ETA are able to occupy a similar role, the effects of terrorism as evidenced in the Western world are not like the situations described above. The terrorist activities are nowhere as extensive or complete. Yet even if they were, the evidence would suggest that their effects would not be best expressed in terms of some general concept like terror. Such dramatic effects clearly do not characterise the consequences of terrorist actions on the general public in the contemporary western democracies.

Unlike the situation of actual occupation of a country by a foreign power, where contact with the repressive regime cannot be avoided, it is of some significance to note that most members of the public *never* encounter any direct form of terrorist action. The only way in which it does become evident is through the media. Most members of society, their relatives or friends, are very unlikely to be shot or bombed, nor are they likely to be involved in a hostage incident. The statistical probabilities of encountering a terrorist incident are very low, and this is even the case amongst what might be thought to be relatively vulnerable sections of the community (airline passengers, for example). The general public is in fact much more at risk from road accidents, rather than terrorist incidents. Thus, members of the public are unlikely to be the direct victims of terrorism; nor in the course of our daily lives do we see people smitten by 'terror' (in any psychological sense) after the latest terrorist outrage.

However, that terrorism has an effect upon the public cannot be denied and it may well be that fear, or panic *in extremis*, might, in some sense, characterise some part of that effect, rather than terror. As we have already noted, the role of the media in this cannot be overemphasised[30]. We can see this from such incidents as the Provisional IRA car bomb, which exploded outside Harrods department store in London on Saturday 17 December 1983 (killing six and injuring ninety-seven) and had a marked effect upon pre-Christmas shopping that year. But that effect seems to be inappropriately characterised in terms of terror. Rather, its effects might be more appropriately described as temporary fear or intimidation. The effects of the Harrods bombing upon shopping in the West End, for example, did not appear to extend beyond the Christmas period.

However, we cannot simply dismiss the broader psychological consequences of terrorism on the general public. A study of the effects of terrorism on the Israeli public by Friedland and Merari illustrates this[31]. During 1979, 271 terrorist incidents took place in Israel, which resulted in the death of twenty-three people, and injuries to 344. In that year, researchers assessed, amongst other things, the extent of fear and concern for personal safety amongst the Israeli public through a systematic attitude survey in the four largest cities in Israel (Jerusalem, Tel Aviv, Haifa and Beer Sheba). The survey was conducted immediately after a hostage incident in which a young girl, her sister and her father were killed by Palestinian terrorists. The results of the survey (taken four days after the hostage incident) revealed a high level of worry and concern amongst the Israeli public sampled. Results from a survey taken several weeks later confirmed the original results, suggesting that they were not an artifact of the proximity of the hostage incident. These results suggest that terrorist actions do create anxiety and worry on the general public living in terrorist situations; however, this might be said to be most appropriately described in terms of intimidation, rather than terror.

On the other hand, that same survey looked at the Israeli public's attitudes to the Palestinian situation and found that, even in the context of high levels of worry and concern, attitudes to issues such as the recognition of the PLO, or political solutions to the Palestinian problem, were not influenced by the terrorist threat. Indeed, the results suggest that the threat strengthened public resolve to resist terrorist demands, rather than diminishing it. Terrorist action was seen by the vast majority of respondents to be a reason for *not* accepting a political solution to the Palestinian problem. It is interesting to note, in this context, that whilst the *actual* probability of being victimised in a terrorist incident in Israel at that time was extremely low, the majority of respondents to the survey expressed worry about personal involvement in a terrorist incident.

Perhaps a part of the problem is that we are beguiled by the term terrorism itself. The creation of terror within an audience as a consequence of terrorism is clearly not an obvious occurrence and an inappropriate preoccupation with it may serve to obscure from our view those other processes that may have elements in common with the effects of terrorism, which might progress our understanding. Indeed, the consequences of terrorism might well have much more in common with the other kinds of fears which people have of low probability violent events, such as mugging, violent burglary, or just a general fear of victimisation, rather than some particular *special* quality of terrorism itself. Fear of mugging for the elderly, for example, is unquestionably prevalent[32], and such fears undoubtedly influence the life styles of many elderly people. Yet as a group, the elderly, whilst both being perceived and perceiving themselves as vulnerable, are in fact statistically a relatively safe group with respect to violent crimes such as mugging. Their fears are not a reflection of the statistical probability of being victimised themselves.

The media seem to play an important role in this, by drawing attention to infrequent, but newsworthy, violent events. This explanation has considerable appeal, but we should note that the relationship between, for example, television viewing and assessment of risk from violent events (flooding, cancer, terrorist violence) is far from straightforward[33]. Whilst this area clearly needs more investigation, it draws our attention further towards similarities in potential effects of violent events, of which terrorism is one. To concentrate on special qualities in the effects of terrorism may well hide these similarities which terrorism may have, in terms of its effects on the public, with other kinds of event, such as violent crime.

The Political Effects of Terrorism

On the basis of the above, we can say that it would be inappropriate to characterise the public response to terrorism as terror. What then, in psychological terms, might characterise its political effect? In seeking to account for the effects of terrorism, it may well be that the focus should not be on the terrorist act (which by its nature is extranormal, usually dramatic and probably bloody), but on the broader context of the analysis of the effects of events on public opinion and the political process. Analyses of the role of the media are again particularly relevant here.

Analyses have been made of the relationship between terrorism and the media, in terms of violence as a form of communication[34]. The relationship between terrorist activity and the media is undeniable. As far as the terrorist is concerned, it can be argued to be of primary importance. Schmid and De Graaf take a rather extreme position in their statement that '. . . without communication there can be no terrorism . . .' but nevertheless, the operational significance of the media for the terrorist in terms of choice of target, mode of action and so forth, is clearly important. The extent of the *mass* media, and its universality, clearly assumes even greater significance in this respect.

The Palestinian terrorist groups are probably amongst the most effective users of the media. Many Palestinian actions have been explicitly designed to bring to the attention of the world the Palestinian problem, and in this they have been enormously successful. Indeed, one of the most famous (or infamous) terrorists associated with the Palestinian cause, the Venezuelan Illich Ramirez Sanchez ('Carlos—The Jackal')[35], said of the outcome of terrorist actions '. . . violence is the one language the Western Democracies can understand', and this 'understanding', if such it be, is gained through the news media. The Palestinian Liberation Organisation has a well developed Press liaison system to capitalise on the media potential of their actions, as do other effective terrorist groups, such as the Provisional IRA.

There is relatively little psychological work to draw on to understand the role the media might play. The recent resurgence of interest in the work of Le Bon and the social psychology of the crowd[36] may offer some insights into the effects that terrorism, and other similar activities, might have on mass behaviour. (Such accounts may well also offer insights into the nature of the terrorist group, and the dynamics of terrorist decision making). Likewise Touraine[37] may offer valuable insights into the effect of such mass behaviour on 'the public', and the effect that 'the public' might have on the political process. We remain in need of much more work in this area.

The importance of terrorism in political terms cannot be denied. Yet given the relative lack of direct personal effect on the audience of terrorism, it is not particularly clear in psychological terms why terrorism should have the political effect it does. It might be thought that if not terror, then the public concern generated by terrorism is responsible for the political consequences of terrorism. In a simple sense, this does not seem to be the case, however, for as we have noted with regard to the Israeli public, terrorism can actually strengthen resolve to resist terrorist demands. We have little knowledge of the psychological processes that might lead to these effects, and of the relationship between terrorism and the public arena.

We can speculate, however, about some of the forces at work here. Some progress towards understanding has been indicated by Friedland and Merari[38]. They suggest, on the basis of the survey of Israeli opinions on terrorism referred to earlier, that public willingness to concede to terrorist

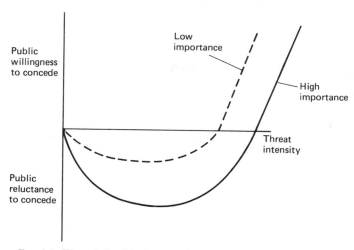

FIG. 2.1. The relationship between importance, threat intensity and willingness to concede to terrorist demands (after Friedland and Merari[33]).

demands (which might find expression in political change) is in fact a complex relationship in which, at least in the early stages, terrorist threats can lead to a strengthening of public resolve *not* to concede. The extent and degree to which such strengthening might occur, they suggest, is related to the importance of the issue; the more important the issue, the greater the strengthening of resolve not to concede in the face of threat. However, the more prolonged the threat, regardless of the importance of the issue, the greater *eventually* is the probability of conceding to the terrorist demands. They suggest that this can be expressed graphically in the form of a 'J' shaped curve, relating willingness to concede to terrorist demands to intensity of terrorist threat. The 'J' shaped curve offers a very useful way of analysing and understanding something of the relationship between the political process, public opinion and terrorist action, and clearly merits further attention. Its features are illustrated in Fig. 2.1. Following the continuous line, it can be seen that the more important the issue, the greater the threat intensity has to be before the public begin to concede. Issues of low importance (broken line) yield concessions sooner, but follow the same relationship. The important point to note is that the relationship between threat and public concessions is not linear and willingness to concede *diminishes* initially in both high and low importance curves.

Whilst we tend to assume that terrorist action has a negative effect on society, Friedland and Merari draw our attention to the capacity for terrorist activity to increase resistance to concede to terrorism. Whilst they suggest in the above diagram that this is a feature of the early stages of a terrorist campaign, in some circumstances, it can be argued that some incidents may strengthen resolve to resist the terrorist demands or intentions, rather than weaken, regardless of the extent of previous incidents. This seems to be the case where especially emotional or other significant issues are involved.

An example of this can be seen in the wave of public outrage which followed Provisional IRA bombings in London in July, 1982. The bombers attacked a troop of mounted soldiers on the edge of Hyde Park and later in the same day a band playing in Regents Park. Eleven soldiers and seven horses were killed, and 50 other people injured. The bombings showed that the Provisional IRA could operate with relative ease in London, and in that sense, from the terrorist's perspective, the incident should have been a success. However, its effects on the public were undoubtedly contrary to those expected by the terrorist group. The principal element which seemed to strengthen public opinion, rather than weaken it, was the death of the soldiers *and* the horses. Public sentiment was such that two years later, one of the horses which survived the attack, Sefton, was given a place of honour in the Trooping the Colour Ceremony to mark the Queen's birthday.

The United States public was similarly affected by the death of an American citizen, Leon Klinghoffer, in October, 1985. Mr Klinghoffer was a passenger on the cruise liner the *Achille Lauro*, which was hijacked by four Palestinian terrorists. United States responses to terrorism had for the few years previous to this point been relatively muted, despite terrorist incidents involving American citizens. The issue of special emotional significance which caught media attention, and seemed to mobilise public opinion in this case, was that Klinghoffer was disabled and confined to a wheelchair. He was shot twice, in the neck and in the back, and then thrown over the side of the ship. His body was found several days later off the coast of Syria. A wave of revulsion and anger swept the United States at the news of this brutal and unmerited murder.

These kinds of limitations on the effectiveness of terrorist incidents are understood by at least some terrorist groups. Writing on the effectiveness of airplane hijackings, Salah Kahlaf[39], at that time a prominent PLO member, observed that 'This weapon too, to our chagrin, was shown to be valueless. Except for the hijacking of the first plane in 1969, which caught Israel by surprise, the Zionist leaders refused as a matter of course to negotiate with the hijackers. . . . Thus we soon realised that hijacking planes did not aid our cause at all. On the contrary, it caused us serious damage in our attempts to have people understand the significance of our struggle for liberation'.

The two examples above illustrate circumstances in which a terrorist incident has (at least in the short term) resulted in a public and political response which strengthens, rather than weakens, public resolve. They both clearly illustrate the complexity of the non-linear relationship between terrorist threat and public response described by Friedland and

Merari. The dynamics of this relationship, however, remain unclear, and this issue requires much more investigation.

There are, of course, more straightforward ways of thinking about how terrorism affects the political process. At a simple and rather cynical level, the politician is himself likely to be a direct target of terrorist violence (or at least may think he is) and this, perhaps, might prove to be for him or her a significant factor in political, as opposed to public, responses to terrorism. Similarly, the terrorist certainly poses an explicit threat to the politician's capacity to exercise power, and may indeed offer an alternative authority to the sovereign government of a state; again, this may prove to be a somewhat cynical important factor, regardless of public opinion however expressed.

We can therefore see from the above that a naive notion of terror does not properly describe the public response to terrorism. Furthermore, we can see that whatever its effects might be, they do not appear to be particularly unique to terrorism. At least, if we move away from these assumptions of a 'special' consequence of terrorism, it then becomes possible to place terrorism within a more general analytical framework, which may in turn offer us help in dealing with the problem. Thus, whilst the label 'terrorism' seems to identify some unique dramatic qualities in terms of its effects upon the public processes of society, on inspection, those effects, whilst complex, seem to refer to qualities that may not be unique; perhaps terrorism differs with respect to quantity and intent in this sense, rather than quality.

Violence and Terrorism

Whatever the role of violence might be as an essential quality of terrorism, in the public mind at least there is a clear association between the two. For some authors the involvement of violence in terrorism would indeed be one of its essential attributes (Hutchinson[40] for example), along with other notions such as qualities of randomness (Kupperman and Trent[41]), and a lack of relationship to 'the just deserts' of the individual victim (Friedlander[42]). In terms of the discussion above, there is a clear link to be made between the term 'terror' and violence, with one assumed to be the inevitable consequence of the other. Probably all the terrorist incidents that come to our attention, via the media, involve some form of violence, either directly in an incident like a bombing, or indirectly through a potential for violence, as in a 'find' of weapons. Given the nature of the contemporary media and their appetite for drama, it is because of the violence that our attention is drawn to a terrorist event.

There is considerable disagreement amongst workers in the field about the attributes of terrorist violence[43]. It may be, however, that the problems encountered in this context, as with the problems of terror discussed above, have their origins in the attempt to identify some *special* quality of terrorist violence that will serve to identify it, and distinguish it from other violent acts. In trying to do this, many definitions focus on the instrumental quality of terrorist violence as an essential attribute. Instrumental is used in this sense to refer to violence undertaken to achieve some specific end known to the terrorist before the event. It might be contrasted with random or mindless violence. Arendt[44] will serve as a typical example of an author who takes this approach. In referring to terrorist violence, she notes that it '. . . is distinguished by its instrumental character'. In a more specific sense, Schmid and de Graaf[45] argue coherently for communication as an important instrumental element in terrorist violence.

But the instrumental qualities of violence and aggression *are not* special attributes of the terrorist use of violence. Many very different and varied individuals commit violent acts in a multiplicity of circumstances. Furthermore, such violence is often commonly instrumental in character and inflicted on 'innocents'. Indeed, one of the few psychological analyses of the ætiology of aggression and violence that continues to be of note makes reference to its instrumental character as an important explanatory tool in understanding the development or learning of aggression and violent behaviour. Bandura[46] drew attention to the extent to which aggressive behaviour is *learned*, both in terms of how to be aggressive, to whom to be aggressive, and when aggression can succeed. The important quality of this view on aggression is its emphasis on the consequences of aggression. If aggression is in some sense rewarding for the individual, it will tend to occur more often, not only in that particular context, but in other contexts as well.

What 'rewarding' might mean in any given situation is, of course, quite crucial here. Furthermore, the nature of the particular reward for the individual may well be unique to that individual. Peer group approval, for example, is a powerful reward for most people, and aggression which results in peer group approval may well be instrumental in character. Within the context of the terrorist group and its extreme group pressures, this example may be of some significance. As an explanation of violent behaviour, an approach emphasising learned responses seems to be useful in explaining a wide spectrum of instrumental violent acts, of which terrorist violence may well be a part.

It can be argued that we lack a clear understanding of the nature and determinants of violent behaviour in a general sense, but we can be quite certain that instrumental violence is not a special attribute of terrorism. Terrorism may differ only in intended focus and consequence (given its likely political agenda) from other forms of violence, rather than in any qualitatively different way. The consequences of a failure to recognise this can be seen in van der Dennen's[47] analysis of terrorist violence. By failing to recognise the importance of consequence for the individual in understanding *any* violent behaviour, he illustrates the difficulties that can be encountered in seeking to identify a special category of violence (special to the terrorist) that has qualities of purposiveness, that in some way distinguishes terrorist violence from other, presumably more reflexive violence.

The failure to recognise the instrumental qualities of violence may lie in the assumption made by many authors of frustration as a principal factor to account for aggression. Very often, that this is an assumption, and that there are alternative ways of thinking about the problem, seems to be unrecognised. In psychological terms, the relationship between violence and frustration has been coherently expressed in what has become known as 'the Frustration-Aggression' Hypothesis[48]. This Hypothesis has a long history in psychological explanations of aggression. In its original form it proposed that frustration *always* leads to aggression, and that aggression is *always* the result of frustration. The authors of the theory express it as follows: '. . . the occurrence of aggressive behaviour always presupposes the existence of frustration, and contrariwise, that the existence of frustration always leads to some form of aggression.' There is a problem with this view, however; quite clearly, not all aggression is the result of frustration. The kind of instrumental aggression characterising terrorist violence discussed above, for example, does not easily fit in with this hypothesis, unless the notion of frustration is stretched beyond its original meaning.

In response to problems of this kind, a revision of the hypothesis was proposed by Berkowitz[49] where he inserted the concept of anger as the consequence of frustration, which, given appropriate cues, might become evident as aggression. This revision still does not really help explain instrumental aggression, however, unless we assume the instrumental features of circumstances giving rise to aggression to be directing agents, rather than casual agents in their own right. Yet we know that events do act as *causes* of aggression, not just features to direct aggression. The insertion of anger into the account adds little to our understanding, but does serve to push the level of explanation away from the observable.

The concept of anger has been used in a more general sense as a means of describing the development of ideologically committed individuals[50], and in this discussion, we can see some of the weaknesses of explanations of this kind. In this discussion, Adams has interpreted the development of the peace activist in terms not that dissimilar to the above, making similar assumptions. Based primarily on biographical information, Adams describes the role that 'anger' might play in turning the uncommitted observer into the committed *peaceful* activist. Although Adams discusses this within the context of the peace movement, a similar analysis might well be applied to other committed individuals. Herein lies the principal weakness, however, for as in many of these kinds of explanations, its value lies only in *post hoc* analysis.

A further difficulty with the frustration-aggression hypothesis lies in how we might identify appropriate frustrating circumstances which give rise to aggression. In carefully controlled experimental settings which have been typically used to explore this view, the notion of frustration can be reasonably clearly defined. In the more complex environment in which we find terrorist behaviour, however, recognition of appropriate frustrating circumstances becomes much more difficult. Given the complexity of human behaviour, and the variety of backgrounds to which we are all exposed, we have to accommodate to a very broad range of events giving rise to frustration, many of which may be unique to the individual. If we are to sustain the frustration-aggression relationship, we have to call on very general kinds of explanations of frustration which retain their consequences over long time periods. These contrast dramatically with the kind of specificity shown in laboratory contexts. Where the kinds of circumstances we want to identify as frustration are about essentially unique personal conditions, we lose our ability to predict the occurrence of frustration, and become dependent on essentially *post hoc* analyses. This of course greatly limits their value.

A yet further problem can be identified with this approach that makes it difficult to apply in terrorist contexts. By relating aggression to frustration, this theory can appear to suggest a reflexive character to aggression. Aggression becomes the inevitable and unavoidable consequence of frustration. This diminishes the role of the consequences, or the instrumental qualities, of aggression. In fact many commonsense explanations of terrorism often seem to suggest a reflexive element to terrorist violence, by referring to concepts like instinct to account for violence. When applied to terrorism, this kind of explanation serves to distance us from the situation, reinforcing the notion of the 'specialness' of terrorism. Terrorist violence, however, is clearly not reflexive, and it is only necessary to place it in a special category of explanation if we fail to appreciate alternative approaches to the problems of understanding aggression and violence.

Notwithstanding, ideas relating frustration to aggression have wide currency in explanations of political change and revolution in Political Science. Despite the above kind of reservations, the assumption of a relationship between something like the psychological concept of frustration, and violent political change expressed as revolution, seems to permeate many theoretical approaches to revolution. This seems to apply as much to social analyses as it does to personal analyses. Theories that stress the importance of relative deprivation in the origins of revolution, for example, draw heavily on the frustration-aggression model. We have noted above some of the difficulties in applying the concept to individual terrorist acts; how much greater should the caution be, therefore, in attempting to apply the concept to broader, less clearly specified, social conditions.

This is not to say that we should dismiss the role of frustration in the analysis of violent behaviour. In spite of the relatively naive use of the frustration-aggression hypothesis by many authors in this area, there may be grounds for including frustration as *a factor* in the development of terrorist aggression[51], although not necessarily yielding to it a dominant explanatory role. As an element in explaining the setting conditions of terrorism, or the context out of which terrorism might grow, then the notion of frustration seems to have some use. But as an explanation of the *particular* act of terrorism, explanations in terms of frustration need not necessarily be of help.

Violence is of course not the special prerogative of the terrorist, and neither is its purposiveness. It may be that the intention of terrorist violence may distinguish it from mugging, for example; but again this hardly yields the necessary attributes of specialness in this sense. Both mugging and terrorism are extra-normal in character, but are not necessarily pathological. The social context of terrorism is clearly important, in that it contributes to both the essential attributes and the identification of the purposiveness of terrorism. But rather than seek 'meaning' for the violent acts in terms of some inaccessible special quality of violence, perhaps we might find greater utility in looking at what the effect such activities have in terms of their consequences. 'A social stimulus, like any other stimulus, becomes important in controlling behaviour because of the contingencies into which it enters'[52] is a view that might have as much relevance in analysing the effects of terrorism (as a social stimulus), as it does in the analysis of social interaction and facilitation.

Terrorism as a Label

When we use the term terrorism to describe an event, we are also using the term as a label. Unless we are careful, however, when we do use it in that way, the label terrorism is often as much a term of abuse as it is a descriptive term. It is used in all sorts of inconsistent and varied situations, and such promiscuous use, allied to the emotive and complex content of the term greatly adds to the problems of analysis. It is an attention getting term for the media, who sometimes use 'terrorism' to describe any violent act ('Husband terrorized wife' in an account of domestic violence, for example). It has become in Jenkins' terms '. . . a fad word, used promiscuously and often applies to a variety of acts of violence which are not strictly terrorism . . .'[53].

Scanlon[54] describes an incident which illustrates this added complexity of use. In 1981 in Calgary, Canada, a man took his wife and children 'hostage' as part of a well prepared and planned protest against the actions of a local bank. It would appear that his family took part in the preparation and planning. The local police took the incident seriously, and treated it as a major incident. But it seems unlikely that he actually intended harm to his essentially co-operative family; rather he sought publicity (which he amply received). This incident lacked as far as can be seen a general social or political context, and addressed the individual's dispute alone. It was violent only in potential, and arguably had willing hostages.

Is this properly described as a terrorist incident? The police response to it certainly was appropriate to a terrorist incident. Does it perhaps illustrate a confusion of tactics and intent implicit in the term terrorism itself? Or is the problem really again something to do with the assumption of 'specialness' in the concept, and that the promiscuous use of the term is only possible *because* a specialness is implied which seems to remove the act in question from other kinds of explanations? When we move out of the general into the political arena, we seem then to make assumptions that imply specialness.

Another way in which the term terrorism might be used as a label can be seen in situations where we lack sufficient information about an event, but need to classify or describe it, either for purposes of attempting to understand it, or for use by the media. We might classify by analogy, labelling an unusual act as terrorist because that seems to be the only way we can make sense out of it. However, sense might become more evident if we look more closely at the act itself, examining it in terms of its consequences, and exercise some caution in immediately seeking to label it. An example which illustrates this can be seen in the events of February 23, 1984 at Beirut airport. A security guard at the airport seized an aircraft as it prepared for take off. During the emergency evacuation of the aircraft, which resulted from the hijacking, a passenger was killed. Minus its passengers, and under the direction of the security guard, the plane was flown from Beirut to Cyprus, and back to Beirut, where the hijacker was eventually persuaded to give himself up.

At first sight, this looks to be an example of an all too common Middle-Eastern hijacking, and we assume a political motivation of some form, probably related in some way to either Palestine, or the factional fighting in Beirut. Press reports of the incident did indeed describe it as a terrorist hijacking, and initially speculated about which group was responsible. The accidental death of a passenger of course served to add to the impression of a terrorist incident. However, in this particular case, it emerged that the Security Guard who performed the hijack was not acting in the interests of any broad political movement; he merely wanted to draw attention to essentially local and personal grievances related to pay and promotion. On termination of the hijacking, he was not arrested, and indeed airport workers subsequently went on strike in support of his demands.

Using the term terrorism to describe an act like the above seems to offer a form of explanation. We may not understand the act, nor its context, but to label it as an act of terrorism sounds as if we have explained it. The event was certainly *like* a terrorist incident, but when we know more about it, we find it lacked what seems to be the *crucial* element required — the broader political aspiration. Labelling this incident as terrorism in some senses, would clearly be inappropriate.

It may be that one of the problems is that we are using the term terrorism in the sense of what Skinner[55] refers to as an 'explanatory fiction'. Explanatory fictions are words that when we use them sound as if we have explained something; but we have only described the word through labelling, and in fact know no more about the situations that have given rise to it. We may, for example think that the answer to the question 'why do we eat?' is supplied by the response 'because you are hungry'. There is a sense of completeness about the question and answer, but when you examine it more closely, you have not actually added to your knowledge, because you are left in ignorance of the factors that determine 'hunger'. 'Hunger' sounds like an explanation, but in providing an answer like that, we are simply pushing the explanation farther away. The term that sounds like an explanation but does not offer one only serves to confuse and obscure. The way in which the term terrorism is sometimes used does just that.

We can identify another sense in which using the term 'terrorism' or 'terrorist' as a label may have unrecognised consequences. Categorising a behaviour can itself, through labelling, determine how society might regard an activity. Describing and labelling an act as 'terrorist' immediately places it in a particular context, outside of those things we normally encounter. The precise attributes of the term may be in some doubt, but they certainly involve violence and illegality. It can also result in the individual so labelled adopting the stereotype of the label, enhancing and reinforcing those attributes. By labelling someone as a terrorist, he may in fact then become one, or become an exaggerated version of one. The expectations in the term can actually influence the individual's behaviour, and result in something rather like a self-fulfilling prophecy. We might also, in the same sense, find that labelling of this kind can imply a legitimacy which further enhances a commitment on the part of the individual to terrorism.

Specialness?

Frequently in this chapter, the term 'specialness' has been referred to as a quality the terrorist is assumed to possess, but which on examination we find he does not. Indeed, throughout this book, there is an implicit rejection of the qualities of 'specialness' of the terrorist, whether in terms of mental health or fanaticism, or in terms of other psychological structures. The term 'specialness' has been used to describe the persistent tendency to describe unique qualities or attributes of the terrorist, attributes that might set him aside as being fundamentally different from other people who might share some of his attributes.

Without necessarily eliminating all of the notion of uniqueness in the concept of terrorism, our discussion has served to raise doubts, *from a psychological perspective*, about the usefulness of attempts to set the terrorist aside from other people, in a number of important areas. It has also served to illustrate some of the problems of definition inherent in the term, which may help to explain why it can be so difficult to understand the effects of terrorist acts.

Perhaps the important point to make is that whilst terrorism may well be special and perhaps unique in the mix of attributes it displays, those attributes are themselves not necessarily unique to terrorism—they are shared by other kinds of situations and events. Similarly, neither can the terrorist be conceptualised in unique terms—whatever qualities he has, and whatever forces he might be exposed to, they are shared by others. Many of the explanations for terrorism, however, seem to be premised on either explicit or implicit assumptions of uniqueness (or specialness); where this is the case, we can see that they are unlikely to be helpful.

We can see how this search for specialness can hinder our analysis of terrorism from another, rather different perspective. One recurrent theme of many contemporary analyses of terrorism is the assertion that it is a modern phenomenon, related to the availability of weapons, explosives etc. Scientific development and the technology of modern living are seen as providing its basis and methods. This represents another way in which terrorism is distinguished in terms of a dimension of 'specialness', because it attempts to distinguish (and by so doing *make special*) the political violence we presently experience from historical political violence.

However, from that historical and comparative perspective, the technologically related specialness so often ascribed to modern terrorism can be questioned. In an important paper by Rapoport[56] the links and similarities between contemporary terrorism and the historical terrorism associated with religious groups are discussed. The nature of the doctrine and methods of the Thugs, Assassins and Zealots-Sicarii, revolutionary groups in the ancient world, show many similarities with the attributes of the modern terrorist, in using violence in support of the propagation of their doctrines. Indeed, each of these groups lasted longer than any contemporary terrorist group has done (at least so far), and were responsible for much greater destruction than their more modern counterparts. Their activity, in contrast to the essentially secular contemporary movements, was essentially religious in character, and has been termed 'holy or sacred' terror. Given the existence of these, amongst other historical terrorist (or terrorist like) movements, Rapoport concludes that terrorism as we experience it today is far from a modern phenomenon, although its non-religious basis may be. Whilst we tend to emphasise the technology of the modern terrorist, social and doctrinal issues may well prove to be more important in explaining the rise (and fall) of such movements. By undertaking this analysis, Rapoport therefore questions assumptions of the relationships between modern technology and the incidence of terrorism. In a comment relevant to the above discussion, he notes that 'When the history of modern terrorism is written, the cyclical character of modern terror will be conspicuous', and he relates such cyclical changes 'not so much to technological changes as to significant political watersheds . . .'[57].

Once more, we see a special quality of the concept of terrorism that seems critical, which on further examination proves to be less unique and significant. Yet, whilst it is clearly possible to question the adequacy of the concept, and to point to its complexity, nevertheless, we still use it meaningfully. The actual acts of terrorists may be difficult to identify; does this mean therefore that we can say little about the nature of terrorism? The next chapter examines this issue.

CHAPTER 3

The Nature of Terrorism

The previous chapter examined some of the issues that lead to complexity in the analysis of Terrorism. Our uncertainty about how we use the term reflects our uncertainty about the concept, and the actions it describes. The essential social ambiguity of the terrorist adds to these problems. Nevertheless, we use the term, and it does have some meaning. If we can peel from it the complications (of the notion of specialness, for example), then we will see that it refers to something which relates violence to political change. This chapter continues the examination of the concept from that perspective, and tries to identify attributes of terrorism that might be of value in our analysis.

The discussion is developed initially through a consideration of State Terrorism. It is worth pausing a moment to elaborate on the reasons for this starting point. We have discussed at length the uncertainty surrounding the effects of terrorism, and drawn attention to the problems of its recognition. We are worried by it, but are unclear as to its attributes and characteristics. A consideration of State Terrorism allows us to examine the problem from a different and rather less familiar perspective. In doing so we will see more clearly some of the contradictions inherent in the term. We will also, and more importantly, develop a more sophisticated notion of the nature of terrorism. By 'peeling away' the complications arising out of our everyday view of terrorism as the activity of a secret or underground society, we can better come to look at terrorism as a process, and attempt to identify the particular kind of acts that characterise it.

State Terrorism

Thus far, we have considered terrorism largely in the context of the small violent group committed to political change. Terrorism has been presented, therefore, as a feature of groups marginal to society, who operate in an essentially clandestine manner. This corresponds to the broad public perception of terrorism, and is the kind of view most evident in Western newspaper coverage. Terrorism is not, however, necessarily confined to

40

clandestine groups, and if we see the term as referring to the attributes of certain kinds of acts, then other sorts of agencies, including state agencies, can show evidence of terrorist behaviour.

It is useful to begin this discussion of the nature of terrorism from the perspective of the State, for if analysis of notions of specialness referred to in the previous chapter have questioned our assumptions about terrorism, so issues related to State Terrorism may also serve to clarify some of our assumptions. The essential quality of terrorism adopted here is its use of violence in the furtherance of political ends. If this is so, then it follows that terrorist actions can be committed by a variety of agencies concerned with the management of the political process in order to produce, or attempt to produce, or to forestall such political change. In this way state agencies, just as much as secret societies or dissident groups, may commit terrorist acts in an attempt to produce or maintain political objectives.

On the other hand, we should note that there is some potential for confusion in understanding the relationship between state terrorism and other forms of terrorism. Hacker[1] describes state terrorism as terrorism from above, and asserts that as a matter of principle, it is totalitarian. It would certainly appear that state terrorism is most easily perpetrated in the context of authoritarian or military regimes, where the terrorist acts seek to maintain a ruling group in power. Control over the armed forces and the media which might characterise a totalitarian state clearly make easier attempts at coercive control of society. One of the most excessive examples of such state terrorism in recent times was in Uganda under the rule of Idi Amin. With the assistance of his 'Public Safety Unit', between 50,000 and 250,000 Ugandans out of a population of ten million are thought to have disappeared, the result of torture and assassination.

The world has, of course, a long history of states maintaining coercive control over their citizens, and in a historical context, the excesses of Amin present little problem of recognition. The most extensive example of this in recent times probably occurred in Germany during the period 1937 to 1945. A structure of concentration camps was established to intimidate opponents of the Nazi regime, as well as to provide the bases for the death camps and slave labour camps. Explicit programmes of intimidation were conducted against what were regarded as dissident groups as *examples*. No one knows how many people died in the concentration camps. Probably some six million Jews were killed, and probably as many again (or more by some estimates) of other kinds of camp inmate[2]. The Nazi extermination programmes were more complex than simple intimidation—they also involved strange ideas about racial superiority and a form of totalitarianism unrivalled in its extent and aspirations. Nevertheless, we can see in it, perhaps, the extreme of State Terrorism.

Terrorism becomes more difficult to identify when the target of terrorism is not the broad population of the country, but an identifiable and specific section of that population. It presents special problems of recognition when the society in which that population lives lacks the attributes of totalitarianism. State terrorism in democratic societies presents us with the greatest difficulty of objective analysis.

Policing

Terrorism arises out of attempts to influence the political process through violence. In developing this analysis in a State context, we must inevitably focus on the role of the police. The police are one of the principal sources of coercive power available to the State, and must inevitably be drawn into state activities involving the use of force. Paradoxically, it is worth noting that the customary (and generally accepted) objectives of policing in the democracies may add to this potential. In general, it is broadly accepted that one of the fundamental requirements of a police force in a democratic society is that it 'keeps the peace'. This is usually interpreted to mean not only the detection and pursuit of criminals, but also the prevention of crime. The maintenance of public order, when failure to maintain it is seen as crime, presents particular problems. Whilst the right to protest is an essential attribute of most democratic states, there is no right to undertake violent protest, or incite others to violence. In states of civil unrest, and in times of political protest, there is a very thin line to be drawn between appropriate policing to control civil unrest, and coercive state control and repression, which may well be regarded by the recipients as 'terroristic'.

The policing of industrial disputes and strikes illustrates this problem outside of the context of totalitarian attempts at social control. From the perspective of strike organisers, the exercise of legitimate protest, and picketing to sustain the strike, is a fundamental quality of a dispute. If thwarted in this, strikers and strike organisers will react with vigour in defence as they see it of their rights, curtailment of which may well hinder their capacity to win the dispute. From the police perspective, (and perhaps from a Government perspective), the need to maintain order, and perhaps to enforce the rights of others legally going about their business (which might include strike breaking), seem paramount. In order to enforce those rights, the police may well have to resort to the use of force (a defining quality of police work[3]). These inherent tensions of industrial disputes are inevitably contradictory, and can in their turn lead to inevitable disputes, often resulting in escalating violence.

Examples of this on a large scale could be seen in the Miners' strike in the UK during 1984[4]. Mass picketing of working coal mines became a controversial feature of this dispute, which in its turn resulted in the mobilisation of massive police resources to counter the pickets. Because the nature of the dispute was itself intensely political, inevitably, the confrontations that developed between the striking miners and the police acquired political overtones. Any response of the police to the situation may well itself have unintentionally contributed to the development of tension, and violence. An article in *The Times* of 2nd April, 1984, noted that '. . . The very pervasiveness of the police presence is beginning to displace picketing as the locus of the argument. And that shift plays into the hands of the left . . .'.

Excesses are reported to have been committed by both sides in this dispute. It is very difficult to reconstruct accurately the events that might have occurred, but quite clearly, the standpoint from which those events are viewed may well be dependent on one's political perspective. From the view of the participant striker, however, receiving perhaps unintentional and minor (in the broader sense) violence may well have the attributes of state terrorism. The following incident, related by a National Union of Mineworkers Branch Secretary, illustrates this:

> It were a bit rough, like; a minority were chucking things at police then riot squads with truncheons charged at us. Well it were bloody chaos; people running in all directions. I saw coppers—they got this chap on ground and kicked hell out of him. Later on, I was walking back home with two mates when police van pulls up and out gets four or five coppers and they just laid into us. I got cut lips and big bruises—others were worse. Eric's nose got broke—we didn't resist at all. All of us were in our fifties. Its destroyed what little faith I had left in the police I can tell you.

Equally violent incidents against police officers on the picket lines, it should be noted, could also be quoted, for the extent of violence on both sides was considerable. This, however, is not the point. The maintenance of order requires a consensus for forceful enforcement to be acceptable. Where the recipients of forceful law enforcement have a clear political aspiration, and where the politics of confrontation (accidentally or deliberately) are encouraged by either side, the outcome may well be seen as repression and terrorism, by the recipients of those attempts at maintenance of public order.

Where management of public order requires the deployment of army personnel, as opposed to civilian police, the above situation can occur with even greater ease. The military are, in the main, not trained to be responsive to the subtle needs of a population. They are often armed, and dress in what for the ordinary citizen may well appear to be intimidating uniforms. The British Army in Northern Ireland is accused frequently of repressive actions, accusations which are undoubtedly accurate from the perspective of some recipients. If you regard searching for arms in a house as a legitimate activity, for example, a thorough search may well seem more important than the avoidance of damage to furniture, and inconvenience of the occupants. If it is your house, or your friend's house, or you think possession of arms in the circumstances is appropriate, you may well have a different interpretation to place on it.

Because the maintenance of public order is such a political aspect of law enforcement, it can inevitably become the focus for political violence. The example used above to illustrate the potential for repressive action (on either side) of public order policing in strikes may not seem like an example of state terrorism. The reader's perspective and own political views will colour this judgement, which is of course precisely the point; the acceptability of the term is dependent on the perspective from which you view the problem. Clearly, the example above is unlike the kind of repressive murder that characterised the maintenance of order in Uganda. It might be argued that if the above properly falls into the category of politically motivated use of force, it represents state repression, rather than terrorism. However, if we focus on the *process*, we can see that it shares elements in common. If not itself terrorism, it is clearly a step towards it.

State Repression and Terrorism

A relatively recent and dramatic example of state terrorism applied to the specific political end of social control can be seen in the recent history of Argentina. In this case, *both* the process and outcome of repressive political control are more readily recognised as state terrorism. It is estimated that during the period of military rule from 1976 to 1983 some 20,000 people were arrested, two million fled the country, and at least some 11,000 'disappeared'. This extensive period of coercion was ostensibly directed at Communists, and members of the terrorist organisation, the Montoneros. There is good evidence that this period was characterised by an organised programme of arrest, torture and murder, expressed in terms of anticommunism and Christian virtues[5].

The establishment of State Terrorism as policy may well result in it providing its own justification[6]. The logic of State Terrorism was illustrated by the Argentine Minister for Foreign Affairs, Admiral Cesar Guzetti, in a speech at the United Nations in August, 1976.

> My idea of subversion is that of the left wing terrorist organisations. Subversion or terrorism of the right is not the same thing. When the social body of the country has been contaminated by a disease which eats away at its entrails, it forms antibodies. These antibodies cannot be considered in the same way as the microbes. As the government controls and destroys the guerrillas, the actions of the antibodies will disappear. This is already happening. It is only the reaction of a sick body.

A slogan was painted at a notorious prison, the unfortunately named Villa Joyosa, where many executions appear to have been carried out. 'We will carry on killing until people understand'[7]. It is doubtful that the essence of terrorism, state or non-state, could be better expressed.

This example of State Terrorism qualitatively differs from the example above of the state's response to industrial unrest, but parallels can clearly be drawn. The extent of the violence used, and resort to the use of deadly force, are obvious differences. In both these examples, coercion was directed against a large section of society which, in some sense, held views contrary to those of the government. In this respect, they both differ fom most non-state terrorist actions, which usually have a more focused intention and are often aimed at discrete targets.

State Terrorism, however, can also take this more specific form. An example which illustrates State Terrorism directed against a particular small group, rather than at a large section of society, is the action which the French Government took against the environmental group, Greenpeace, in 1985. The Greenpeace ship, the *Rainbow Warrior*, intended to lead a flotilla of small ships into the French nuclear testing zone around Mururoa Atoll in the South Pacific to protest against planned French nuclear tests. The French Government mounted an extensive operation to hinder the Greenpeace protest, which eventually resulted in the sinking of the *Rainbow Warrior*. There is some evidence that this was initially intended to occur whilst the ship was at sea, presumably with the loss of both ship and all hands. This plan was subsequently modified, and the ship was, in fact, sunk in Auckland Harbour, New Zealand, on July 10, 1985.

The *Rainbow Warrior* was sunk after two limpet mines, attached to its hull, exploded. The second explosion killed a Dutch crew member, photographer Fernando Pereira. Although a team of French agents seemed to have been involved, only two were subsequently arrested for the crime. They were eventually sentenced to ten years imprisonment for man-slaughter. The involvement of the French Government in this seems to be beyond doubt, and to have been confirmed by the subsequent release of the prisoners into French custody and the payment of seven million dollars compensation to the New Zealand Government by the French Govern-ment. The Secretary General of the United Nations acted as mediator in the negotiations between the two governments, and accounts of the contents of the Secretary General's report said 'the damages were to compensate for the cost of the investigation and court proceedings, the infringement of New Zealand sovereignty and the sentiment of indignation suffered by New Zealanders.'

The French Defence Minister at that time, Charles Hernu, was forced to resign, and the Chief of Intelligence, Admiral Pierre Lacoste was fired. There were some newspaper reports that the French President himself, Francois Mitterrand, was aware of it. Indeed, there is also some evidence that the incident was actually financed by a special fund administered from the offices of the President. This incident seems to illustrate very clearly a form of terrorism, and is properly termed State Terrorism, in that it appeared to have explicit Government sanctioning and was a deliberately violent act addressing the political arena. It parallels closely numerous examples of non-state terrorist action designed to intimidate.

With the exception of Argentina and Uganda, the examples chosen above have been from democratic countries. This is a quite deliberate selection. It has been done to challenge and to illustrate the complexity of terrorism, and the extent to which if we are systematic and consistent in our usage, it can be seen not to necessarily be a feature of totalitarian regimes, but rather the consequence of mixing violence with the management of political events. In this way, State Terrorism can be seen as parallel to other forms of more individual terrorism, where the logic of violence predominates the political agenda.

It is a feature of most States that they reserve unto themselves the right to indulge in the use of force. Not all State violence, however, is necessarily State Terrorism, and it may be useful to develop further a systematic notion of State violence. Surprisingly, this area has received relatively little attention. Three forms of political violence originating from the State have been identified by Stohl and Lopez[8]. These are *State Oppression*, where social and economic privileges are denied to whole classes, regardless of their support for a regime; *State Repression*, where coercion, or the threat of coercion is used to weaken political opponents; and *State Terrorism*, where violence is used to create fear and compliance, amongst a particular group or amongst an audience. It may not necessarily always be easy to distinguish between these, especially in terms of 'coercion' and 'violence', but this distinction does serve to refine further our notion of the limits of terrorism when used by a State. The difficulties of analysis are apparent, however, when these distinctions are applied to the examples given earlier.

Accepting the above, further distinctions within the notion of State Terrorism in an international context have been made[9]. *Coercive Diplomacy* is used to refer to efforts to make non-compliance with a particular political demand 'terrible beyond endurance' for the non-compliant State. The extensive bombings of Hanoi and North Vietnam at Christmas in 1972 would be an example of this. *Covert Behaviour* refers to the terrorist actions of clandestine agents of government (the sinking of the *Rainbow Warrior* is a good example of this), and *Surrogate Terrorism* refers to the encouragement and supply of materials to another State, or organisation, to enable it to undertake terrorist acts broadly consistent with the policy objectives of the supplying State. Libyan sponsorship of various European Terrorist groups would be an example of this form of State Terrorism. The analysis of State Terrorism discussed above may help in the development of conceptual order in this area. We can see the term may well be used to apply to many forms of activity in which States indulge.

Perspectives

A substantial difficulty encountered in the analysis of terrorism stems from the perspective of the reader. 'One man's terrorist is another man's freedom fighter' is an oft-quoted cliché that nevertheless illustrates the difficulty. From some perspectives, the actions of a terrorist may seem a legitimate action of defence, or an attempt to control criminal threats or acts. From other perspectives, such legitimate defence may be seen as oppression. Therein, of course, lies one of the major paradoxes and difficulties facing any observer of terrorist action. In the example of State Terrorism given above, the views taken by the French and New Zealand media of the blowing up of the *Rainbow Warrior* were very different and illustrate these important differences in perception. In New Zealand, a wave of anger and bitterness swept the country at both the loss of the ship and the affront to sovereignty; in France, there was relatively little public and media criticism of the fact that the boat was sunk, but a wave of outrage at the capture of the agents!

The ambiguity and ambivalence of political violence also constitutes one of the great strengths of terrorism, especially non-state terrorism, for the terrorist. In attempting to control the threat of terrorism, a government can be led deliberately into situations where controls applied become increasingly coercive and increasingly impinge on members of society who have no direct involvement with the terrorist organisation. What for a government may be a legitimate response to terrorism can become terroristic. The logic of escalation is well expressed above by Admiral Guzetti; and in the chilling slogan of the Villa Joyosa, 'We will carry on killing until people understand', we see clearly the logical spiral of repression, State or non-State.

The introduction of the 'Diplock Courts' in Northern Ireland similarly illustrates a logical response to the problem of intimidation of jurors, which nevertheless seems to infringe one of the important elements of living in a democracy—the right to be judged in a trial by a jury of fellow citizens. In 1972, a committee under Lord Diplock recommended that in Northern Ireland, terrorist suspects should be tried by judges sitting alone without juries. At the time, there was considerable concern at intimidation of witnesses and jurors by various paramilitary groups. It was also related to the phasing out of internment without trial of terrorist suspects, and was seen at the time as a preferable alternative. Since then, it has been the focus for protest by paramilitary sympathisers and civil libertarians. Where the terrorist seeks to sustain the rationale for his actions by the reaction of the authorities, initiatives such as the Diplock Courts, however logical they may appear, clearly become counter-productive.

The discussion in Chapter 2 drew attention to problems of 'specialness' associated with terrorism. That discussion was largely in terms of the difficulties such assumptions present for the analysis of the problem. However, in terms of both the police and military response to terrorism, the discussion assumes much greater significance, for the assumption of specialness can have important operational consequences, which may exacerbate the problems outlined above. The setting aside of terrorism as 'special', from those activities with which the police normally deal, for example, can become the justification in turn for, and may well even predispose, extra-normal and special responses by the police to deal with the problem. These responses, if they involve the use of force or violence, can result in the very outcome they are designed to avoid.

It is not by any means clear however that the State's response to terrorism should differ qualitatively from the response to other kinds of societally damaging behaviour. Epstein[10] describes the qualities of success-ful anti-terrorist policing, for example, in terms that look very similar to the qualities of successful policing in *any* policing environment—patrolling, investigation, intelligence gathering, human relations, police self-regula-tion. It may well be that the nature and extent of the police effort may differ from that normally undertaken, as might the balance of effort between the various areas. Similarly, measures to ensure self-protection may become more important and evident. But there is no necessary reason for qualita-tive differences in response which, for example, take the form of excessive violence or repressive measures against a community. The identification of the problem as different *in principle* from other demands on police time can legitimise responses that actually contribute to the furtherance of the ends of the terrorist, by unnecessary violence and harassment, victimising and radicalising an otherwise uncommitted community. In the context of the earlier discussion above of the 'repressive' consequences that any police action might have (in for example the policing of public order) this becomes a very serious issue.

Kinds of Terrorists

State terrorism is of course one kind of terrorism which we can identify (in contrast to non-State terrorism). However, other more complex ways of categorising terrorism have been developed by Wilkinson[11]. Four kinds of terrorist action have been identified which are helpful in placing some order on the situation, and may aid our understanding of the conceptual issues involved. As a means of developing the concept of terrorism, it is worth discussing these categories in some detail. The four kinds of terrorism identified are Criminal Terrorism, Psychic Terrorism, War Terrorism and Political Terrorism. The types vary according to the form and intention of the violent acts.

The first of these, *Criminal Terrorism*, is characterised by the systematic use of terror for material or monetary gain, as distinct from political gain. From the perspective adopted in this book, this form of terrorism would not seem to merit the term, for it makes no reference to political aspirations. Many of the examples of the promiscuous use of terrorism may well fall within this category. The extortion of money from shopkeepers and club owners, that may have characterised the actions of 'The Mob' in Chicago in the 1930's might attract the term terrorism. But such actions lack a political motive, and were conducted for purely financial gain. Promiscuous use of the term terrorism in this way simply confuses.

On the other hand, in order to maintain supplies of arms and weapons (generally bought outside of the country) to provide an income for members of imprisoned terrorists' families, or to supplement the income of active terrorists, a terrorist group may well have to become involved in crime. Such crimes will often involve theft or robbery, because this is the most convenient and easiest way for terrorist groups to acquire funds. In contrast to the above, this is, in one sense, a form of terrorism, in that it is a necessary secondary activity to other forms of terrorist action. The crimes themselves, however, may also serve a political purpose in terms of the political aspirations of the terrorist group, by demonstrating their power to operate in a broader arena without interference from the security forces. This is clearly a more complex issue than it might have appeared at first sight, and a fuller discussion of some of the points raised here is given below (under the section 'Terrorism and Criminal Fund Raising' on page 50).

The second form of terrorism, *Psychic Terrorism*, is characterised by religious or magical ends (as practised by a religious cult to enforce compliance with beliefs, for example). Sectarian killings, as practised by both Nationalists and Loyalists in Northern Ireland, would also presumably fall into this category. A more obvious historical example of Psychic Terrorism would be the medieval Inquisition which attempted to enforce adherence to the Roman Catholic faith. Given the diminishing role of religion in contemporary society, recent examples in the broader context of terrorism are rather rare, although the efforts of some recent religious cults to maintain control over their members might well merit the term terrorism (such as the Jonestown massacre referred to in Chapter 5).

The third form of terrorism, *War Terrorism*, involves the use of terrorist action in pursuit of war ends. This presents some difficulties of identification, however, for it is not always possible to distinguish between formal warfare and informal warfare, a distinction that has a bearing on the attribution of the term 'terrorism'. Conventionally, a distinction is drawn between terrorist action, and guerrilla warfare, the latter being generally thought of as a form of explicit 'warfare', the former not. Both are types of anti-government action, and may well share common ends; both may also share what might be termed an aspiration to 'social' warfare, as opposed to 'international' warfare in a more traditional sense.

At one level, the notion of War Terrorism seems an appropriate category of terrorist action, but the precise attributes when examined in detail become somewhat obscure. Perhaps the difficulty here is that warfare is not something that occurs in social isolation, and more particularly, does not occur outside a political context; perhaps it might be more properly subsumed under the next kind of terrorism Wilkinson identifies, Political Terrorism.

The fourth form of terrorism, *Political Terrorism* involves the use of, or threat to use, violence for political goals. Most of the examples given in this book illustrate aspects of Political Terrorism, and this perspective has been adopted as reflecting the fundamental attribute of terrorism. Its principal feature is that the event itself, and perhaps the victims, are incidental to some broader political aspiration. This aspiration is expressed in terms of influencing either directly or indirectly the political process. Warfare, as a feature of the political process, clearly might fall within this category, drawing together war and Political Terrorism.

Quite clearly, these categories are not mutually exclusive. In one sense, all the above can be interpreted in terms of Political Terrorism, in that they may impinge in some way on the political process. Psychic Terrorism is in some senses about the acquisition of power, spiritual or temporal, and from that perspective might well be a form of Political Terrorism (in that power over society is expressed in the political arena). On the other hand, the categories do offer a useful way of organising the diverse range of events we refer to as terrorism, and we can use them to develop a more extensive analysis of the nature of terrorist acts.

Terrorism, Crime and Criminal Fund Raising

Criminal Terrorism, because it lacks the political and change elements which might be thought to characterise terrorism, may well seem to be easily discernible from War and Political Terrorism at first sight. Hence violent crimes like extortion or kidnapping undertaken for the personal gain of the perpetrator, whilst often described as 'terroristic' might not be properly regarded as examples of terrorism. There may well be problems here, however, in that the ordinary criminal may well seek to justify his actions by reference to some broad 'political' generalisations. Even a general reference to 'they can afford it' by the burglar might suggest a degree of political justification to an otherwise straightforward criminal act. The ordinary criminal might also, seeing the relative success of terrorist tactics, adopt those tactics for his own ends. This is sometimes referred to as 'Quasi-Terrorism'[12]; the distinctions here however may sometimes be difficult to make.

Whilst the dividing line between terrorism and acquisitive crime can be difficult to make, by examining that line, we can gain a better understanding of the rationale behind some terrorist acts. As we have already noted above, non-state terrorist organisations may well have difficulties in raising sufficient finance to maintain their organisation or activities. Thus bank robberies for money, raids on arsenals for arms and the like, may become part of the hinterland of terrorist activity. Whilst such crimes may not themselves have political aspirations, they may well be a necessary foundation to more obvious political violence, by providing funds, on which other acts might be built. A good case can be made for the inclusion of such activities within the category of terrorism.

The scale of fund raising undertaken by terrorist groups can be enormous. In 1981, United States Treasury figures showed that the Provisional IRA raised in excess of $500,000 from the USA through their support group Noraid, with contributions also coming from other groups. The actual annual figure needed to sustain the activities of the Provisional IRA probably exceeds one and a half million pounds to support operational activities alone, so it can be seen that the financial needs of such a group are very considerable. During the hunger strikes of 1980–81, the turnover of that organisation probably exceeded four million pounds. It follows, therefore, that a sophisticated facility to raise, monitor and control such funds becomes a necessary part of the terrorist organisation[13].

The large scale of funds needed to sustain activity of a group like the Provisional IRA exceeds the capacity of voluntary fund raising, and alternative means of raising funds have to be developed. A large number of the armed robberies committed both in the Republic of Ireland and Northern Ireland appear to be the responsibility of paramilitary groups, and are undertaken to raise funds. The Official IRA, for example, are thought to have been responsible for theft of £10,000 from the Larne to Stranraer ferry in Northern Ireland in September, 1984. This money was used to support the activity of its political wing in the Republic of Ireland, the Workers Party, and to finance its operations in the North of Ireland. The Official IRA were also responsible for the theft of £250,000 in cash and cheques from a security van in Newry, Northern Ireland. The proceeds of this robbery were subsequently disposed of in Dublin. An Official IRA robbery gang is also thought to have been responsible for an extensive series of armed robberies in 1977 in the Republic of Ireland including £25,000 from a Bank of Ireland Branch in Dublin, £11,000 from the Allied Irish Bank, £6,000 from a builders and £30,000 from a meat packing company. £150,000 was stolen, probably by the same group, from the offices of the Irish Transport Authority (CIE) in 1978. More recently, Official IRA gangs have been involved in the hijacking of drink consignments and attempts at extensive forgery of currency notes[14].

In fact, all the various terrorist groups operating in Northern Ireland are in some sense involved in crime of this sort, both in Northern Ireland and, the Republic of Ireland. We can think of this in one sense as a matter of economic survival. One of the notable attributes of many such crimes is their degree of preparation and 'competence', in terms of forward planning and effective execution. This feature often serves to distinguish paramilitary activities from other kinds of similar criminal activities. An example of this can be seen in an armed robbery in 1983 in the South of Ireland of a van conveying a large quantity of money, thought to be carried out by the Provisional IRA. The night before the robbery, a roadside farmhouse was taken over by a number of armed men, who held the householders hostage. The robbery itself was effected the following morning by driving a tractor and trailer between the van carrying the money and the police escort, after skilfully using a roadworks diversion sign. The robbery appeared to have been planned in detail before being executed, with lookouts posted in radio contact with the armed men to give warning of movements of the van and police escort. Well prepared escape routes were used, with cars stolen for the purpose. The robbery netted in excess of £130,000, as well as a number of police automatic weapons.

Crimes of this sort are distinctive in the context of armed robbery in Ireland, in terms not only of their very evident forward planning, but also of the use of weapons and the types of weapon used. At least in the Republic of Ireland, the use of weapons in robbery is relatively infrequent, (although of rising incidence), and armed robberies lacking this terrorist dimension, even if weapons are used, are often poorly planned and executed. A further notable feature of such terrorist robberies is generally a failure to recover any of the proceeds of the robbery.

The Northern Irish terrorists are not alone in undertaking crime to finance their operations. ETA, the Basque terrorist group, is also known to have undertaken robberies and other crimes to raise funds for its operational needs. Clark[15] reports that in the period 1967 to 1977, more than sixty million pesetas (around one million dollars) were raised by bank robberies. In 1978 alone, the organisation is thought to have committed some fifty robberies, yielding in excess of 250 million pesetas (four million dollars)[16].

Kidnapping has been a traditional method used by terrorist groups to raise funds to further their political ends. A notable early example of this can be seen in the kidnapping of an American missionary, Ellen Stone, in the early twentieth century, by a group calling itself the Internal Macedonian Revolutionary Organisation. The church group which supported Ellen Stone's missionary work in Yugoslavia paid a ransom of sixty-six thousand dollars for her release. These funds are known then to have been used to support a revolution aimed at Macedonian independence in 1903 by the group that kidnapped her.

More recently, kidnapping for money has become an increasingly popular terrorist strategy. Many groups have resorted to this to raise funds, with considerable success; business targets have on the whole proved to be the most lucrative, although where relatively weak governments have been involved, or where the politics of the situation has weakened government resolve, governments have from time to time paid ransoms. During the period 1968 to 1982, an astonishing 3,162 individuals have been the subject of terrorist hostage taking[17]. Nationals of the United States, France, the United Kingdom, West Germany and Italy were the most likely to be victimised. Most countries have experienced hostage situations, although they were in the main concentrated in Latin America and Western Europe. The countries appearing most frequently as hostage locations were Lebanon, El Salvador, Mexico, Guatemala, Colombia and Ethiopia, where more than a third of all attacks took place. It is of some consolation to note that in only four percent of the situations were all or some of the hostages killed.

The Basque terrorist group, ETA, has been responsible for a number of hostage takings which have been resolved by the payment of a ransom. Such ransom income has played a considerable role in financing its activities. Its first explicit kidnapping for money took place in January, 1973, when Felipe Huarte was abducted[18]. His family paid a ransom of fifty million pesetas for his release. From then onwards, kidnapping of Basque industrialists became a feature of ETA's fund raising activities, yielding in 1978 alone in excess of a quarter of a million dollars. In January, 1981, Senor Luis Suner was kidnapped for a period of ninety days before being released. Senor Suner met one of the principal attributes attractive to the terrorists; he was wealthy, and indeed was one of Spain's richest men. It is widely thought that a payment of 2.6 million pounds was made for his release. Whilst the Spanish Government condemned the negotiations, it did little to hinder them, nor the exchange of money.

Hostage taking for ransom places a government in a difficult position. Whilst the public rhetoric of 'no negotiation' with terrorists has an appeal, the reality of contributing to the possible death of the hostage, or at least continued imprisonment, by hindering negotiations, places enormous pressures on the political will of governments to maintain their position. The situation is made even more complex by the role of the insurance industry in this area. It is possible to acquire insurance cover against being taken hostage. This is of course an attractive proposition for industry, seeking to protect its senior executives, and for the families of wealthy individuals. Premiums range from one half percent of cover to five percent, depending upon risk, with cover extending to as much as twenty million dollars, making it a reasonably priced protection[19]. In a sense, however, such cover could be argued to be criminogenic, for it ensures a readily available supply of funds to the hostage taker, at no cost to the hostage. Insurance cover may well smooth the path in negotiation and help to protect the hostage, but instead of diminishing the extent of hostage taking, it offers a positive inducement.

Kidnapping, if successful, may well be a highly lucrative activity for the terrorist group, but it is undertaken at some risk. To be effective in raising large amounts of money, the individual concerned must be of some financial stature and probably of some importance in his own community. Inevitably, a kidnapping will result in an increase in the activity of the security forces, activity which may well compromise other operations planned by the terrorist group. As the sophistication of the security services has grown, so has the difficulty in sustaining hostage situations. Inevitably, therefore, terrorist groups would be expected to turn to other means of raising money.

A lucrative activity, of low risk, is the levying of so-called 'revolutionary taxes'. More commonly known as protection money, this form of intimidation and extortion is widely practised by the Basque group ETA, and all the paramilitary groups in Northern Ireland. In essence, the procedure is very simple; on payment of an amount, the individual or organisation is 'protected' from some unpleasant consequence. As a form of extortion, it has much to recommend it. It is difficult to detect in the absence of explicit information, and even more difficult to prove. In Northern Ireland, a lucrative source of protection money has come from pubs and clubs. This 'trade' is conducted by both protestant and catholic paramilitary groups, raising a steady income.

ETA has a well-established programme of extortion. In 1976, ETA demanded payments of between twelve and a half and twenty-five thousand dollars from several hundred individuals[20]. Death was threatened on failure to pay. This was continued in 1977 and 1978, and was estimated to have intimidated some 800 wealthy Basques into paying. The threat of death was no idle threat; Javier de Ybarra, a well-known Basque industrialist, refused to pay. In May, 1977, he was kidnapped and later murdered. In the period from 1978 to 1980, Clark[21] describes some 3 killings, and 6 woundings, which appear to be connected with enforcement of intimidation threats. The people involved were all leading financial or industrial figures in the Basque country. Such intimidation appears to have been effective, for in the first four months of 1980, over 800 million pesetas were thought to have been collected.

More subtle crimes are also committed by the various paramilitary groups in Northern Ireland. Extensive tax fraud involving building sites have been perpetrated on a massive scale, involving both Republican and Loyalist paramilitary groups. The income in such cases is raised by not declaring earnings to the tax authorities, with the workers involved paying a weekly sum to the organisers of the fraud. The scale of such frauds is difficult to estimate; one such effort thought to be organised by the Official IRA in October 1983 would have yielded up to three million pounds in the year it was intended to run had it not been broken up. On top of the extensive intimidation and protection rackets operated by all groups in Northern Ireland, the scale of income involved is enormous[22].

Criminal fund raising is not, of course, confined to Irish and Basque terrorist groups. Probably all groups have necessarily undertaken theft of one kind or another to raise funds to sustain their activities. The morality of theft or extortion is easily dealt with in revolutionary rhetoric as expropriation; the Tupamaros referred to it as 'requisitioning'.

The first requirement that must be strictly observed . . . is that only capitalists or the State may be expropriated, and in order to underline this, goods must be returned or damages compensated whenever the interests of the workers are affected[23].

Attractive as this notion might be, it would be difficult to find examples of such restitution in the activities of European Terrorists.

There are intriguing reports of another area of terrorist involvement in illegal money raising activities — drug trafficking[24]. This, at first sight, may seem rather surprising, given the almost puritanical view of life which often characterises the terrorists' interactions with the community in which they live. Various terrorist groups have from time to time been implicated in the drug trade, (notably ETA and the Red Brigades), but evidence is difficult to come by. However, perhaps the clearest evidence exists to show the involvement of the Provisional IRA in the movement of drugs. The Provisional IRA may well have been involved in the smuggling of drugs into the United States in exchange for arms, through intermediaries with Mafia connections. This is denied by the Provisional IRA leadership, but given the extent of international contacts necessary to supply the weapons and explosives used by them, and the kinds of individuals involved in the illegal international arms trade, the accusation appears plausible. Accounts of more systematic involvement of terrorist movements in drug dealing from time to time emerge, often implying international links, and possibly State sponsorship[25]. By their very nature, such accounts are almost impossible to check.

These activities present great difficulties when we try to identify attributes of terrorism. Are the illegalities described above terrorist acts? In so far as they seem to be necessary activities to support the politically motivated violence and aspirations of the groups, then in a sense they clearly are. On the other hand, in many ways, the activities of, for example, all the paramilitary groups in Northern Ireland closely resemble those of the Mafia, or United States organised crime in the 1930s. Very often, they differ from them only in terms of a secondary political aim; secondary in the sense that the crimes themselves yield not personal profit, but profit to the terrorist organisation. Even this, however, is not strictly accurate. Given the amounts of money involved, occasional 'free-lance' operations can occur, in which the individuals involved use the cover of terrorist organisation membership to commit straightforward acquisitive crime. This serves to complicate the issue even further, for the same participants may be involved in crime, both sanctioned and non-sanctioned, by the terrorist organisation.

Illegality in the Community

The relationship between terrorism and illegality is complex. In one sense, terrorist acts which merit the term are by definition illegal. But in sustaining their presence in a community, illegality of another form can characterise terrorist groups. The terrorist functions within a broader non-terrorist community in some sense. Issues of scale of course determine the size of the community—small left wing groups operate in different kinds of communities from large scale groups, such as ETA or the Provisional IRA. But in both cases, the terrorist must exercise some control over that community to protect himself and his organisation, however large or small. In exercising that control, he may well develop systems which involve the coercive control of that community, which will almost certainly be illegal with respect to broader societal rules. Interestingly, however, such illegal coercive control may well have attributes in common with the 'normal' criminal justice system, and might even be premised on a notion of 'justice' in a sense which the broader society might recognise. They might also show attributes which are similar to those we have described above as state terrorism—an irony indeed!

Evidence related to this kind of issue is difficult to obtain, for it involves detailed knowledge of the community in which the terrorist operates, not an easy thing for the researcher to acquire. However, Morrissey and Pease[26] describe what they refer to as the 'Black Criminal Justice System in West Belfast', which illustrates the nature of the control exercised by the Provisional IRA over its community. In the same sense that there exists a 'Black Economy' (an economy that refers to a system of exchange, theft and purchase of goods and services outside the official economy), Morrissey and Pease describe the existence of a parallel terrorist based criminal justice system. The Provisional IRA have been active in West Belfast for many years and the area has been subjected to intermittent civil unrest for many decades, a period characterised by political crises, communal rioting and challenge to the legitimacy of the state. The extent of 'normal' policing is limited[27], and the inhabitants of the area, as well as experiencing a high degree of social disadvantage, have little resource to, or confidence in, the normal organs of the state to effect crime control. The Black Criminal Justice System seems to be an attempt to exert (at one level at least) some degree of social control.

The following, issued from the Republican Press Centre, Belfast, on 5 June, 1982, illustrates the kinds of thinking underpinning the role of the terrorists in this area in providing an alternative to State social control. It refers to the general principles, but resulted from a particular incident in which a young man was 'punished' for theft.

> Belfast Brigade (of the Provisional IRA) would like to make it clear that the physical punishment of criminals by shooting is only undertaken as a last resort. We take no pleasure in having to turn our weapons away from the imperialist enemy onto young Irishmen, who have, for whatever reason, turned to crime.
> Other forms of deterrent are used by us in dealing with the problems posed by the 'hoods'. However, our policy is one of trying to persuade young people that their criminal actions are in a majority of cases a consequence of the repressive and deprived society they have grown up in.

> We point out to them that their actions only further increase the suffering resulting from poverty, bad housing and unemployment, discrimination, etc. already so widespread within the Nationalist community, and we explain how the British State makes use of their criminality as a counter-revolutionary force in opposition to the national liberation struggle . . .
>
> Unhappily, in spite of the methods we already employ, the ongoing debate we have with youth and our actively seeking new and effective alternatives, we are forced on occasions to make use of the weapons of physical punishment.

Such physical punishment may well include death. On 22nd April, 1982, the Provisional IRA shot dead a 19-year-old man; the Republican Press Centre issued the following statement as justification:

> In spite of repeated warnings, and having been punished last year, Devlin continued to engage in armed robberies, hijackings and the physical intimidation of the nationalist community.

The sentence of death may well seem excessive for the crime, in the context of the kinds of punishment such crimes might attract from the State Judicial system in Northern Ireland, but perhaps this is a feature of such unofficial justice. A more common form of punishment which has attracted much media attention is 'knee capping', (shooting through the knee), although other lesser forms of punishment are also used, such as forms of community service or curfew. Morrissey and Pease draw our attention to parallels that can be seen to exist between the 'official' system and the 'black' system. These include the determination of sentence, taking into account the severity of the offence, the recognition of mitigating factors, and prior offences.

The above draws together a number of different issues related to the notion of terrorism. Its illegality is often related to its denial of the legitimacy of the State and its processes. The development of alternative structures of justice is clearly an element in that denial, where its very illegality serves to reinforce the inadequacy of the state. Not only does it serve the terrorist group in maintaining control over its community, but it also, therefore, directly challenges the regime against which the terrorism is directed.

Political Terrorism

Whilst we can identify various kinds of terrorism, its essence, as it seems to impinge on us and worry us, lies above all in its political aspirations and relationship with violence. These things together seem to constitute its particular power. It is widely assumed that a vital quality of this aspiration has its origins in psychological mechanisms, rather than physical action[28]. However, the mechanisms that might be involved remain obscure, and analyses rarely extend beyond the level of speculation. Wardlaw[29] seeks to refine our notions in this context by distinguishing between political terror and political terrorism. In his view, the essential difference between them lies in their relationship to an expressed policy of political change. *Political terrorism* he characterises as a sustained and organised policy employing terror of some form within an ideological context. *Political terror* in contrast occurs as isolated acts, perhaps in the form of indiscriminate or arbitrary violence. The distinction between the two is useful, but is essentially *post hoc*, requiring the recognition of links between events, often on the part of the perpetrators of those events. It may well also be the case that political terror becomes political terrorism in this sense through the process of media (or other) incrementation.

A perhaps more useful way of developing our understanding is to explore the three sub-types of political terrorism identified by Wilkinson[30], sub-revolutionary, revolutionary and repressive terrorism. *Sub-revolutionary Terrorism* describes terrorism aimed at the production of limited change, designed perhaps to force a government to change its policy on particular issues, or to punish a public official or agency for some action. The damage to property that has characterised the Welsh Nationalist protesters in the United Kingdom, for example, might fall within this category. Groups such as *Meibion Glyndwr* (Sons of Glyndwr) and *Cadwyr Cymru* (Defenders of Wales)[31] have claimed responsibility for a series of arson attacks on holiday cottages in rural Wales in the period 1979 to 1986. Up to 1986, over eighty attacks, of increasing sophistication, have been carried out in protest against the summer use by visiting urban English people of second-home holiday property in Wales. Such arson attacks have not yet injured anyone and can best be seen as a protest aimed at changing the planning process that allows the purchase of second homes and at deterring the purchase of second homes. It is in a sense a 'single cause' protest, although it should be noted that it exists in the context of much broader notions of Welsh nationalism, and the value of the Welsh language. It has a very real social basis which, for those communities involved, is very important. It addresses the issue of the lack of availability of local housing (resulting from holiday homes) for local people and the consequent depopulation of rural villages.

However, terrorism that at any one particular time addresses limited issues, such as the above, might also become part of a more coherent and extensive programme of political change, when the limited objectives fail to be reached, or if they are reached and other more ambitious objectives become possible. Where this is the case, it represents a second form of political terrorism, *Revolutionary Terrorism*. Wilkinson defines this as the use of 'systematic tactics of terroristic violence with the objective of bringing about political revolution'. It is characterised by a number of attributes: it is essentially a group activity, rather than an individual acting on his own; the actions are informed and justified by a revolutionary ideology; leadership functions are exercised within the group; and as the terrorist campaigns develop, an alternative political structure develops to organise and direct its actions, and to plan actions in relation to the terrorist's ultimate goals. An important attribute of political revolutionary terrorism, as defined here, is its emphasis on organisation and that organisation's alertness to the consequences of its actions in furthering the movement's objectives. The activities of the Provisional IRA in Northern Ireland, for example, clearly fall within this category, given its sophisticated alternative political and social structures (as illustrated, for example, by Morrissey and Pease[32]), and its associated political wing, Sinn Fein.

The third form of political terrorism identified by Wilkinson is *Repressive Terrorism*. This is characterised by the systematic suppression of individuals or activities regarded as undesirable. We have already noted what might be regarded as an example of this within the context of the Provisional IRA's activities in the area of criminal justice. But this form of terrorism seems to be most obviously evident in state activity, and might be thought to be an important element in what has already been referred to as State Terrorism. In this sense, it is often characterised by the use of specialist units to undertake the repressive measures—the *Tonton Macoutes* in pre-1986 Haiti or the SS of Nazi Germany in the Second World War.

Revolutionary and Repressive Terrorism

The interrelationship between repressive terrorism and revolutionary terrorism has already been noted, and clearly both can exist together *within* the same organisation. In this context, it is not really possible to separate coercive enforcement as a means of controlling society from its consequences. Skinner[33] has drawn our attention in psychological terms to the by-products of 'aversive' or coercive control, and Cronbag[34] has discussed this issue, from the State's perspective, in the context of the law as an instrument of aversive control. 'The aversive stimuli . . . generate emotions, including predispositions to escape and retaliate'. Coercive action may control, but it also has inevitable consequences, often expressed in emotional terms. Thus repressive control itself can be one of the contributing factors in the development of violence and perhaps revolutionary terrorism.

Indeed, in psychological terms, it might even be asserted that attempts at coercive control will almost always result in some form of aggressive consequence in the recipient of the control. It is well established that relatively limited physical or verbal provocation is capable under some circumstances of producing aggression. Because aggression is often met with aggression, this may well result in escalation of aggression on both sides. To help us understand this, the psychological process of *attribution*[35] is important. There is good experimental evidence to show that when we are subject to provocation, even in a mild form, we seek to attribute reasons for that provocation to the person causing the provocation. Where attribution is related to external factors, such as accident or conditions beyond the control of the person concerned, then we react with low levels of violence. On the other hand, if we attribute internal factors to the cause of such provocation, such as intention, then we tend to react with violence and anger. We can see this process at work in many examples of the use of force to effect social control, whether by terrorist or state use of force.

Chapter 5 discusses some of the psychological features that might characterise extreme behaviour, and draws attention in particular to the rigidity and focused nature of terrorist views. Given such a particular perspective, the contributory factor of repressive terrorism to the development of further terrorism through the process of attribution cannot be underestimated. The consequences of such aversive and coercive control (aversive stimuli referred to above) can be profound and important.

Wilkinson's suggested categorisation of kinds of terrorism is undoubtedly useful. A given terrorist act, however, may not necessarily fit within one of the various categories, and in particular when looking at the *effects* of terrorism, confusion can exist between revolutionary and repressive terrorism. A source for such confusion can arise if the creation of repressive terrorism is itself an objective of revolutionary terrorism (as indeed it might well be). Indeed, in some respects, this may well be the obverse of the process described above, and may also be amenable to explanation in terms of attribution.

The above discussion of attribution factors may have particular relevance in the analysis of the effects of the security forces when working in terrorist environments. Most of the work undertaken by the Police, for example, is of an essentially personal nature, even when undertaken in difficult or hostile environments (see Taylor[36]). Whilst we tend to think of the actions of the security services in terms of large-scale activities as in public order situations, most police work is conducted either by an individual or, at the most, a small group, and involves interaction with members of the public. If we consider the process of attribution referred to above, provocation offered by a householder whose house is being searched by the police, which is attributed by the police officers to deliberate intention to offend or injure, may well result in a response of aggression by the police officer. The control of effects like this represents one of the greatest challenges to police work in difficult environments.

We can see evidence of the same process at work in broader social contexts. This is particularly evident in Northern Ireland. The provocative killings of security force personnel in the presence of their families, (members of the Royal Ulster Constabulary or the Ulster Defence Regiment), a not unusual feature of Provisional IRA activity in Northern Ireland, seems designed to engender, amongst other things, aggression in the security forces through the process of attribution. Unless there is careful management of the situation, an unending spiral of escalating violence can ensue, which only serves the terrorists' ends. A similar process (with probably a similar intention) can also be seen in the way the Basque terrorists selectively victimise the Spanish Police.

An example of the very effective use of terrorism to goad and produce repressive terrorism on a broad scale can be seen in the actions of the Cypriot terrorists during the 1950s in their efforts to remove British forces. Assassination of British soldiers produced reprisals against the population, which both served to radicalise the Cypriots, and attract international attention. The terrorist organisation, EOKA (*Ethniki Organosis Kyprion Agoniston*), was never a serious military threat to the British Forces, but the consequences in political terms of the escalation of violence were quite profound, and materially contributed to the eventual departure of the British Administration. Indeed, informed observers have suggested that the success of EOKA in fact lay less with its own actions, and more with the failure of the British Authorities to actively follow measures against EOKA. Of course, this analysis is partial, and omits the importance of the international political situation at that time, and the particular domestic issues faced by the British Government. It does illustrate, however, the potency of repressive action on the part of the State in paradoxically contributing to the change it is designed to prevent, given the right circumstances.

Terrorism, Warfare and Legitimacy

The notion of warfare, its attributes and legitimacy, is one of the important elements of ambiguity in analyses of terrorism. If terrorism is a legitimate form of warfare, as is often claimed in some circumstances, then it might be argued that its legitimacy, in some sense, extends to the overall conflict of which terrorism is an aspect. Terrorism, for many people, contrasts with commonsense notions of warfare. These probably reflect the dominant technology of the time, and assume State protagonists; memories of the past two World Wars, for example, probably condition Europeans to a notion of warfare reflecting those conflicts.

What do we mean by warfare? Perhaps the first point to make is that in the context in which we are discussing it, the term 'war' is often used as a label, in the same way that 'terrorism' is. War has certain implicit connotations (principally legitimacy) which can on occasions confuse and mislead. If however we pursue what we mean by war further, we will see that terrorism can, in fact, be argued to be a form of warfare. One of the most influential thinkers in this respect is the military theorist, Clausewitz[37]. In his treatise 'On War', his analysis of 'What is War?' has been enormously influential in shaping both conventional and revolutionary concepts of warfare. It led him to two assertions about the nature of war which are probably as relevant now as they were in the nineteenth century. The first is '. . . war . . . is an act of violence intended to compel our opponent to fulfill our will . . .'. The second assertion is '. . . War is a mere continuance of policy by other means.'

These ideas greatly influenced Engels and Marx, and subsequently Lenin, and have permeated contemporary thinking about both conventional and unconventional warfare. Indeed, Lenin quoted the latter of those two assertions adding the parenthesis . . . i.e. violent . . . to read 'war is a continuance of policy by other (i.e. violent) means'. He also noted that war seems more 'warlike', the more political it is. Mao Tse-Tung similarly extended Clausewitz, in his assertion that military activity is subordinate to its political objectives. 'War cannot for a single moment be separated from politics . . . politics is war without bloodshed, while war is politics with bloodshed'[38].

The logic of terrorism is of course entirely consistent with these views about warfare. As we have noted, terrorism is the explicit use of violence to further political ends and, by these accounts, so is warfare. Terrorism may be seen, therefore, in these terms, as a form of warfare and the rhetoric of the terrorist, which frequently seeks justification for acts of violence in terms of the logic of warfare, appears to be accurate at one level.

A significant difference between the 'model' of war envisaged by Clausewitz and our concept of terrorism, however, (and probably one shared by most lay observers), is that warfare is something which takes place *between States* in pursuit of their objectives. Furthermore, there is a sense in which such State wars are 'symmetrical'; technically sophisticated armies match other sophisticated armies. Clausewitz makes reference to 'reciprocal actions'[39] which implies either some measure of equivalence on the part of the protagonists, or the development of measures to achieve equivalence. Such equivalence, along with other issues becomes a critical issue in achieving victory. In the main, this does not characterise terrorism as warfare. The terrorist is rarely in a position of superiority in any military sense, and indeed, paradoxically this may be one of his greatest strengths, giving him flexibility, and relatively low financial commitments.

We can see in this one of the more important ways of distinguishing terrorist aggression from warfare. We can also see that in another sense, Clausewitz's analysis does not help in the conduct of 'warfare' against terrorism. Where war has '. . . the compulsory submission of the enemy to our will [as] the ultimate object . . .'[40], this may be difficult to achieve in the case of the terrorist where his identity may not be known, or where he is so well hidden within a community. Who then is the enemy? How do we identify him? Who, then, is to be subjected? In this case, the war solution of subjection fails to achieve political ends unless pursued to its ultimate limits (which may perhaps be genocide) and, indeed, where attempted, even in a lesser way, might radicalise paradoxically an otherwise uncommitted community.

There is a broadly held assumption that a State has the prerogative of employing war as an instrument of policy, in the same way that it generally claims the monopoly of the use of force in the maintenance of its internal affairs. Implicit in this assumption is the notion of legitimacy in some sense. Allied to this concept of legitimacy is the notion that States conform to broadly accepted rules or 'norms' in their exercise of force. These have been expressed with respect to warfare in the 4th Geneva Convention of 1949, for example, where the deportation of individuals or groups, for whatever reason, the taking of hostages, torture, unjustified destruction of property, collective punishment and reprisals, outrages against personal dignity, discrimination on the basis of race, nationality, religion or politics, are all forbidden as acts of war. The terrorist, who is almost by definition unrepresentative, lacks that legitimacy, and on these grounds alone might be said not to be able to claim his actions as 'warfare'. This lack of legitimacy in warfare is also enhanced by the terrorist's frequent focus on his own State, and his aspiration to influence the internal political processes of that state through violence. By definition, the terrorist does not obey the rules of war, through non-combatant bombing, taking hostages, sectarian attacks, and the like. These illegitimate features of the terrorist's claim to be conducting a war are all quite critical in our assessment of terrorism within the context of international law.

Unfortunately, the rather obvious logic to the above is undermined by the actions of States themselves. Warfare this century has been distinguished by its disregard of the kinds of rule expressed by the Geneva Convention. This assertion applies as much to post-1949 (the date of the signing of the Convention) as pre-1949. Wilkinson[41] concludes in a discussion of terrorism and the Laws of War that 'even though the laws of war are not entirely defunct, they are so gravely debilitated as to be in danger of expiry'. This gives little confidence for the future.

When we look at the theoretical political context within which the terrorist typically locates himself, we can see that the issue of legitimacy as expressed above is largely meaningless. Revolutionary theories, from which most terrorist movements derive their rationales, to a large extent invert the kinds of assumptions discussed above. In a world where 'ends justify means' the issue of legitimacy is just one more aspect of 'means', to be used or discarded as appropriate. Analysts of terrorism might learn from that!

Pursuit of war ends (and therefore political ends) by revolutionary means is not of course a new phenomenon; contrary to popular belief, terrorist-like attacks and guerrilla warfare are not nineteenth or twentieth-century inventions. Records exist of the use of guerrilla-like tactics by the Emperor Hang in about 3,600 BC, and tactics that we would refer to as terrorist or guerrilla were analysed by Sun Tzu, a Chinese military historian in the sixth century BC. The term 'guerrilla', however, has its origins in the Peninsula war of 1808 to 1814, and in origin, like terrorism, it gained currency in use in the period following the French Revolution.

Guerrilla warfare and terrorism may well have a great deal in common, but we may be able to distinguish between them. A useful definition of guerrilla warfare has been provided by Huntingdon (from Laqueur[42]). 'Guerrilla warfare is a form of warfare by which the strategically weaker side assumes the tactical offensive in selected forms, times and places. Guerrilla warfare is the weapon of the weak ... Guerrilla warfare is decisive only where the anti-guerrilla side puts a low value on defeating the guerrillas and does not commit its full resources to the struggle'. Many terrorist groups would offer justifications for their activities consistent with this definition, and it may be argued that if the distinction between terrorism and guerrilla warfare is real, any difference is only a matter of scale, rather than principle. The rhetoric of terrorism often makes great play with the term 'warfare', which would lend support to this view.

On the other hand, distinctions between guerrilla activity and terrorism are made. The terrorist on the whole is largely anonymous, and operates essentially within clandestine settings; the guerrilla, in contrast, is usually thought to be more open and less clandestine. Inevitably, however, this is not necessarily the case; some of the most infamous terrorists of our time (the Baader-Meinhof terrorists in Germany, for example) were far from anonymous. But certainly, they can be seen to operate clandestinely within an existing society, rather than openly within a 'liberated zone' which might more properly typify a guerrilla group.

Perhaps a more significant distinction might be made in terms of the size of the operating unit. The terrorist group is usually small, and because of the nature of the environment in which it works, it must operate in even smaller units; the guerrilla acts more like an informal but conventional army where the operational units are large. Unfortunately, however, this again is not necessarily the case. The Vietcong, for example, might be thought of as a typical guerrilla army. It certainly operated in large units, not unlike a regular army; indeed, the principal difference between the Vietcong and a more normal army lay in its tactics, rather than organisation. But other groups, commonly referred to as guerrillas, have been much smaller. EOKA, the Cypriot group that was active in gaining the independence of Cyprus, rarely operated in units of more than eight or ten men.

A more significant difference is that the guerrilla takes as his principal target the armed forces and security services of the country in which he is active. Whilst inevitably, civilians may become involved, the principal target remains the State's defence forces. In a sense, therefore, in conflicts of this kind we might expect to see some evidence of Clausewitz's 'reciprocity' and relative equivalence in the dynamic of the opposing forces. It might be argued that the terrorist is not focused primarily on the security services, and regards the civilian as an appropriate target, regardless of links with the security services. Again however, particular circumstances seem to question this distinction. More deaths were caused amongst Cypriots by the EOKA guerrillas in Cyprus than amongst the British Army; more Africans than whites were killed by the Mau Mau in Kenya.

Other distinctions may be made in terms of rural and urban activity, the latter representing terrorism, the former guerrilla warfare. This distinction may be useful, insofar as it draws our attention to the extent to which the environment may be seen to condition the nature of insurgency.

A further area where a distinction is sometimes made is in terms of respect for the rules of conflict. The terrorist often displays a callous disregard for innocent civilian non-combatants, using them perhaps deliberately as the vehicle for attaining some political end. The guerrilla, in contrast, is often portrayed more like an army, showing respect for the civilian context in which he operates, taking prisoners and so on. If we regard the terrorist as being at the end of a continuum of a dimension of regard for the rules of warfare (showing extreme disregard), we may well locate conventional armies at the other end (showing regard for the rules of combat), with the guerrilla located somewhere in the middle.

This is an attractive notion in many ways. It offers a degree of order to the situation, and it also allows us to express implicitly negative judgements about the terrorist and perhaps the guerrilla (by contrasting them in terms of adherence to 'civilised' rules of conduct with conventional armies and conventional warfare). Like many such convenient analyses, however, it is inaccurate. The leaders of conventional warfare might well express adherence to rules of combat, and indeed, prisoners might be taken and relatively well cared for. But modern warfare, as we have noted above, no more confines itself to the antagonists' armed forces than any guerrilla or terrorist movement does. Indeed, a striking tendency of modern warfare has been the increase in civilian casualties in proportion to military casualties. Saturation bombing of cities like Coventry and Dresden in the Second World War, and the nuclear bombing of Nagasaki and Hiroshima seem to offer poor precedents for conventional warfare's respect for the civilian.

Indeed, we might note that the scale of violence inflicted against civilian populations in the Second World War, especially arising out of saturation bombing, exceeded by an enormous factor the scale of casualties produced by any contemporary non-State terrorist incident. In Chapter 2, we discussed the inappropriateness of the term 'terror' when used to characterise the public response to contemporary terrorism. Terror, however, seems to be a very appropriate term to apply to this scale of attack against targets known to have no military or economic significance.

Some authors have drawn terrorism and guerrilla warfare together by seeing them as related developments in the process of achieving social change through violent means. Thus terrorism is regarded as a step in the escalation of revolution, which itself results in the development of guerrilla warfare[43]. In this respect, we again see terrorism and guerrilla warfare as merely an element of the extension of war as a means of achieving political change.

The historical context to the notion of guerrilla warfare noted above is a specific example of the more general issue of the role of violence and fear in the production of political change. Although we can identify ancient antecedents, the sense in which contemporary terrorism is associated with violent political change most probably has its origins in the French Revolution of 1789. Although the revolution itself owed little to 'terrorism' in the sense that we might recognise it, as the revolution developed, the role of 'terror' became increasingly more important in the maintenance and consolidation of social control. Opponents of the regime (either actual, or 'class' opponents such as aristocrats) were ruthlessly hunted and executed, in order to maintain the revolution. As Robespierre said, it was necessary to 'force men to be free', a familiar enough sentiment in contemporary terrorist and revolutionary rhetoric. However, we should note that, as a model for the *development* of large-scale revolution (as indeed the French Revolution has served), terrorist-like activity seems to have little role.

Indeed, the inappropriateness of 'terror' in the initiation of revolution was recognised by both Marx and Engels, and subsequently Lenin. (We might note that this view was not necessarily shared by all revolutionary theorists of the time, notably Kropotkin[44].) The social and repressive political consequences of terrorism certainly were thought to have a role in the execution of revolution once resistance had begun, but terrorism, as such, was not regarded as having a causal role. Interestingly, however, State Terrorism was recognised as having a role to play in setting the conditions for revolution.

Contemporary revolutionary theorists no longer share these views. Since the Second World War, experience in Cuba, China and Iran have all tended to shift the emphasis of political theorists on terrorism away from consolidation to initiation of revolution, and such theorists have increasingly seen terrorism as part of the developmental process of revolution. Mao Tse-Tung[45], for example, has proposed a three stage theory of revolutionary warfare characterised by a stage of preparation, a stage of establishment of a guerrilla movement which expands to control increasingly large areas, and finally a stage of transition from guerrilla bands to armies capable of defeating the 'occupying' armies.

Terrorism has a part to play in Stage 1 by destroying confidence in the Government's capacity to exercise control, thereby making it possible for a guerrilla army to recruit with some semblance of potential success. It also has a part to play in Stage 2, by both consolidating the destruction of confidence and by offering an example of how blows against the government can be struck with limited resources. Terrorism also can be used to destroy local opposition to the development of guerrilla forces. Thus terrorism is an essential element in Mao Tse-Tung's concept of revolutionary progress.

Experiences in Cuba, as described by Debray[46], further developed Mao Tse-Tung's concept of the relationship between terrorism, guerrilla activity and revolution. Debray places much greater emphasis on the role of a committed nucleus of revolutionaries, who lead rather than facilitate. Citing his mentor, he says that 'Fidel Castro says simply that there is no revolution without a vanguard'[47] and it is the task of that vanguard both to develop the circumstances for revolution and to facilitate and consolidate it when it develops. In a sense, that vanguard is a terrorist group.

These ideas have greatly influenced the contemporary political terrorist, who thereby sees a rationale for his actions in the writings of Mao Tse-Tung and Debray. Whilst both have written about their own experience of successful revolution, thus far these ideas when applied to contemporary European or American society seem largely to have failed. Facilitating links between terrorism and the development of revolution may well be a theory on which some terrorist movements draw to legitimise their actions. It may be an aspiration to guide participants, but experience seems to suggest that such links, if they exist, are somewhat tenuous. Broader guerrilla warfare, for example, has not been a consequence of the terrorist activity in Germany in the 1960s and 1970s, nor indeed in Northern Ireland or the Basque country.

Of course, in particular settings, the distinction between guerrilla warfare and terrorism becomes very difficult to make. Are the Provisional IRA involved in guerrilla warfare in Northern Ireland? They regard members of the security services as legitimate targets, but they do not confront the security services in battles in the sense that the Vietcong, for example, fought the United States Armed forces in Vietnam, or the partisans, on occasions, fought the Nazi forces in Europe and Russia in the Second World War. They show, therefore some of the attributes of a guerrilla force, but not others. In targeting an occupational group who are predominantly (but not exclusively) Protestant, they also serve to sustain sectarian ends, at any rate as perceived by the Protestant community in Northern Ireland. Their victims, however, are not confined to members of the security services, nor do the Provisional IRA appear to be particularly concerned at placing civilians at risk. As with all such analyses, however, the particular circumstances and historical context of Northern Ireland must be taken into account[48].

The Role of the Media

Terrorist groups are often small, and rarely can be said to command popular support. Indeed, in the liberal democracies it may be asserted that the terrorist group *by definition* does not command popular support (as evidenced by its failure to gain popular representation); other means of obtaining power would be available if this was the case. This is a striking problem for Sinn Fein, the political wing of the Provisional IRA, for example, who have consistently failed to achieve electoral success on any significant scale in either Northern Ireland or the Republic of Ireland. It is worth noting that the terrorist may not regard this as a problem, for the revolutionary rhetoric of terrorism often rejects the legitimacy of the democratic process. Yet in the light of this, a problem faced by any terrorist group is the propagation of its ideas *and* the mobilisation of popular support to further develop social change. Repressive terrorism may play an important part in the strategy of gaining such public support in its effects on the community in which the terrorist operates, or which he aspires to represent, but the facility most readily available to achieve this is the media. The media, as the 'oxygen of terrorism', is a real force in directing and sustaining terrorist action.

Given the importance of the media in publicising terrorist actions, and its apparently inevitable focus on violence, widespread dissemination of terrorist ideas and propaganda can be relatively easily achieved. The Weathermen, a small splinter group in the United States of the Students for a Democratic Society, attained enormous publicity for their cause through bombings in the environs of the Pentagon and the Capitol. The massive media attention they attracted even extended to placing an article opposite the editorial page of the *New York Times*. They attained widespread media coverage and their message was undoubtedly widely dispersed; but they failed to achieve any significant degree of popular support. One reason for this may be that their actions failed to elicit large-scale repressive change in American Society.

The role of the media may indeed be of enormous importance in understanding terrorism. It has been argued that an essential attribute of the terrorist is his violence; but it is also clear that in most cases, such characteristic violence is not random. Rather, it is clearly specific and directed and as such, it may be argued to be a form of communication. By its very nature it is intimately dependent upon the media. Thus to see the media as the *arena* in which terrorism is performed may be a helpful way of conceptualising the issue and in helping us to understand the nature of terrorist action.

From this perspective, we can identify and distinguish the terrorist from others who use violent acts, as one who uses violent communication strategies (Schmid and De Graaf[49]). For violence to become terrorist violence, therefore, it needs witnesses, provided and mediated by what we loosely term the media (television, newspapers, radio, etc.); the Chinese proverb 'Kill one, frighten ten thousand' seems particularly appropriate in this respect. In this context, therefore, the victim and the enemy are not identical, and this lack of identity may well constitute one of the important attributes of the modern terrorist.

The actions of the Palestinian terrorists seem well suited to this analysis. They, more than any other terrorist group, have deliberately developed strategies aimed at effecting and influencing media coverage. One of the most significant terrorist actions which illustrates the role and uses of the media by Palestinian terrorists was the hijacking of the three airliners and 276 passengers in September, 1970. This event attracted enormous media attention, with press and television reporters from all over the world attending Dawson's Field in Jordan, the scene of the hijacking. The press conference organised with the hostages and the blowing up of the aircraft, were viewed by many millions of television viewers throughout the world. They had an enormous effect on the public awareness and knowledge of the Palestinian problem and of the particular terrorist group involved (the Popular Front for the Liberation of Palestine). A later statement by Bassam Abu Sherif, a local Popular Front leader, illustrates the logic behind this action: 'It was a direct assault on the consciousness of international opinion. What mattered most to us was that one pays attention to us'.

An even greater act of horror, which nevertheless seems to have been explicitly aimed at generating media coverage, was the attack, and subsequent taking of hostages, on the Israeli team at the Munich Olympic Games in 1972. Eleven Israeli athletes were taken hostage by eight Black September Palestinian terrorists in a drama played out in front of an estimated 800 million spectators. In perhaps the first effective use of the global capacity of satellite broadcasting, negotiations for the release of the hostages were set against the release of 200 Palestinians in detention. It seems likely, however, that the release of the detainees was never a high priority, with influencing opinion and gaining media coverage being much more important. In military terms, the action was a failure, for five terrorists were killed, and three captured. The overt 'demands' of the terrorists were also not met, in that the detainees were not released and, indeed, the eleven athletes were killed. But in the terms set by the terrorists themselves, this rated as an enormous success, because of its effectiveness in gaining publicity.

Drawing attention to the role of the media complements the analysis given in this chapter. In terrorist violence we see a complex series of interrelated actions on political and public processes. These effects are focused and developed by the media, and control of the media will clearly serve to control the broader public effects of terrorist action. The use of this by States subjected to terrorism can be seen very clearly in the way in which the German authorities managed the news, and the subsequent reporting of events, of the kidnapping of Hanns Martin Schleyer, a German businessman, in September, 1977. Members of the Baader-Meinhof group not in prison sought to obtain the release of Andreas Baader, Gudrun Ensslin and nine other detained group members. Herr Schleyer was kidnapped in an attempt to force the German authorities to negotiate. However, the Government held its ground and did not negotiate, imposing instead a news blackout. The terrorists sent some 140 communications to more than thirty-six media outlets, most of which failed to reach the public.

There was no wave of public pressure to negotiate the release of Herr Schleyer, and in these terms, the news blackout was clearly a success. The German Government held firm and resisted the terrorist's demands. Unfortunately for Herr Schleyer, it may well be that the very success of the Government's resistance to negotiation cost him his life, for after forty-five days of captivity, he was killed. Such is the risk of resistance to the demands of hostage takers.

Concluding Comments: A Form of Definition

The above discussion has largely centred around the nature of terrorism. In that discussion, the importance of the political context of terrorism is apparent. The term 'Political Terrorism' has been used to describe the kinds of actions that are of principal interest, and within that broad category, what Wilkinson refers to as Revolutionary Terrorism seems to be the area of most relevance. As a perspective from which to view terrorism, the attribute of violent political act is helpful in developing our understanding. However, the complexity of the issue cannot be overstressed. Our efforts to identify simple criteria to describe and identify both terrorist actions and effects are clearly ineffective, and we should note Schmid's[50] comment that:

> ... we cannot offer a true or correct definition of terrorism. Terrorism is an abstract phenomenon of which there can be no real essence which can be discovered or described.

It has to be accepted that the boundaries of definition of the concept of terrorism are blurred.

Given the discussion in Chapters 2 and 3, however, we can, after Schmid[51], identify a number of features of terrorism in the sense that we are concerned with, that are important and which assist in our recognition of the problem. These features, in one sense, constitute a form of definition, in that they provide attributes to help us both to describe and to categorise. But we should note that not all the features we will describe need obtain in any given situation for an event to be termed terrorist. Indeed, given the discussion of terrorism in this and Chapter 2, it would seem inappropriate to attempt to create an all-embracing definition. A series of descriptive features has the advantage of flexibility in use, and breadth, and can accommodate the inherent ambiguity of terrorism.

A terrorist action involves *violence*, or *force*, or *threat* of force as a *method of combat* directed towards some *political* end. That end is normally but not necessarily expressed as the action of a *non-state group* or *organisation*, and may be achieved through *coercion, extortion, intimidation*, or *induction of compliance* in some area of policy, addressed to either a government, organisations or third parties. It is essentially *criminal* in character, using the *publicity* generated by its acts as a potent weapon. In the public perception of the event *fear, apprehension* or *terror* is emphasised, through actual or potential *threat*. The threat intended is the result of *purposive, planned, systematic*, and *organised* action, where the threat is expressed in terms of *extranormality*, and is *in breach of accepted rules without humanitarian constraints*. The violent actions undertaken by terrorists are often *repetitive*, or *serial in character*, and a critical element of the choice of action is *victim-target differentiation*, where *civilians, noncombatants, nonresisting, neutrals, or outsiders* are the principal *victims*. Terrorist action shows an *arbitrary, impersonal*, and *random* character, where *indiscriminateness* in the choice *innocent victims* is emphasised. Through its *clandestine* or *covert* nature, *incalculability, unpredictability*, and the *unexpectedness* of occurrence of violence constitutes an important feature (after Schmid[52]).

This rather lengthy description of terrorism serves to draw attention to the most critical and fundamental attribute of terrorism, which is the use of violence, or threat of violence, by the terrorist to achieve political ends. Furthermore, that violence is expressed as the action of some kind of organisation. This latter point is an important one to make, for it allows us to distinguish between the occasional acts of violence of individuals against society (or other individuals) and acts undertaken by some form of political movement. That there may well be difficulties from time to time in making this distinction does not diminish its significance. The other features which are noted above are all, in a sense, subsidiary to these characteristics. Drawing attention to them in this way, however, enables us to recognise in the complexity of events, those aspects that we should focus on in using the term terrorism.

Psychological Approaches

The previous chapters have been primarily concerned with the attributes and nature of terrorist action and have enabled us to clarify the concept of terrorism. The individual who undertakes that action has so far received relatively little attention. There is little point in attempting to examine the psychological features of the terrorist, until we can say with some certainty what terrorism is. A major difficulty with our undertaking is of course now apparent—there is no single essential attribute. What our examination has revealed is a multitude of attributes, focusing around violence and political change, but having very little else in common.

Whilst the terrorists' actions may be varied, we have identified some features of the way in which we describe terrorism that shows consistency. In particular, we have noted that our use of the concept of terrorism often draws on a notion of 'specialness', perhaps as an attempt to try to make some sense out of an inherently ambiguous concept. In particular, Chapters 2 and 3 have presented evidence to suggest that the 'specialness' that we so often try to ascribe to terrorism is probably inappropriate. This is an important point to make, for as we have seen, that assumption of specialness can influence not only the way we think about it, but also the way in which we act.

We can develop this issue further, however if we examine terrorism from a more personal perspective; so far, our discussion has in the main been concerned with 'terrorism'; we must now examine the 'terrorist'. In the next two chapters, we continue the line of argument presented so far, by examining two often held assumptions about the nature of the terrorist. Through looking at the notion of the terrorist as someone who is mentally ill, and as someone regarded as a fanatic, we progress in Chapters 6 and 7 to attempting to develop some understanding of why, in psychological terms, he might commit the acts that he does.

CHAPTER 4

Terrorism and Mental Health

We have seen in the earlier chapters that the attributes which we use to identify terrorism are often inconsistent. The boundaries are necessarily fuzzy, and although problems like this do not necessarily reduce the importance of the concept, nor its utility, they do provide a caution against promiscuous use.

When we come to examine the individuals who commit terrorist acts, we encounter problems of a similar kind. Because terrorist acts are apparently unnecessarily violent, we seek an understanding of the people who commit them in terms of explanations that set them apart from other people. Because terrorist acts are unusual, we assume that people who commit them are also unusual. Two broad categories of explanation are used to do this: the terrorist as someone who is ill, and the terrorist as fanatic. In this and the next chapter, we will examine these concepts.

Terrorist acts are often abhorrent, and we try to understand them in terms of the abnormality of the individual perpetrating the act. This is a very powerful explanation of terrorism, that has wide currency. Whilst much psychological research in this area has also shown this influence, another approach has been to emphasise the terrorist's rational qualities, the cool, logical planning individual whose rewards are ideological and political, rather than financial[1]. It is easy to see why these views have predominated. We are rarely in a position to consider terrorism outside the context of some horror or other, and inevitably, we focus on the violent consequences of the act, rather than its other features. The view of the terrorist as mentally ill seems to reflect a concern with the events and outcomes of terrorist action; the notion of the terrorist as fanatic reflects a concern with violence and perhaps a preoccupation with the terrorists' sometimes sophisticated rhetoric and political analysis. Both of these views can be seen to have a common basis in that they draw on notions of 'specialness' again, and try to separate out the terrorist and his actions, from those of other people.

Mental Illness

The notion that the terrorist is in some sense mentally ill is one that has wide currency. The acts committed by the terrorist are in a sense extra-normal. They are unusual in our society, although not unique. However, the nature of the violence, and its expression against symbolic rather than individual targets greatly influences our view, and we feel that the terrorist is not just extra-normal but abnormal. We see his behaviour as patho-logical and therefore he is in some sense mentally ill. By taking this perspective, we also tend to place the terrorist within a clinical context, because in our society this is how we conventionally deal with mental illness. In some ways, views of this kind parallel those held about crime and deviance in general—because these behaviours are out of the ordinary and inflict damage on people and society, the individual undertaking such acts must be in some sense disturbed, and therefore ill. Terms such as psycho-path or sociopath are then used in the case of the terrorist (and in other situations involving less dramatic events) to diagnose and identify the specific features of this presumed abnormal behaviour state.

A characteristic of many terrorist acts which make them very disturbing to us is that they 'break the rules of engagement'. (A better way of expressing this may be to say that the terrorist operates to *different* rules of engagement, for many terrorist acts are suggestive of rule following). We find it very difficult to have much sympathy, for example, for what appears to be the random killing of civilians. Indiscriminate killings are not necessarily a feature of terrorist action, but they do occur from time to time, with worrying regularity. An extreme example of such an apparently indiscriminate and as far as the victims were concerned, motiveless terrorist killing occurred in November, 1986, when Sikh extremists in the north Indian state of Punjab shot dead twenty-four Hindu bus passengers, and wounded eleven others. This incident embodies many of the attributes of terrorism that we find most frightening. Soon after dusk, four Sikh terrorists hijacked a local bus near the village of Khudar in the Hoshiapur district. After ordering the driver to take a side road, the terrorists dragged the Hindu passengers off the bus and machine-gunned them.

This incident seems to be part of the campaign of Sikh extremists to gain independence for a separate Sikh state. There is no suggestion that those killed were in any way active in politics, or in any sense opposed the Sikh extremists' aspirations; it was sufficient that they met the attribute of being Hindu. As far as the victims were concerned, (and indeed as far as the terrorists were concerned) the killings were without any motive in a personal sense. It appears that the twenty-four victims were an incidental part of a campaign to discredit more moderate Sikh leaders and of an attempt to exert political pressure.

Murder on this scale is repulsive to most people, for many reasons.

Whilst we may well have complex and at times inconsistent views on conflict, most of us have grown up in a world where conflict is regulated by broadly accepted rules—The Marquis of Queensberry Rules, The Geneva Convention—which seek to place limits on the extent and focus of conflict. Innocent bus passengers are not usually thought to be participants in conflicts, nor do we expect particular racial or religious groups to be killed for purposes of some distant (to the victim) political manoeuvring. There is, however, as far as the terrorist is concerned, a logic to such acts, which is usually located in some broader political context. The victim is both incidental and instrumental; the ends justifying the means.

A somewhat similar example of ruthless and apparently motiveless killing can be seen in the death of three church officials at Darkley, Northern Ireland, in November, 1983. Two hooded gunmen broke into the Mountain Lodge Pentecostal Church in Darkley, Co. Armagh, during the Sunday evening service. Two church elders welcoming late-comers were immediately killed as the gunmen burst into the church, firing from the hip at the congregation. Another elder was killed, sprawled beside the plain wooden altar. The Pastor of the Church, Bob Baines was reported as saying: 'We had almost finished the opening hymn when one of the congregation came staggering down the aisle bleeding from gunshot wounds. We thought we'd heard shots over the singing. He staggered and fell and the gunmen came in spraying bullets everywhere. People have been brutally murdered in a place of worship'. About twenty-four young children were thought to be in the Church at the time.

The only apparent motive for this incident seems to be sectarian. This was a protestant congregation in a predominantly Roman Catholic area. Responsibility for the incident was claimed by a hitherto unknown group called the Catholic Reaction Force, but forensic evidence from spent shell casings scattered around the Church indicated that the weapons used had previously been involved in the murder of two policemen in the neighbour-hood of the Church in 1982 and in two further ambushes of the security forces that year. Those latter incidents had been claimed by the Irish National Liberation Army (INLA)[2] and it is a reasonable assumption that the Catholic Reaction Force was nothing more than a name of convenience for the INLA. The incident took place in the context of a concerted series of attacks against protestants and members of the security forces in the area and presumably had a justification in raising tension and fear amongst the protestant community. Within the particular context of Northern Ireland, the fact that it involved the killing of people at worship adds to the horror, (and of course the effectiveness of intimidation).

The ruthless shooting of twenty-four innocent Hindus in the Punjab, and three Church Officials in Northern Ireland certainly breaks the rules of what we normally regard as acceptable political behaviour. We are inclined to argue that the people who do this kind of thing must be abnormal and mad! The drama and horror of the situations can, however, blind us to a more general point. Failures like those described above to follow 'accepted' norms are not in themselves sufficient grounds for ascription of mental illness to the participants. Indeed, in some contexts (but not those described above) failures to follow accepted rules might be termed 'innovative' or 'creative', and therefore applauded! But the breaking of rules, in the way they occurred in the incidents described above, is very disturbing to us. This is well recognised by the terrorist and provides an important element in his rationale for such actions. He knows that the very fact of his actions not following these accepted rules constitutes one of his major weapons (however this might be legitimised and rationalised by revolutionary theorists, such a Marighella[3]).

Explanations in Terms of Abnormality

A basic problem in looking for explanations of terrorist behaviour in terms of abnormality, or mental illness, lies in the uncertainty that surrounds such concepts. The notion of abnormal behaviour is one fraught with difficulty, and a number of conflicting views on its nature can be identified. However, to understand this issue better, we need to examine what we mean by mental illness, or abnormal behaviour, and to see the extent to which it can be applied to terrorist behaviour.

Four kinds of criteria can be identified by which we might detect abnormal behaviour[4]. One view which has gained wide currency is termed the **statistical view**. Abnormality can be defined, for example, in terms of the statistical incidence of a particular behaviour in the public in general. The incidence of most behaviour states might be seen as varying along a continuum, with few people showing none or very little of a particular behaviour in their everyday lives, and a few people showing an extreme incidence of that behaviour, with most people, somewhere between these two extremes, in the middle. Those people who are at the extremes by this kind of definition might well be labelled as abnormal. (It is important to note that *both* extremes of the distribution merit the term by this view.) If we take violence as an essential characteristic of terrorist behaviour, therefore, we might like to locate the terrorist in the abnormal range because he displays extreme violence.

Abnormality of course is not something that can be identified by reference to a single behavioural or psychological dimension even if we knew what the appropriate dimensions were, and this represents a major weakness of this kind of view. Socially unacceptable acts, like extreme violence, are not regarded as evidence of abnormality in certain circumstances. Warfare condones killing the enemy; an individual is entitled to defend himself against another if he is assaulted. The circumstances, rather than the act itself seems to be the critical thing in this respect.

If we take the excessive use of violence as an essential characteristic of terrorist behaviour, therefore, we might want to locate the terrorist in the abnormal range because he displays violence beyond that which most people might show. In doing so, would we also include others who are involved in occasional extreme violence in one form or another which is sanctioned by society — the military perhaps? Equally, would we want to include the opposite end of that dimension — the pacifist — within the category of abnormal, because he uses no violence, whereas most members of society use some?

Violence is socially unacceptable only in some circumstances, not all. Warfare condones killing the enemy; an individual is entitled to defend himself against another if attacked; in the event of warfare, every citizen may be required to become involved in the armed forces. In thinking about the terrorist in this context, the circumstances are as important an element as the act itself. (We might also feel that there are some absolute standards we might want to bring to bear as well; this approach to abnormality has little or no room for them).

Developing the theme of the importance of circumstances, an alternative approach to the identification of abnormal behaviour can be expressed in terms of a **social definition** of abnormality. This approach emphasises the importance of consensual agreement in the ascription of abnormality, rather than the frequency (or infrequency) of the behaviour. Put simply, this view might be characterised as 'abnormality is whatever society says is mental illness or psychological impairment'. Thus behaviours that violate social norms are likely to be labelled as abnormal. We need to make a number of distinctions here, however. We must first of all distinguish between those rules that we use to judge criminal behaviour and the notion of social norms used in the sense that they are used here. Social norms may well incorporate criminal laws but will probably go beyond them, involving implicit expectations of how people will behave. At least in contemporary secular societies, religious or moral rules which might give rise to expectations about particular kinds of behaviour also tend not to find equivalence in legal expression. Thus, not going to work regularly or having long periods of absence for no physical reason, exhibiting extreme moodiness which is contrary to people's expectations, drinking excessively, not wanting children, are all examples of activities that might break social norms as identified by some sections of society, and therefore might be regarded as abnormal.

A further distinction may also need to be made here between social norms and moral norms. For some sections of the community, moral laws might well acquire the status of social norms, and of course, by this view of abnormality, transgressions of these morally-based norms would also constitute 'abnormality'. Our mental hospitals still contain examples of this use of abnormality, in the unmarried parents or their illegitimate offsprings, who in the early part of this century were committed to mental hospitals in need of moral protection, with the implication that this was in some sense a 'mental' deficiency.

It follows from all of the above that, from this view, someone has to be bothered or concerned about a behaviour for it to be labelled as abnormal, for the social context implies some form of social interaction for the 'abnormality' to become evident. Thus, behaviour which impinges on no one might well not be regarded as abnormal, regardless of what it was. Deviant behaviour, therefore, is defined in relation to the standards of behaviour and expectations of those with whom the individual functions; such standards for a *particular* group within a larger society may appear absolute, but as far as society in general is concerned, such standards may not be absolute.

Sometimes this kind of view is also termed a **relativist** approach, in that normality is a relative, rather than absolute concept. It gains support from anthropological studies, which describe behaviour states which, in their own context, are normal but which, in another cultural context, might be regarded as abnormal. Ambition, for example, might well be regarded as an essential attribute for a 'healthy' person in the modern world, and conversely, someone who shows no ambition, to the point of allowing his economic state to decline dramatically (the drop-out) might well be regarded as abnormal. That these are socially defined qualities can be seen by looking at the Zuni Indians of New Mexico, where ambition in the Western sense is viewed with revulsion and repugnance, and is regarded as 'abnormal'.

The relativist view emphasises conformist and non-absolute qualities and, as such, has received considerable criticism. Many people may want to say that there are absolute standards against which individuals might be judged; they might also perhaps want to distinguish, in a rather more subtle way, between the innovator, the nonconformist, who might make a major contribution to society, and the negative nonconformist who contributes little. We might also want to argue for diversity for its own sake, as a healthy challenge to society.

We also face another kind of problem with this view. Even if we accept the notion of social definition of deviance, how do we deal with someone who has been brought up in, and knows nothing more than, what we might describe as a deviant environment? Or what of the person who deliberately chooses an alternative lifestyle? Is that individual's behaviour abnormal, (as it may be with reference to society in general), or is it normal (as it may be with reference to the society in which he lives or grew up in). This is a very real problem when considering terrorism, in that very often the terrorist rejects the political and also (perhaps necessarily) the social rules of society. He can seek sustenance, justification and legitimacy from the alternative society which he might either create or aspire to.

A third view of abnormality can be developed from a **medical** perspective. The behaviour which we see that troubles us is, by this view, a symptom of some underlying disorder; thus the presence of certain specific symptoms might be said to define abnormality. This view seems to be most appropriate when the abnormal behaviour which we see is the result of some biological disorder. Such *organic* states (like those that might result from brain damage) clearly are best explained in these terms; but problems arise when we consider states that have no clear organic basis. This applies to most of the activities which we might want to label as abnormal. Notions derived from psychoanalytic theories, which emphasise unconscious processes in the control of behaviour, are of this kind. They adopt an essentially medical model of explanation, describing symptoms of hypothesised underlying pathogenic states.

In the main, this approach tends to neglect the importance of the social context in which behaviour might occur. Because in some senses, designation of psychological impairment *is* related to other people's reactions, we clearly need to go beyond the restrictive medical model. This is particularly the case when we seem to be involved in situations where *adjustment* to some life event, or developmental stage, is important. The medically based notion of mental illness does not seem appropriate when we attempt to understand the adolescent's reactions to growing up, for example.

The final approach to the understanding of abnormal behaviour which we need to consider is the **behavioural** approach. This approach is radically different from those described above, in that it views both normal *and* abnormal behaviour as the result of the learning history to which an individual has been subjected. Thus all behaviour is caused by the history of the learning that an individual experiences; the particular qualities of behaviour we encounter reflect the environment to which the individual has been exposed. Deviant behaviour, therefore, is the result of faulty learning experiences. *Why* such deviant behaviour should worry us is another issue, perhaps the result of *our* particular learning experiences. This view is particularly attractive in helping us to understand terrorist behaviour, although it does not particularly help us identify the attributes of those behaviours that worry us. It is an explanation of why a particular behaviour is there, rather than a judgement as to its status with respect to the notion of abnormality.

A simple example will help to clarify this approach. Disruptive behaviour in a classroom, for example, is a common problem in many schools. There are a number of possible explanations of this kind of behaviour, drawing on the models of abnormality discussed above, which are almost always expressed in terms of some underlying cause like loss of a parent or family upset. In contrast, a behavioural approach would examine the situation to identify those events that follow the disruptive behaviour. These events reward, or *reinforce*, the disruptive behaviour; they are responsible for its maintenance and the behaviour will not change until these rewarding events are changed. At first sight, this may seem an unlikely explanation of disruptive behaviour when its only consequence is disapproval in some form from the teacher! But we also know that attention, even if negative, is a very powerful reward for children. In many situations where disruptive behaviours occur, the child is actually being rewarded *by attention for being disruptive*.

The behavioural approach emphasises the role of learning in the development and maintenance of behaviour. The critical element in a situation that produces learning is reward, or reinforcement. Thus, in undertaking a behavioural analysis of any problem, the task is to identify the rewards in the situation that follow the behaviour you are interested in. The approach has many links with the relativist account above, in that one way in which culture or social norms exert their pressure is through the individual learning about them as he grows up.

In general, most commonsense explanations of the abnormality of terrorists lack the sophistication of these different approaches and seem to draw upon notions based upon the medical model. Because the terrorist is a distant and rather shady figure and because he does things which are outside the 'normal' rules of conflict (by inflicting casualties on innocent bystanders, for example), it is very easy for us to seek to explain his actions by making reference to some form of illness that sets him aside from other people and helps, therefore, to 'explain' his unusual acts. We are well used to this kind of explanation, and the trivialising of terms like illness and the inappropriate use of 'psychological' explanations of deviant behaviour which has characterised much criminological thinking over recent years, thereby encouraging the public to place terrorism within the ambit of mental illness. Thus terms like 'sociopath' and 'psychopath' recur in the literature on terrorism.

'Sociopath' and 'Psychopath', and similar terms, present considerable difficulties in understanding as we will see later. They reflect a view of human behaviour that subsumes deviance within a medical, rather than social or behavioural model. We have briefly discussed the significance of this in terms of the concept of abnormality, but we should also note that how we conceptualise the terrorist in this sense may well have implications for members of the security services who are faced with terrorist acts in some form, and the operational strategies they might develop to deal with them. By assuming abnormality, there may well be a temptation to assume equally 'abnormal' strategies are appropriate for dealing with them. But, describing terrorism within a medical framework makes assumptions about motivation, and other factors which may be inappropriate and counter-productive. It also places terrorist behaviour within the context of 'illness' and, as such, somehow outside the normal rules of behaviour and the process of law. Ascription of abnormality can serve to legitimise acts of repression against individuals or communities, which, if committed in other contexts, in themselves would be viewed with abhorrence.

The Legal Context

The relationship between terrorism, the law, and mental illness is important, and we cannot consider the issue of abnormality as an explanation of terrorism without reference to its legal context. In one sense, almost any terrorist act that we notice is by definition a crime, and illegal. However, from a psychological point of view, the significance of the relationship between terrorism, the law and mental illness lies in the extent to which the terrorist can be held responsible in law for his actions. Indeed, we might well add this way of thinking about the 'abnormal' qualities of terrorism to the notions of abnormality discussed above, for it constitutes an important way of analysing terrorism in a social context.

The courts offer a way of determining social norms, as expressed both by the legislature and, in countries whose legal systems are based on that of the United Kingdom, common law. When considering issues related to responsibility, the law applies a test of 'insanity' in circumstances where there may be doubt about the status of a defendant. This is almost exclusively applied as a defence in cases of murder, but could be applied to other crimes.

Common law testing of sanity has been expressed in what are termed the M'Naghten Rules. Daniel M'Naghten was tried for murder in 1843. A jury acquitted him on the grounds of insanity, so that instead of being hanged, he was sent to a psychiatric institution, where he remained until he died some twenty years later. The judges in the trial, whilst noting the presumption of sanity and responsibility for actions, expressed the position as follows: ". . . to establish a defence on the grounds of insanity it must be clearly proved that, at the time of committing the act, the accused was labouring under such a defect of reason, from disease of the mind, as not to know the nature and quality of the act he was doing, or, if he did know it, that he did not know he was doing what was wrong." In legal terms, this may appear to be a relatively clear direction, but in psychological terms, the judgement as to whether someone can 'know the nature and quality' of an act, and whether it is 'wrong' is of course very complex.

Within a legal context, the notion of *intention* is of fundamental importance in both the determination of guilt and the defence of insanity.

Similarly, the notion of intention is important in both the psychological and political analysis of terrorist acts. We have well-developed concepts that limit the extent to which limits on capacity to form judgements amend the ascription of intention in any particular situation. Foremost amongst the limiting factors is that placed on intention by mental illness. Within this context, the legal concept of *mens rea* is a fundamental element in the determination of the guilt of a crime. This is a legal concept addressing what is essentially a psychological problem, and its analysis illustrates the difficulties of interpreting concepts from different perspectives.

In simple terms, *mens rea* refers to the necessary intention associated with an act before guilt can be established; a 'guilty mind' must be established. Quite clearly, the insane or incapable may commit acts which for ordinary people would constitute a crime, but by virtue of the nature of their affliction, we probably would not want to regard them as guilty and deserving of punishment. In a similar context, accidental commission of a crime where negligence is not at issue, would seem to be an inappropriate event to occasion conviction or punishment. The important point to note is that to sustain a conviction for an offence, both *actus reus* (the offence) and *mens rea* (guilty mind) must be established (Cronbag[5]). Placing the terrorist within the context of the mentally ill immediately, of course, raises issues as to *mens rea* in any attempt at prosecution, and by extension, in the way we think about terrorism. The appropriateness, or otherwise, of this in particular cases is, of course, a matter for analysis within that particular context, but, clearly, locating terrorism in general within the ambit of mental health raises this problem.

The problems of recognition of responsibility in terrorism are not confined to the determination of *mens rea* alone. There are circumstances where, because of our uncertainty about the notion of terrorism, there can be other kinds of considerations that lead us to have doubts perhaps about *mens rea*, or even *actus reus*. This can lead to confusion between *intention* and *motivation*. This can be best illustrated with respect to international law, and the notion of extradition for terrorist offences between countries. Hannay (1980) has discussed this issue, and drawn attention to the problems of dealing with terrorism in international extradition treaties.

The principle of exchange of criminals between countries has always been a feature of international relations. Perhaps the oldest known diplomatic document is a peace treaty between Ramesses II and the Hittite prince Hittusli III in 1280 BC, which provided for the exchange of the criminals of one nation found in the territory of the other. Later developments of this concept gradually began to recognise the legitimacy of attempts to gain freedom from oppressive rule and the constraints that this might place on the extradition of a person seeking the freedom of his country. These notions began to develop in something like their modern form during the eighteenth and nineteenth century in Western Europe and were, to a large extent, associated with the development of democracy and the revolutionary movements of those times. A landmark in the development of the concept can be seen in 1855, when a Belgian court denied a French request for the extradition of someone who attempted to bomb the Emperor Napoleon III. Whilst consistent with Belgian law, this decision provoked outrage in its day and led to an amendment of the 1833 extradition law to limit the crimes recognised as political offences, excluding from that category attempts at murder, assassination or poisoning upon the person of the head of a foreign government or of members of his family. This clause, known as the 'attentat clause' has been widely accepted as a limit on the political offence exception, and continues to have force.

Most international treaties providing for the exchange of criminals exclude extradition for 'political offences'; the interpretation of 'political' is however usually left to the courts to decide. The case of Castioni in 1891 has generally been regarded as a guide in this respect in most English speaking common law countries. In this case, the courts decided that however deplorable, cruel or irrational the act, the furthering of a political goal was enough to establish the necessary political *intention* sufficient to avoid extradition. United States courts have appeared to rely on this interpretation in a number of proceedings to deny extradition to the United Kingdom of a particular IRA activist accused of committing bombings in the United Kingdom. An example of this was the case of Joseph Patrick Doherty, a Provisional IRA member who was accused and convicted in the British courts of murder and a number of other serious offences. He escaped from prison two days before his conviction and fled to the United States, from which the British Government sought his extradition. This was denied by the United States courts, on the basis of the political crimes exception.

In contrast to the above, however, rulings subsequent to Castioni on the political offences exception in the United Kingdom have tended to follow another test case established in 1894, where an English court tempered the Castioni ruling, by asserting that violent acts against private citizens rather than political entities cannot be regarded as political offences. In this case the French government were seeking the extradition of a political activist, Meunier, who had carried out bomb attacks on a crowded cafe, and on army barracks. It was ruled that for an act to merit the political offence exception:

> . . . there must be two or more parties in the State, each seeking to impose the Government of their choice on the other.

Meunier was judged to be an anarchist and the enemy of all organised society, and therefore not subject to the political offence exception; he was therefore extradited.

More recently, the apparent enormous increase in terrorist activity especially in an international context, and the problems it presents for the issue of extradition of terrorists, has figured prominently on the political agenda, and efforts have been made to change the legal situation. One notable attempt to do this was the signing of the US–UK Supplementary Extradition Treaty in 1986[6]. This treaty identifies particular crimes that shall not be regarded as of a political character, regardless of the context in which they were undertaken. Thus, aircraft hijacking and sabotage, crimes against internationally protected persons (including diplomats), hostage taking, murder, manslaughter, malicious assault, kidnapping, and specified offences involving firearms, explosives and serious property damage will no longer be exempt from extradition on the grounds of political intention.

The enactment of this Supplementary Treaty has not been without considerable controversy in the United States, illustrating the political and emotional complexity of the issue, which has drawn together civil rights workers, Irish nationalists and others to protest against the measure. The fact that this was a contentious issue and that *political intention* may still remain grounds in some circumstances for denying extradition illustrates the ambivalent position society takes in making judgements about violent terrorist acts.

The ambivalence we have noted above with respect to extradition for terrorist offences is, of course, merely an aspect of the broader ambivalence we feel about terrorism which we noted in Chapter 1. It has received expression on the international stage in the extensive, and ultimately largely fruitless, discussion in the United Nations in 1972 and 1973 on 'measures to prevent terrorism and other forms of violence which endanger or take human lives or jeopardise fundamental freedoms', an attempt at the production of an International Convention on Terrorism. This UN initiative followed the Lod Airport massacre in Tel Aviv, and the death of hostage Israeli athletes at the Munich Olympics, but was largely negated by the insistence of Third World countries who resisted any attempts to limit the forms of violence used by 'liberation movements'. We can see in the debates in the UN around this issue, a clear commitment on the part of some States to the use of war, and unconventional violence, as the expression of politics and national interest.

The Indonesian Representative to the United Nations expressed this as follows:

> . . . A distinction should be drawn between terrorism perpetrated for personal gain and other acts of violence committed for political purposes. Although recourse to violence must ultimately be eliminated from relations between peoples, it must be borne in mind that certain kinds of violence were bred by oppression, injustice, the denial of basic human rights, and the fact that whole nations were deprived of their homeland and their property. It would be unjust to expect such people to adhere to the same code of ethics as those who possessed more sophisticated means of advancing their interests.

We can see expressed in this extract, the denial of guilt for a violent act when that act has a political intention. It would seem that, on occasions, political intention still seems to abrogate *mens rea* and denies *actus reus*.

Psychopathy and Sociopathy

The use of abnormality in the discussion about terrorism clearly presents difficulties. These difficulties become more apparent when we consider what we mean by two terms that are often used to refer to the nature of terrorist's abnormal state—psychopath and sociopath. The two terms refer to similar concepts, and the third edition of the American Psychiatric Association Diagnostic and Statistical Manual (DSM-III)[7] includes the terms 'psychopath', 'sociopath' and also 'antisocial personality' to describe individuals who come into conflict with society because they refuse to conform to established rules of conduct. Cleckley[8] has identified some sixteen characteristics of psychopathic behaviour which include such things as superficial charm and intelligence, poor judgement and failure to learn from experience, lack of remorse or shame, unreliability, insincerity, absence of delusion, pathologic egocentricity and incapacity for love, unresponsiveness in general interpersonal relations, sex life impersonal, trivial and poorly integrated. Violence or aggression in some form is often a feature of their behaviour. Other authors[9] have largely confirmed this listing of the attributes of psychopathy. A feature of the psychopath which is of importance to this discussion is the emphasis placed by many commentators on the apparent absence of guilt or remorse for his actions. This may seem to apply particularly to the terrorist.

The actions of Nezar Hindawi, an Arab terrorist, who sent his pregnant girlfriend on an attempted suicide bombing of an El Al airliner in April, 1986, seems to illustrate aspects of psychopathy as we have described it. Hindawi was a journalist employed in London, who had links with Palestinian organisations. He met his Irish girlfriend, Ann-Marie Murphy, at the Hilton Hotel in London, where she worked as a chambermaid and he stayed as a guest. They became lovers, but Hindawi seemed to have dropped out of her life when she became pregnant. Six months later, however, Hindawi suddenly reappeared, apparently begging forgiveness, and wanting to marry her, and used her pregnancy to persuade her to agree to a quick marriage in Israel. He even appears to have bought her a wedding dress. He also made arrangements for her to travel to Israel, where they would be married within days of her arrival. However, for reasons which remain unclear, these arrangements involved Ann-Marie travelling alone to Israel. Hindawi took Ann-Marie from her home in London by taxi to Heathrow Airport, and saw her check on to Flight 016 to Tel Aviv. He arranged to join her by a later flight.

When passing through the security checks at Heathrow, Ann-Marie was found to be carrying explosives in a false bottom to her hand luggage, luggage supplied by Hindawi. Had she boarded the plane, the bomb would have gone off in mid-flight, killing herself, her unborn baby, and the other 369 passengers. Ann-Marie seems to have known nothing of the attempted plane bombing, and could in no circumstances be regarded as being anything other than an unfortunate and innocent dupe of Hindawi.

Hindawi's actions seem to show clear evidence of what might be termed psychopathy. He had little regard for Ann-Marie's welfare, his own unborn child, or the other passengers on the plane, and appeared to show no remorse or emotion for his actions at his subsequent trial. An unusual feature of this incident which seems to make the term psychopath appropriate is the use by Hindawi of his girlfriend as the vehicle for the bombing. Most terrorist action by definition involves innocents, but usually innocents without any connection to the terrorist; fortunately both for society and for our view of ourselves, the kind of thing Hindawi did is relatively rare.

The concept of 'psychopathy' is one that has a somewhat mixed conceptual status, and not all authorities agree on its usefulness[10]. The main reason for this is that the term seems to depend upon the idea of a cluster of attributes, of which any given individual may have some, but not necessarily all. This inevitably means that the term has both a very broad meaning, and loose usage because of that breadth of meaning. Also because of this, the term psychopath has, on occasions, been used to refer to any antisocial individual who does not fall into any other diagnostic category. (This reveals the dependence on the medical model in thinking about psychopathy, for it clearly makes the assumption that there has to be a recognisable underlying abnormal personality state to correspond to the behavioural 'symptoms'.) However, given the above, there is no necessary reason for psychopathic behaviour to fall within the category of illegal. Indeed, violent acts that show psychopathic attributes may well be more common than we realise or care to notice. The repeated use of excessive physical punishment to discipline children within the family, for example, may well show attributes on the part of the parent that are psychopathic in character, but we may well only do something about them when faced with explicit evidence of physical injury of children. The worrying rising incidence of non-accidental injury amongst children seems to justify concern in this area.

Some characteristics of the terrorist clearly do fall within the above listing of psychopathic attributes, and this has led some authors to concentrate on the relationship between aspects of terrorism and presumed deviant characteristics of the individuals concerned. This is evident in, for example, Lanceley[11] who describes the hostage taker as the Antisocial Personality. The term 'antisocial personality' is related to the concept of psychopathy, and appears in The American Psychiatric Association Diagnostic and Statistical Manual (DSM-III) under the general heading of 'non-psychotic mental disorders'. The term antisocial personality is reserved for individuals who are 'basically unsocialised, and whose behaviour pattern brings them repeatedly into conflict with society.' An important quality is that they are incapable of loyalty to individuals or groups, and are grossly 'selfish, callous, irresponsible, impulsive, and unable to feel guilt or learn from experience'.

Lanceley is able to draw on his experience in the development of hostage negotiation programmes for the FBI to highlight significant features of hostage situations. For example, part of the aetiology of the antisocial personality suggests a role for deviant family relationships, especially with parents. Hostage takers often demand that family members be brought to the scene, but on the basis of knowledge about the characteristics of the antisocial personality, Lanceley suggests that negotiators do not fulfil such requests. Family members, he thinks, may add unpredictable elements because family relationships may well be laden with emotion and therefore complicate the negotiation process.

Another feature of the antisocial personality is his stimulus seeking. The hostage taking situation itself may well be a source of such stimulation, an 'expressive act'. It may well follow, if this analysis is correct, that who ever controls the sources of stimulation in the hostage situation may gain control of it. Thus, the hostage negotiator may be in a position to control the flow of information and stimulation; but it is, of course, important that the negotiator is able to exercise this control, and that the hostage taker does not obtain stimulation from the hostages, either through assault or other abusive acts.

If the typology suggested by Lanceley offers predictive utility, clearly this kind of approach has value. However, not all hostage takers fall within this category, and it may well be positively harmful for the assumption to be made that this kind of approach characterises *all* kinds of hostage takers. These reservations may be particularly appropriate with respect to politically motivated hostage situations. We have noted already the complexity involved in the analysis of any terrorist situation, and the hostage taking situation is no exception to this. Simple minded application of what appear to be general rules are unlikely to be useful.

Indeed, when more general statements about the relationship between psychopathy and terrorism are attempted, the difficulty of the undertaking becomes clearer. Cooper[12] in his discussion of psychopathy and terrorism concludes that whilst psychopathic behaviour and some forms of terrorist action have elements in common, there are sufficient important differences between them to lessen the utility of this point of view. He notes that 'Terrorism, like any other serious undertaking, requires dedication, perseverance and a certain selflessness. These are the very qualities that are lacking in the psychopath'. Whilst this quotation serves to illustrate the inappropriateness of the notion of psychopathy in some circumstances, it must be pointed out, however, that all these qualities are not necessarily evident in all terrorists either. It is probably necessary to examine the role of the particular terrorist in question before making judgements about these attributes.

Many authors refer to the psychopath's inability to profit from experience; this alone may well serve to distinguish most political terrorists from the psychopath. Another, and rather important difference between the psychopath and the terrorist is that whilst both are manifesting behaviour outside the normal moral and legal framework, for the psychopath, the purposiveness of the behaviour, if it exists, is essentially personal. This is clearly not the case for the terrorist.

To illustrate this, it might be useful to contrast the kinds of actions already discussed, with those of someone who has killed violently in non-political circumstances. A recent murderer in the United Kingdom who might well merit the term psychopath is Denis Nilsen[13]. He admitted to the killing of 15 men during the period from 1978 to 1983; the possibility remains that he was also responsible for the death of others, and a number of men are known to have narrowly escaped death at his hands. Typically, he picked up homeless men in London in what appear in the main to have been homosexual encounters.

He was put on trial for six murders and two attempted murders in October and November, 1984. A feature of the trial was not whether he had committed the offences which he admitted, but a debate between prosecution and defence expert witnesses about the state of Nilsen's mind — whether Nilsen could be held responsible for his acts at the time when they were committed, or whether he might be said to be suffering from diminished responsibility. He was eventually found guilty by a majority verdict and sentenced to life imprisonment, with a recommendation that he serve a minimum of twenty-five years.

Nilsen's offences clearly differ from most terrorist acts. Whatever his reasons were for committing them, they did not have any aspiration to a broader ideological context; his reasons were essentially personal. In most cases, this is not the case (at least ostensibly) with the terrorist who often has a very coherent and consistent rationale for his actions. The terrorist's actions are to a large extent independent of his particular victim, and given the use of bombs and similar devices which distance the terrorist from the victim, the terrorist may well have no direct personal experience of the damage and mutilation caused.

We should note, however, that there are acts committed by the terrorist which may well have some of the horrific qualities similar to those committed by Nilsen. The personal nature of the violence is the important feature to note. Examples of this seem to be especially evident when the terrorist is concerned to discipline his own members, or occupants in his territory, rather than make a political point. Numerous examples of savage beatings, torture and death have been committed by the Provisional IRA in Northern Ireland, for example, either against its own members who are suspected of breaking some organisational rule, or against members of the communities they claim to represent and defend when they transgress the Provisional IRA's rules. These acts range from tarring and feathering of Catholic girls suspected of having relationships with members of the Northern Ireland security forces, to the beating, or shooting and injuring of individuals accused of crime, to the shooting and killing of people who transgress.

This chilling statement from the Republican Press Centre in Belfast issued on 23 April 1982, gives a brief account of the reasons behind such an incident when a young man was executed for alleged 'antisocial behaviour':

> . . . In spite of repeated warnings, and having been punished last year, Devlin continued to engage in armed robberies, hijackings and the physical intimidation of the nationalist community . . .

A prominent Catholic priest, Father Dennis Faul, who is closely involved with the Catholic communities in Northern Ireland, but who has also been critical of the Provisional IRA, said of the incident:

> A 19-year-old crippled boy murdered on allegations of hijacking and intimidation . . . actions in which his murderers indulge on a large scale . . .

Acts of this kind inevitably raise issues about the mental state of the individuals who undertake them. This becomes even more the case when examples of excessive beatings as punishments are considered. The quality here that gives rise to most concern is of course the very personal nature of violence. A shooting in an ambush, or a bombing, is an act undertaken at a distance. Horrific as they may be, the terrorist never sees the victim close to, and therefore never sees the effects of his actions. It is a form of de-personalised killing. A beating, however, is a much more personal activity, where not only does the terrorist see and interact with his victim, but also the severity of the beating is directly under his control; a graded response is possible.

Frightening examples of this can be seen in the actions of members of the Official IRA in 1985, who inflicted 'punishment' beatings on two youths, Liam Fitzsimmons and Tony Knocker[14]. The youths were accused of attempted theft of materials from a building site controlled by the Official IRA in Belfast. In the case of Liam Fitzsimmons, he was held down by one man, whilst another broke both his hands with a hammer; Tony Knocker was attacked by two men wielding iron bars who attempted to break both his legs. The nature of these activities may well lead us to distinguish acts of this kind from bombings and shootings. It is difficult to see such barbarous beatings in the context of normal behaviour, and it is hard to see the perpetrators of such acts as anything other than abnormal.

It may also be important to distinguish here between the rationale and motives of the terrorist leader, and those of the active terrorist. This may well have a considerable bearing on the extent we might want to use terms like mental illness or psychopathy in describing terrorist behaviour. The individual member of a terrorist group may well not have a *particular* rationale for his act. The individual Provisional IRA terrorist, for example, may well have no knowledge of the significance or otherwise of the individual he seeks to shoot. He will be detailed for the assignment with relatively little warning and given limited information, if any, about the broader significance of the target. In a general sense, he presumably subscribes to certain beliefs about his actions which he can express, perhaps in ideological terms. In the particular circumstance, however, he is probably acting on instructions from his leadership. It may also be appropriate to distinguish between *post hoc* rationalisation and actual influencing conditions at the time. In the examples above, the individual terrorist may well be able to rationalise his actions; but without knowledge of the particular rationale *before* he attempts to kill (or whatever) his intended target, he is merely acting on instructions. The distinction is less than clear but an important one to make.

One of the more worrying consequences of attempting to locate the terrorist necessarily within the ranks of the mentally ill is the assumptions this makes about terrorist motivations. It has the dangerous consequence of placing terrorist behaviour outside of the realms of both the normal rules of behaviour *and* the normal process of law. Taylor[15] concluded that the notion of mental illness is not one that has particular utility with respect to most terrorist actions. Just because the behaviour of the terrorist seems extra-normal, it need not necessarily follow that the explanation of that behaviour must be expressed in terms like abnormality.

This is not to say, of course, that some acts that seem to be of a terrorist nature are not committed by individuals who are mentally ill, or that some members of terrorist groups are not abnormal in this sense. Indeed, it might be argued that the nature of terrorist acts offers excellent vehicles for the expression of paranoia and other abnormalities. The examples of atrocities in Northern Ireland, committed by both nationalist and loyalist paramilitary groups, are evidence of the capacity of terrorist action to attract people who perhaps take pleasure from the infliction of death, or physical mutilation.

Terrorism can itself appear to offer a means of expression of mental illness. A different example of this is described by Hacker[16] in an account of his client, Muharem Kurbegovic, who, during 1973 and 1974, was responsible for a series of violent incidents involving fire raising and bombings in Los Angeles. In 1974, a man claimed that the 'Aliens of America' organisation would be responsible for a series of outrages. The man, who called himself Isaac Rasim, became known as the Alphabet bomber, because he claimed that bombs would be placed at major locations signifying each letter of the group's name. Tape recordings were found which described the Aliens of America organisation as a 'powerful military group', and its leader would take over the Government of the World 'if the immigration and naturalisation laws of the United States were not abolished, and if the United States did not deal with Russia in a more decisive manner'. On August 6, 1974, a bomb exploded in a locker at Los Angeles International Airport, causing the death of three people, and considerable damage. This was claimed by Aliens of America as its first bomb.

'Aliens of America' and 'Isaac Rasim' appeared to be figments of Kurbegovic's imagination. He had a history of previous attempts at bombing people who had in some sense thwarted his wishes, and Aliens of America seems to be a development out of a history of paranoia. He was followed and arrested at a hamburger stand in Hollywood, where he had deposited a tape recording. He, as Muharem Kurbegovic, denied all responsibility for the bombings. He did this in writing, for as Kurbegovic he claimed to be mute: he spoke only as Isaac Rasim. After initial conviction for these offences, Kurbegovic was finally dealt with as criminally insane.

The obvious pathology of Kurbegovic, however, contrasts starkly with the lack of clinical pathology in other cases. Perhaps the most notable terrorist group that has been studied in this context is the Baader-Meinhof group[17]. Rasch, a professor at the Institute of Forensic Psychiatry of the Free University of Berlin, examined some eleven subjects suspected of involvement in terrorist activities in the Federal Republic of Germany, at the request of the authorities. 'None of the men and women I encountered could have been diagnosed as "paranoid". This applies particularly to the four main defendants who died in Stuttgart prison: Baader, Meinhof, Ensslin and Raspe.' Nor could Rasch diagnose them as psychotic, fanatic, neurotic or psychopathic. Nor in a further study of forty persons wanted as terrorists in the Federal Republic of Germany was there any indication of psychological disturbances.

These comments by Rasche are of some significance in the light of the eventual outcome of the imprisonment of the Baader-Meinhof group. This is referred to in Chapter 5 in the context of political suicides, for the members of that group eventually killed themselves in what can only be described as acts of terrorism against themselves: using their bodies '. . . as our ultimate weapon' as Gudrun Ensslin put it. The lack of obvious pathology in members of that group lends added weight to the arguments presented later.

This view seems to be confirmed by other clinically oriented investigations of terrorists. Ferracuti and Bruno[18] for example noted of Italian terrorists they studied that '. . . a general psychiatric explanation of terrorism is impossible. To define all terrorists as mentally ill would be an easy way to solve the problem, simply by invoking evil spirits in order to exclude from normality those from whom we want to be as different as possible . . .' Evidence from studies of IRA terrorists in Northern Ireland, notwithstanding the examples of particular barbaric acts given above, also tend to support the notion that psychopathology is not a useful account of terrorist behaviour.

Lyons and Harbinson[19] examined the case records of 106 individuals charged with murder in Northern Ireland during the ten year period 1974 to 1984. Of the 106, forty-seven were charged with offences related to political activity. Although the study suffers from some methodological flaws, the overall conclusions are that the political murderers were generally 'more stable' than the non-political murderers, and interestingly, in the light of discussions later, they suggest that non-political murderers have rather more unstable family backgrounds, and show a greater incidence of mental illness.

Concluding Comments

We try to understand behaviour by making sense of it in whatever way we can. In doing this, we can, in a sense, be said to try to place structure on a disorderly situation. Attempts to locate the terrorist amongst the abnormal seem to be an aspect of this process. The actions of the terrorist are difficult to understand, probably frighten us, and are outside our everyday experience. In a sense, because the terrorists' actions are infrequent, the terrorist is clearly in this sense abnormal, but is not necessarily mentally ill. This is a distinction which we must make, for the abnormal and the mentally ill in this context are clearly not synonymous. We have seen from the above discussion that it may be inappropriate to think of the terrorist as mentally ill in conventional terms. His acts are frequently barbaric, but this in itself does not seem to be a sufficient attribute to enable us to use the term mental illness. Much of the problem here seems to lie in the term 'illness' and its implicit assumption of abnormal cause.

We noted above Ferracuti and Bruno's[20] comments about the Italian terrorists they studied. They draw our attention to an important quality of mental health explanations of terrorism, which is that they represent '. . . an easy way to solve the problem, simply by invoking evil spirits in order to exclude from normality those from whom we want to be as different as possible.' The terrorist is clearly different from the rest of us in some senses, and placing him in the category of the mentally ill allows us to express that difference in an almost 'comfortable' way. It is comfortable in the sense that it does not challenge us; we can accommodate then to his actions without paying attention to the reasons for them.

A separate issue from the above is the extent to which the *nature* of the terrorist life has implications for the terrorist's mental health. In simple terms, whilst his mental health might not be in question when he becomes a terrorist, do the acts that he becomes involved in eventually impinge on his mental state? Terrorism brutalises the individuals involved. Terrorism is not unique in this respect, and other occupations in some circumstances may do so as well, such as being a butcher, serving in an army or being a social worker. But an important difference may lie in the covert context of terrorism. Terrorism is often conducted in the environment in which the terrorist lives; he does not 'go to war'. Nor does he operate in an environment that can help him deal with the personal consequences of the acts he undertakes. The supportive context of terrorism extends to maintaining terrorist behaviour, rather than offering counselling or more explicit intervention to deal with these problems.

The covert context of terrorism also contributes to the psychological stress the terrorist experiences. The nature of terrorism, its illegality and its antagonism towards the state inevitably places the terrorist under considerable pressure. We know that prolonged and severe stress adversely affects people, and there is no obvious reason to exclude the terrorist from this analysis. The kind of lifestyle which appears to characterise ETA membership[21], for example, seems to have adverse social and psychological consequences. Relationships with family and friends are said to show considerable deterioration, and the ETA member shows a preoccupation with membership which seems to extend into his everyday life. In his reports of interviews with ETA members, Clark[22] notes that they were not particularly happy men, although their lifestyle was 'not sufficiently stressful to exceed the limits of normal and healthy personalities'. The extent to which this generalisation might apply more broadly is, of course, a matter for speculation. It seems reasonable to conclude, however, that whilst mental illness may not be a particularly helpful way of conceptualising terrorism, the acts of terrorism and membership of a terrorist organisation may well have implications for the terrorist's mental health.

To use the term 'mental illness' to apply in a general way to terrorists is to use a label, with connotations which are, perhaps, pejorative. But as we have seen, as a label, 'mental illness' might make us feel better, but it does not seem to be very useful in aiding our understanding of terrorism. What of other labels? One which seems particularly appropriate is the term 'fanatic', for is not the fanatic characterised by the kind of activity the terrorist undertakes? We will examine this issue in Chapter 5.

CHAPTER 5

Fanaticism

[Terrorists are fanatics and fanaticism frequently makes for cruelty and sadism.[1]]

Fanaticism is often assumed to be one of a cluster of attributes of the terrorist. It is also a way of rationalising, for the onlooker, the disturbing qualities of terrorist violence. Rather in the same way that mental health is used to 'explain' terrorism, so fanaticism is sometimes offered as a causal quality of terrorist behaviour.

In this chapter we will examine what we mean by the term fanatic and the ways in which it might reflect our understanding of terrorist behaviour. We will first do this by considering the concept of fanaticism, and then by looking in detail at a particular kind of fanatical act — suicide to achieve some political or war end — which may have links with terrorism.

Historical and Contemporary Context

Historically, the term fanatic appears to have made its appearance in the English language in the seventeenth century, and was used to refer to 'excessive enthusiasm in religious belief[2]. In origin, the term reflects its religious focus, having its roots in the latin fanum (temple). Religious expression seems to lend itself particularly to the expression of fanaticism, and before the term itself came into common currency, religious practices existed which we might now refer to as fanatical. An example of an historical movement from which the concept of fanaticism grew, and which we would today refer to as fanatical, can be seen in the flagellant movement of the Middle Ages. Its distinctive feature, which located it outside of the rituals of self-punishment and mortification of the flesh common to many religious traditions, was its public excesses and group qualities.

The 'Brotherhood of the Flagellants' was an extraordinary mass religious movement which appeared to have its origins in Eastern Europe in the Middle Ages[3]. It gained its firmest ground in the area we now know as Germany. Members of the brotherhood had to promise to scourge themselves three times a day for thirty-three days and eight hours. The

Flagellants moved from town to town in groups of several hundred. On arriving at a town, they held their rituals in the open air, which centred around the beating of those amongst the flagellants guilty of particular moral crimes, followed by collective self-flagellation. Each flagellant carried a heavy scourge with thongs tipped with metal studs, with which they whipped themselves, causing considerable damage. Death was not uncommon amongst the flagellants, the injuries being exacerbated by the rules of the brotherhood, which forbade the washing or changing of clothes.

Although the origins of the term 'fanatic' lie in the excesses of religious practice, such as the flagellant movement, subsequent modern usage seems to have moved the term out of the religious context, to refer to more generally held extreme beliefs. Such beliefs can result in apparent contradictions, (which appear to leave the fanatic untouched). The religious fanatic for example, might well espouse a doctrine of love, but, as in the adherents of the Reverend Sun Myung Moon, abandon family and kin, much to the family's very evident distress. The beliefs that characterise the fanatic become so central a part of his life that other things are devalued or dismissed. This is not to say that the fanatic is not aware of the problem, such as the distress of his family, but that the solution to the problem is seen as lying not with his own actions, but with others.

The focusing of belief on, say, a single overriding theme does seem to characterise the enthusiasts of some terrorist movements, (but not necessarily the terrorists themselves). Supporters of Sinn Fein, the political wing of the Provisional IRA at their annual conference in 1986 passed a motion supporting the 'right to life', with the exception that it should not apply to what they term the 'armed struggle'. This astonishing piece of double-think perhaps typifies the kind of logic which can characterise both the fanatic's and some terrorist's rationales. The overriding concern is with the single issue, or group of issues, around which the group defines itself; other issues become defined in those terms, and become subservient to them.

There is clearly a sense in which fanaticism might characterise terrorist behaviour. But if fanaticism is a meaningful account of some forms of terrorism, is it an account unique to terrorism? Of course not. Whatever the aetiology of fanaticism might prove to be, whether it reflects a 'pathology of perfection'[4], elitism[5] or a flight from fallibility[6], it is not something unique to terrorism. This is an important point to note, for as we have already seen, the attempt to classify terrorism in unique terms such as mental illness is not useful. The terrorist may well be a fanatic, but so are many other people, and what is more, in some circumstances we sometimes applaud them for it!

We do not necessarily always regard the fanatic in negative terms. Indeed, some 'fanatics' receive great social approval. Eckman[7] describes 'the fanaticism' of the athlete who, whilst performing in a different arena from the terrorist, arguably shows common attributes in a psychological sense. Unlike the terrorist, of course, the 'fanaticism' of the sportsman is something we might probably applaud and even envy. Eckman's account is very interesting, for it offers reflections not only on the state of fanaticism, but on the way in which it might develop. Eckman was a notable American football player and self-confessed fanatic. In pursuit of physical fitness and sporting achievements, he describes his introduction to sport from an early age in terms of the rewards and status it conferred on him. The 'rigidity' of the fanatic, he feels, could equally well describe his own behaviour, and he seeks to explain this in terms of personal consequences, the role of the team, and the broader relationship of the team to sport in general. As is inevitable in the form of sport he played, he began to develop injury problems which resulted in considerable pain. 'The risks I took seem dumb to me now. But that's exactly the point. What seems right depends on the time frame and the context you're in.'

Eckman's account may well be useful in helping us to understand the nature of fanaticism better, in that it gives some indication of how his particular state developed and was sustained. He draws attention to the context (social and personal) in which he developed his football skills. Indeed, perhaps the most significant feature is his emphasis on the importance of the personal context that supported and developed his sporting skills. His colleagues, team managers, fans, all defined a world that supported and encouraged his actions. An achievement orientated society might also be said to contribute to this supportive context. We will see later in this chapter that the irrationality of the fanatic becomes much easier to understand if we have regard to the overall context in which he lives.

A critical feature of the concept of fanaticism which complicates our analysis is, as Milgram points out[8], that fanaticism, (like terrorism) is a pejorative term, and 'is applied to the state of mind of those who are wholeheartedly committed to a set of beliefs and are condemned for it.' But similar belief systems can attract terms such as 'passionate involvement, undaunted commitment, and profound religiosity'[9], if we feel agreement in some sense with those beliefs. Is the Pope a fanatic for adhering to beliefs on contraception in the knowledge of the problems associated with the spread of AIDS? Is the Reverend Ian Paisley a fanatic for holding extreme views about the Province of Ulster? Was De Gaulle a fanatic for holding nationalistic (and sometimes romantic) views about France? As with terrorism, perhaps the concept lies in the eye of the beholder.

Psychological Aspects of Fanaticism

In psychological terms, the concept of the fanatic is not clearly understood. It carries with it some implications of mental illness, and indeed might be thought to be a symptom of some particular abnormal states.

However, unlike the diagnostic terms used in Chapter 4 (such as psychopath and sociopath), fanaticism is not a diagnostic category in mental illness. The concept refers in part to rigidly held ideas and beliefs, expressed as actions that seem to be little influenced by the immediate context. We are, however, inconsistent at times in the attributes we use when making judgements about fanaticism. Sometimes we use the term to refer to the expression of beliefs or attitudes alone, sometimes we use the term to refer to actual behaviour of some form.

The failure to distinguish between behaviour and attitude can be important. Whilst we often assume that attitudes are related to behaviour, in practice they frequently prove not to be. Thus, attitudes to smoking, for example, can be changed by advertising campaigns, but such campaigns are notoriously poor at actually changing smoking behaviour. One of the distinguishing features of fanaticism may be that there is a closer link between attitude and behaviour in the fanatic than in ordinary people. Thus the fanatic's belief systems (a term related to attitude) may well have a greater role in the determination of behaviour.

Indeed, one thing that does seem clear is that the fanatic often seems to have a clear view of the world from a particular perspective, usually closely allied to a view widely held by others, but lying at the extreme of a continuum. This particular view provides a base from which everything is interpreted *and* which determines the fanatics' actions. This may not be unique to the fanatic; in a way, we all have elements of this, but we seem often to reserve the term fanatic to refer to extreme views of this kind held about moral, political or religious issues. A further important feature of the fanatic seems to be his unwillingness to compromise, and his disdain for alternative views. In contemporary usage, the fanatic can be of the political right or left, or he can focus around a more complex ideology, (like anti-colonial nationalism), or around a religious idea.

We may be able to identify links between fanaticism and other psychological processes. In particular, fanaticism seems to have a number of qualities in common with prejudice and authoritarianism, two related processes. The fanatic, for example, seems to share with the prejudiced and the authoritarian a tendency to rigidly held views, which seem resistant to any change through rational argument. Furthermore, we can see similarities here with the terrorist as well. We can pursue this discussion further by elaborating on the process thought to underlie prejudice, and in doing so we may be able to progress our understanding of both fanaticism and terrorism. Prejudice for our purposes refers to an attitude or attitudes towards members of some specific group, leading the persons who hold it to evaluate others in a characteristic fashion (usually negative), solely on the basis of membership of that group[10]. Its corollary, discrimination, refers to the expression of negative actions or behaviours against these individuals.

If prejudice is defined in these terms, it can be seen to refer to a means of organising, interpreting and recalling information about the particular group prejudiced against. It makes reference, therefore, to a particular form of cognitive structure. Thus, the prejudiced person tends to notice and remember only certain kinds of information about the prejudiced group, regardless of the actions of that group. The cognitive components of prejudice seem to be organised around stereotypes, which once formed, result in very persistent preconceived notions about the prejudiced group. The prejudiced individual therefore has a way of looking at the world which is highly selective and resistant to change, regardless of actual event. The fanatic may not be prejudiced against groups defined in terms of personal attributes like race, and there is no intention here to suggest this; but the rigidity of cognitive structures, and the *process* of assimilation and use of information clearly shows elements in common between the fanatic and the prejudiced.

An important aspect of prejudice which also has a bearing on the understanding of the fanatic is the self-confirming nature of prejudice. The fanatic and the prejudiced share an insensitivity to circumstances that might be expected to change their views. At least some of the basis for this may be the way in which holding extreme views exerts an impact on behaviour. The prejudiced may treat those who they dislike in special ways, which in turn may well result in those subject to prejudice to respond in particular ways, each of which may well sustain and fulfil each participant's expectations. There is soundly based experimental evidence to confirm that this process does in fact occur, and furthermore, that negative features seem particularly susceptible to this 'spiral'.

There is also some evidence to suggest that persons who are prejudiced share certain common personality characteristics, which have been termed authoritarian. Adorno and her colleagues[11] have made a considerable contribution to this debate in their identification of the 'authoritarian personality'. Highly authoritarian individuals show patterns of submissive obedience to authority, which are paradoxically associated with punitive rejection of groups other than their own. Allied to this is a tendency to see the world in rigid black-and-white terms. The authoritarian has, for example, been repeatedly shown to be more likely to use punishment in dealing with other people. It is of significance to note that the initial work on authoritarianism was undertaken to try to understand the rise and development of the Nazi movement in Germany in the 1930s and 1940s. We can see, therefore, in the authoritarian personality many of the attributes of what we term the fanatic; the tendency to see things in black-and-white, the rigidity of belief, and the personalised structuring of perceptions of the world.

We can extend this discussion further, by considering analogies of what happens when circumstances appear to challenge the fanatic's interpretation of the world. Like the fanatic, most terrorist's rhetoric claims moral superiority. Yet the innocence of most victims of terrorism (in any direct sense) is one of the clearest features of terrorist violence. The apparent paradox between the often moralistic claims in the rhetoric of the terrorist (and the fanatic) and the disregard for the victim is often resolved in two related ways; either by reinterpreting the qualities of the victim, making him or her conform to the overriding world view, or by denial of responsibility because of some other agency's inaction. We might term this the *paradox of morality*. Rapoport[12] illustrates how victim qualities might be reinterpreted by quoting a horrific and frightening speech from a Ku Klux Klan activist at a meeting justifying to other Klan members the death of four children:

> I'll tell you people here tonight, if they can find those fellows who threw the bomb, they ought to pin medals on them. Someone said, "Ain't it a shame little children was killed." Well, they don't know what they're talking about. In the first place, they ain't little. They're fourteen or fifteen years old, old enough to have venereal disease and I'll be surprised if all of them didn't have one or more. In the second place, they weren't children. Children are little people, little human beings, and that means white people. There's little monkeys, there's little dogs and little cats, little apes, little baboons, little skunks, and there's also little niggers. They're just little niggers. And in the third place, it wasn't no shame they was killed. Why? Because when I go out to kill rattle snakes, I don't make no difference between little rattlesnakes and big rattlesnakes because I know it is in the nature of all rattlesnakes to be enemies and to poison me if they can. So, I kill 'em all, and if there's four less little Niggers tonight, then I say, good for whoever planted the bomb. We're all better off.

This is an extreme example, but echoes of the same processes can be heard in a comment of Marie Drumm, an IRA activist quoted by McKnight[13]:

> . . . I don't care how many British soldiers die. I have no compassion in the world for them. I know that it is an awfully callous thing for a woman to say, but it is my honest belief that they've got to go, one way or the other . . .

The second way in which this paradox of morality is dealt with is through placing responsibility for injury or death, resulting after a bombing, for example, on the inaction of others, usually the authorities, in not responding to warnings or threats. Menachem Begin[14] illustrates this in his account of the bombing of the King David Hotel in Jerusalem in 1946 by the Irgun. Begin acknowledges the scale of injury: '. . . the toll of lives was terrible. More than two hundred people were killed or injured.' He also acknowledges their innocence and goes to some pains to explain that this was not an intended feature of the attack. He sees the responsibility for the deaths, however, not in his own actions, and those of the Irgun, in placing the bomb, but in the failure of the British Authorities to evacuate the hotel in response to warnings. Denials of this kind after a terrorist bombing are so commonplace a feature, that they go almost unremarked.

These motifs are common features of terrorist activity, and have been termed 'Guilt Transfer'[15]. The processes involved may be a reflection of underlying psychological processes, but we should also note that denial of responsibility has proved to be a highly effective propaganda technique. It redirects attention away from the violent act towards the actions of others, and by doing this, serves to undermine the moral position often adopted in the response to terrorism.

The psychological origins of behaviour like this may well lie in the cognitive consequences of prejudice, or some allied state. It might also be supplemented by the process of 'deindividuation', a feature of group membership which is discussed in greater detail in Chapter 8, and the process of attribution. In anticipation of that discussion, we might note that features of these states include changes in thought processes.

Another related psychological explanation of the processes underlying the paradox of morality might lie in terms of Festinger's Theory of Cognitive Dissonance[16]. This theory addresses the cognitive problems that arise for the individual when there is a conflict between attitudes and behaviour. Festinger proposes that when such conflict occurs, it creates a state of 'dissonance', which that individual seeks to reduce, thereby eliminating the feelings of conflict. The reduction in dissonance can be brought about in a number of ways, including changes in attitude, behaviour, or more relevantly for our purposes, minimising the importance of the elements involved in the dissonant situation.

In the examples above, the rhetoric of terrorism (and its underlying attitudes) which stresses, for example, the rights of the oppressed, the value of life, or the importance of the individual, is clearly in conflict with the tendency for terrorist activities to embrace, injure and perhaps kill members of the security services who are simply representative victims. The resultant conflict can be reduced for the terrorist in two ways, either by denigrating the qualities of the victim, or by locating responsibility for any injury on another agency. In both cases, the integrity of the attitude structures and their related ideological basis can be retained by the terrorist through reducing personal involvement in the situation, and diminishing the 'value' of the victim. Processes analogous to those which might operate in the terrorist have been experimentally explored, and have generally received confirmation.

We might note in passing that viewing the problem in this way also helps to explain the striking vocabulary of terrorist language, as expressed in communications, which often have reference to 'pigs', 'members of war machines', 'capitalist lackeys' or other emotive but derogatory terms. The use of derogatory language allows the expression of cognitive dissonance reduction (and may indeed be symptomatic of it), diminishing the qualities of the victim, and thereby enabling the terrorist to retain intact his own attitudinal structures.

As can be seen from the above, the basis of prejudiced behaviour may well reflect on the psychological basis of fanaticism, in terms of common or related cognitive structures. There are differences in some respects, especially in the capacity of the fanatic to make evident his fanaticism through action. However, it may be that in this respect the fanatic demonstrates an extreme position on a continuum describing the processes underlying prejudice, where extremity is related to expression, rather than simply holding, extreme views. The differences between the fanatic and the prejudiced or authoritarian may be considerable in terms of the focus of their behaviour, but the processes whereby they are acquired and occur may well be similar. Our knowledge in this area is limited, but the above seems to help us to understand at least some of the factors involved.

Fanaticism and Mental Illness

Whilst fanaticism is not a diagnostic category, nevertheless we have a persistent tendency to place the fanatic within the context of mental health, if not mental illness. The fanatic can be distinguished reasonably easily in clinical terms from the Obsessive-Compulsive state with which it might be thought to have elements in common. The fanatic shares with the obsessive-compulsive a pervasive obsession with a theme, and both may well energetically and compulsively pursue that theme in spite of social disapproval. The fanatic does not, however, perceive his obsessions as irrational or aversive. Such a perception is an important feature of obsessive-compulsive states, and in itself serves to distinguish the fanatic from them. On the other hand, there is a sense in which the fanatic might be said to be 'driven' to do the things he does, which is a feature of compulsive states. Perhaps conclusively, however, unlike the compulsive, the behaviour of the fanatic does not seem to have the stereotyped and ritualistic qualities which characterise compulsive behaviour.

Other kinds of clinical parallels with fanaticism can be developed, which make reference to the delusional qualities of the fanatic, and perhaps the fanatic's propensity to paranoia. Paranoia refers to the holding of chronic, highly systematised and apparently incurable delusions which are held without general personality disorganisation. The delusions often make reference in some way to persecution or some kind of grandiose reinterpretation of the world, and seem to involve interpreting common or chance events from a personal and highly organised viewpoint. The fanatic and the paranoid may well share common elements, and in practice, it may prove difficult to distinguish between them, especially where the paranoid individual expresses his paranoia in some form of extreme behaviour.

An example of a paranoid state that seems to have some elements in common with kinds of terrorist behaviour can be seen in the famous case of Michael P. Mahoney, a 71-year-old Irish emigrant to the United States. In 1914, he made an attempt on the life of the Mayor of New York City, Frank L. Polk. Michael Mahoney firmly believed that he had been the victim of consistent and systematic frame-ups by certain people during the whole of the fifty-two years he had lived in America. He had no known history of other forms of mental illness, neither drank nor smoked excessively, and had no apparent involvement in drugs. When pressed to explain his attempted murder, he eventually admitted that he thought the Masonic Order had consistently conspired against him, stopping him from getting work throughout his stay in the States. Mayor Polk was a Mason, and Mahoney felt that he had used his influence as Mayor of New York to deny him employment. There are circumstances that can be envisaged that would sustain Mahoney's views of conspiracy; there was, however, no evidence that Michael Mahoney had been subject to discrimination, and in the light of this, and in the light of the intensity of his views (culminating in an attempt at murder), the diagnosis of paranoia seems appropriate. There are clearly, however, aspects of Mahoney's circumstances that are relevant to our discussion of fanaticism, in that his preoccupation with the negative role of the Masons and its expression in violence might well be termed fanatical (as well as paranoid).

Anarchism, Fanaticism and Terrorism

In the popular mind, the fanatic is often associated with both the terrorist and the anarchist. Indeed, the terms fanatic, anarchist and terrorist for many will seem to refer to the same things. As a political philosophy, anarchism is often equated with terrorism, and the anarchist is also often referred to as a fanatic. This equation however, is rather misleading, for there is no necessary association beween the anarchist and the terrorist—many anarchists would regard themselves as pacifists, for example, and would abhor violence of any form. Anarchism refers to a particular range of political philosophies that reject the role of the state in the organisation of human life. The various anarchist philosophies hold an optimistic view of human nature, seeking ideal expression in a society unregulated from outside by state, or equivalent, agencies. As with any political view, it might be expressed by an individual in terms that we refer to as fanatical, but as with terrorism, there is no necessary relationship between fanaticism and anarchism.

Anarchistic analyses of society have focused on the inappropriate nature of social organisation. Particular activists or groups might well, therefore, see their aims met by the destruction of social organisation, and this might easily find expression in violence against society. The utopian qualities of anarchist theory may also find expression in fanaticism, especially given the role utopianism might play in some expressions of fanaticism[17]. Thus, links between anarchism, fanaticism and terrorism whilst not necessarily evident may well be possible. The important point to make, however, is that there is no *necessary* link between the anarchist and the terrorist, any more than there is between the socialist and the fanatic, or the fascist and the terrorist. Within the anarchistic context, there has been a tendency to seek expression for anarchist philosophy outside normal society, through the creation of isolated communities aspiring to the utopian form of social organisation envisaged within anarchist philosophies. This is consistent with the views of some anarchist theorists, such as Michael Bakunin[18], who saw social progress being achieved by the creation of 'examples' of future social organisation. In this sense the anarchist would be drawn away from society, rather than seeking to change it through action (a characteristic of the terrorist).

In this respect, however, we can see how the term 'fanatic' might be applied to anarchists. By adopting a deliberately exclusive lifestyle, creating communes that deliberately reject social norms, the observer who accepts those social norms might well see such people as extreme, or seek to label them in a pejorative way, by using the term fanatic. In the midst of plenty, rejection of material wealth (which might characterise some communes) seems to reflect perversity, extremism, and all the other attributes of the fanatical.

There remains, however, a persistent and often expressed association between anarchism and terrorism and the concept of fanaticism serves as a link between the two. In historical terms, this equivalence seems to owe more to a series of events in nineteenth-century Russia and Eastern Europe, rather than some necessary feature of anarchist philosophy. Individual anarchists were involved in an extensive series of assassination attempts and murders in Russia, which extended to other parts of Europe including the assassination of the Italian King Humbert I in 1900 and the Empress Elizabeth of Austria in 1898. These assassinations formed no necessary part of anarchist theory and seem to be the responses of individual anarchists in a series of revenge and counter-revenge chain reactions.

Contemporary with this, and marginally related to it, was the Nihilist Movement. The Nihilist Movement has its origins in the writings of Sergei Nechayev[19], and aspires to the active destruction of society through violent means in preparation for the rise of a more utopian social organisation. Nechayev displays a single mindedness of purpose that might well make the term fanatic an appropriate description. 'The purpose (. . . of the revolutionary . . .) is only one: the quickest and most sure destruction of this filthy system.' '(. . . The revolutionary . . .) knows only a single science: the science of destruction.'

The Nihilist movement, motivated by 'propaganda of the deed' attracted some anarchists. In some ways it might well be seen to complement aspects of anarchist theory, by offering a tangible and more rapid means of progress to the anarchist utopia. Adherents of this view would probably be described as fanatical, and what we now refer to as terrorism certainly formed a part of the strategy of Nihilism. It is *this* link that seems to be the principal point of relationship between terrorism and anarchism, rather

TT—H

than any necessary relationship between the two in terms of fanaticism. The notion of 'propaganda of the deed' is, of course, a concept that now extends beyond the Nihilist philosophies of Nechayev, and might be said to characterise most contemporary revolutionary movements; in it we see the principal link between terrorism and revolutionary political change.

Political Suicides

Our discussion has so far focused on the concept of the fanatic in a general sense and we can now consider particular examples of what we might refer to as fanatical behaviour. In looking at some of the circumstances in which fanatics do things, especially violent things, we might better understand the concept and its links with terrorism. Fanatical behaviour in the context of political violence is clearly our main area of concern. An extreme case of fanatical violence, and one upon which we will focus, can be seen where that violence is directed against the individual himself, rather than others. We find this a particularly disturbing act, which seems both illogical and frightening. However, its extreme qualities allow us to progress our discussion more clearly by emphasising the importance of the context in which it takes place.

The taking of an individual's life by himself has been thought to be indicative in some circumstances of some form of mental illness: it might also similarly be thought to be indicative of fanaticism where the suicide seems to be related to the focus of the fanatic's belief systems. Not all suicides necessarily have a history of mental illness, or any recognisable pathology, and suicide can have a rational and logical basis. Nor is there any suggestion that suicide is necessarily the act of a fanatic. Indeed, suicide can be seen in some situations as a rational response to overwhelming personal distress or circumstance (for example, the individual suffering from an untreatable and painful terminal illness). But suicide can also take place within a political, rather than personal, context and, in this respect, we may well begin to feel that this represents qualities of the fanatic. To kill oneself deliberately for a cause would almost inevitably attract the label 'fanatic'. Because such suicides can also address a political agenda by reference to some cause, and are undertaken in order to have some effect on that cause, they may well also fall within the concept of terrorism — such suicides are, after all, a form of political violence, finding expression not against others, but against the individual himself. They represent a particular form of 'propaganda of the deed'.

One problem, however, we will encounter in our discussion is the confusing and pejorative qualities of the term 'fanatic' when applied to some suicides. We might well admire the individual who sacrifices his own life for another, or for a cause *we* hold dear. The biblical injunction 'Greater love hath no man than this, that a man lay down his life for his friends'

(John, 16:13) expresses this very clearly. Many men and women have soberly and deliberately given their lives for their fellows in acts of self-sacrifice, and sometimes these acts of self-sacrifice might well have political consequences. Depending on our perspective, we might well admire them for it. In the following discussion of political suicides, the essential ambiguity of the concept of 'fanatic' must be acknowledged, and we must also recognise and distinguish between the personal qualities shown by the individual who commits suicide, and the use made of that suicide in a political context. Perhaps suicides merit the term 'fanatic' when the political context is the pre-eminent causal state? This would certainly seem to identify the terrorist-suicide.

Self-Immolation

One example of suicide for an essentially political cause can be seen in the acts of self-immolation described by Crosby et al.[20]. These might well fall within the category of fanatical and they seem to have been undertaken for political purposes, like terrorist acts. Interestingly, societies' reactions to them as political protests differed, however, from those associated with terrorism directed against third parties. Suicide by fire, or self-immolation, is a rare form of suicide, which has an almost unique history of association in the West with political protest. It showed an extraordinary rise in incidence from being almost non-existent in the West pre-1963, to eleven cases between 1964–65 (of which nine appeared to be politically motivated), fifteen cases in 1966 and ten in 1967. Thereafter, the incidence drops somewhat, but remains at levels higher than pre-1963.

Ritualistic self-immolation is not unknown in Buddhist cultures and there is, for example, a long history of burning to death of widows (the rite of *suttee*) in India. There are some hazy historical reports of self-incineration as protest, but the first documented incident seems to be that of Thich Quang Duc, a Buddhist monk in South Vietnam, who on June 12, 1963, doused himself with petrol and incinerated himself, in protest against the continuation of the war. This was followed on August 5, 1963, by the self-immolation of a second Buddhist monk and, on August 16, by that of a further Buddhist monk and a Buddhist nun.

The first Western example of self-immolation as political protest seems to have been Alice Herz on March 17, 1965, an eighty-two-year-old Quaker pacifist who set fire to herself on a street corner in Detroit in protest against 'the arms race all over the world'. She stated that 'I wanted to burn myself like the monks of Vietnam did'. This was followed in November, 1965, by the death of Norman Morrison, a thirty-two-year-old Quaker official, who incinerated himself on the steps of the Pentagon in Washington in protest against the American involvement in Vietnam. Eight days later, Roger LaPorte set fire to himself in front of the United

Nations Building in New York again in protest against United States involvement in Vietnam; he was a twenty-two-year-old member of the Catholic Workers movement.

These deaths, and others that followed, seem to be understood best as extreme forms of political protest. Whilst they occurred in the context of the peace movement, this movement had clear political aspirations in terms of ending the Vietnam war and the withdrawal of American soldiers. The individuals concerned (at least those in the West) appeared to be suffering from no known incidence of psychiatric illness and the drama of the means of suicide seems to be more related to context than their psychiatric state. There is no evidence available to suggest that the people concerned were anything other than rational and aware of what they were doing. Are these acts of terrorism? This is difficult to say, for they are directed primarily against themselves, rather than against other more symbolic targets. They do seem to have at least one of the attributes of what we regard as terrorist acts, however. They are a form of violence explicitly directed at influencing the political process. Are they the acts of a fanatic? The pejorative qualities associated with the term fanatic might well limit its use here, for many would feel a sense of admiration for their acts, without in any way condoning them or the cause they espoused. They certainly were successful *political* acts, and had a profound effect on the peace movement in America at that time and upon public opinion.

Suicide Attacks and Bombings: Islamic Terrorism

Self-immolation leaves only one direct victim — the individual himself. Suicides which fall within a more explicitly terrorist context are those where the suicide is a necessary part of a violent terrorist act. The spate of Middle-Eastern suicide bombings during 1983 and 1984, largely attributed to Islamic Shi'ite groups, illustrates this. From an operational perspective, such bombings are unquestionably successful (in reaching their chosen target, and causing considerable damage), and in some ways it might have been predicted that this method of delivering bombs would have been more widely adopted. In a sense, the suicide attack is the ultimate rational way of ensuring the success of a mission, offering a cheap form of guided missile (in financial terms).

As they have impinged on the West, the principal target for contemporary suicide attacks have been United States installations in the Middle East, principally in Lebanon. Attacks of this form have occurred, however, in other contexts in the Middle East, notably the Iran-Iraq war. As we will see later, we can begin to understand these actions when we think about them within the broader context of Islam and especially the Shi'ite sect and its relationship with the state of Iran. It is the religious basis for what to us appears to be essentially political acts that enables us to make sense of them.

On April 18, 1983, shortly after 1.00 p.m., a van containing approximately 400 pounds of explosives was driven into the side of the United States Embassy in Beirut, after driving across a forecourt. The van was detonated by the driver, and some sixty people were killed, including the driver, and some 120 injured; the dead and injured were mostly American personnel. The consequences of this attack, horrific in themselves, were exacerbated for the United States authorities by the presence in the Embassy of CIA and Defence Intelligence Officers attending a regional conference. About twelve senior members of these organisations are thought to have been killed by the attack. Ironically, the conference was probably held there because it was regarded as a secure location.

Whilst this attack is often regarded as the first of a series of suicide bombings, it was, in fact, preceded by an earlier suicide attack on the Israeli defence forces on April 13, when six Israeli soldiers were killed by a suicide lorry bombing. The American bombing was claimed by Al Jihad al-Ismali, an offshoot of the Lebanon Shi'ite Amal militia, amongst others. In the terms which the terrorist might evaluate this incident, it was a spectacular success, in that a high security perimeter was breached, and considerable damage was done, especially to key intelligence personnel.

The campaign of suicide bombings continued later that year. On October 23, 1983, two similar bombings occurred in the Lebanon, one at the Headquarters of French troops, the other at the Headquarters of the US Marines. The explosions were detonated within twenty seconds of each other, in a well-planned co-ordinated attack. At 6.20 a.m. a truck loaded with some 5000 pounds of explosive crashed into the entrance lobby of the United States Marine Headquarters and detonated. The enormous explosion demolished the building, killing some 260 United States personnel. In an almost identical attack on the French Headquarters at a similar time, a truck carrying explosives crashed some 10 feet into the building before detonating, killing fifty-eight. The drivers of both vehicles who detonated the explosives were killed. Some American observers have described the explosion at the United States Embassy as 'the single largest non-nuclear blast on earth since World War II'. Both these bombings were again claimed by *Al Jihad al-Ismali*. Once more, it has to be said that, from the terrorist perspective, these were very successful attacks, demonstrating precision in targeting, a capacity to penetrate high security areas, and an ability to co-ordinate and plan actions. They also may well demonstrate the involvement of the intelligence services of other regional powers in the Middle East, notably Syria, for it is unlikely that *Al Jihad al-Ismali* (or whatever Shi'ite Grouping that organisation stands as a front for) would have the capacity to find out sufficient details of the buildings, security arrangements, and so forth necessary to penetrate the perimeters.

A subsequent suicide attack on November 4th at the Israeli Army Headquarters in Tyre killed sixty-one after an explosion of a car bomb containing 1100 pounds of explosives. Of the dead, twenty-eight were Israeli soldiers, and thirty-three were Palestinians and Lebanese civilians awaiting interrogation. The focus of the suicide attacks then changed from the Lebanon to other Arab countries. On December 12, in a series of bombings in Kuwait City, a three-storey annexe to the American Embassy was destroyed by a truck driven through the Embassy compound gates, killing one occupant of the truck, and four others. The following year, on September 20th, 1984, an attack on the American Embassy annexe followed a similar pattern to the above. A lorry carrying some 3000 pounds of explosives was driven into the compound, and zigzagged around concrete barriers whilst under fire, apparently aiming for an underground car park. The driver was hit before reaching this objective, however, and the lorry exploded in the compound at the entrance to the building. Some fifteen people were killed. As before, all the above attacks were claimed by *Al Jihad al-Ismali.*

Other suicide attacks have followed. In March, 1985, an Israeli jeep leading a convoy of military vehicles transporting soldiers waved an oncoming pickup truck off the road to allow the convoy to pass. The driver of the truck detonated the bomb it was carrying, killing himself and destroying the troop transport it was passing. The bomb containing some 220 pounds of explosives, killed twelve soldiers and injured fourteen. In September, 1985, an explosive-laden car was crashed into an Israeli-Christian Militia position in South Lebanon. The explosion killed the driver of the car, and killed and wounded thirty militiamen. After this attack, a brief thirty second pre-recorded video of the bomber was shown by the Lebanon Television Service. The young bomber identified himself as Mohammed Awad Masri, and he claimed the attack in the name of the Late Egyptian President, Gamal Abdel-Nasser.

Not all the attacks are claimed by the same organisation but, in the shifting conditions in Lebanon, it is difficult to establish responsibility. What is quite clear, however, is that all the bombings have been undertaken by Islamic groups, many of whom are in close alliance with one another. Islamic religious leaders have expressed support for these bombings. Sheik Sobhi Tofeili, a high official of the radical Islamic Hezbollah, a pro-Iranian group, hailed the bombers as 'holy warrior heroes' who acted in the name of Islam. At a memorial ceremony for three Iranian Revolutionary Guards killed in Lebanon in August, 1985, he said that:

> . . . the names of many of the Mujahedeen (holy warriors) heroes who knocked down the fortress of the infidels and blew up the American Embassy . . . are still unknown . . . Their actions were for the sake of Islam. We must preserve their blood and let the world and history be aware that Islam is the one that destroyed Israel and America.

These attacks were undoubtedly successful, in that they reached their targets, caused considerable damage and, of course, received enormous publicity. Despite intense and sophisticated security provisions, the suicide bomber was able to penetrate the target area with apparent ease. It might also be argued that the attacks had a profound effect on United States policy to Lebanon. Within the broader context of terrorism, however, these attacks stand-out as being unique. Deliberate self-destruction, where the terrorist's death is a necessary part of the act in detonating the bomb, (as opposed to accidental death), is not a feature of much terrorist activity. Only nine percent of terrorist bombing victims from 1977 to 1983 were thought to be suspected terrorist bombers, for example (United States Department of State[21]), and these were largely thought to be the result of accidental explosions, rather than deliberate ones. In contemporary times, suicide attacks are very rare outside of the Middle East.

These acts of terrorism strike fear into most observers and are, to most of us, beyond our comprehension. To the Western observer, such acts can as readily be ascribed to either 'fanaticism' or 'mental illness'; they seem to embody some of the attributes of both. The often violent and extreme rhetoric of the participants increases our concern and seems to the Western ear bizarre and abnormal. Viewed from the standpoint of Shi'ite culture and its Islamic context, however, such acts of self destruction do not seem so pathogenic, and have a clear and appropriate cultural and religious context[22].

There are historical origins for such suicide attacks, which can be seen in the behaviour of religious sects associated with the Shi'ite movement, notably the Assassins. As a form of political terrorists, the Assassins have been well known in the West for many centuries. A German priest, Brocardus, composed a treatise for King Philip VI of France in 1332 for the King's guidance whilst he was contemplating a crusade to recover the lost Holy Places of Christendom. Amongst the dangers Brocardus identified were '. . . the Assassins, who are to be cursed and fled. They sell themselves, are thirsty for blood, kill the innocent for a price, and care nothing for either life or salvation.' As well as giving their name to a particular form of terrorist act, the importance of the Assassins for our purpose is that they illustrate that an historical, religious and cultural context exists for the kind of behaviour seen in the suicide bombings.

The forces that gave rise to the Assassins remain and influence the Shi'ites today. What we might refer to as terrorism (suicide bombings, kidnapping, random explosions in residential areas) are not only features of the present situation in Lebanon but, in some senses, have been a part of the process of politics and diplomacy in the Middle East for many centuries. 'Terrorism' is used as an instrument of policy by States such as Iran to pursue its political ends against its enemies. We can see, in probably the most explicit way, in this Islamic context, the use of terrorism as a form of warfare. In that same context, parallels with Clausewitz's[23] notions of the relationship between war and politics are, of course, obvious. Terrorism is used in the Middle East in the furtherance of political objectives especially by Iran, and we can see this in the way that suicide attacks, for example, are not confined to use against the Western enemies of Iran, but are used also against its regional enemies. In the absence of media attention, however, the Western audience is unaware, in the main, of the scale and effectiveness of these attacks. A spectacular suicide bombing occurred in November 1983, for example, when an Iranian suicide group of what was thought to be two men, destroyed the Iraqi Security Police Headquarters in Baghdad[24].

In a sense, what we see now and label as terrorism is part of the 'normal' process of political activity. Taking hostages, for example, has featured prominently as a political tool in the Middle East for a long time. Failure to recognise this and the social and religious context in which it occurs can lead to serious consequences, as the various attempts to negotiate with holders of Lebanese hostages over the period 1980 to 1987 has shown. Repeatedly it has been seen that making approaches to groups holding hostages using the same assumptions which might be used in the West are met either with incredulity, or disdain.

We can understand this better if we consider a little of the context to the Shi'ite terrorist[25], and in so doing, try to identify areas where Western assumptions seem to be inappropriate. In a sense, Shi'ite terrorism might properly be termed 'fanatical' if we consider the religious roots of the term, for the behaviours which we find so difficult to understand (suicide bombing, for example) have their origins in the kind of religious practice which characterises Islamic fundamentalism, and especially Shi'iteism. The origins of the Shi'ite branch of Islam lie in the very beginnings of that faith. After the death of the Prophet Muhammed in 632, disputes arose over his succession as ruler of the Islamic community. Abu Bakr, an early convert to Islam but not a member of the Prophet's family, was eventually appointed as Khalifa or Caliph (deputy) to the prophet, but there remained residual support for Ali, the cousin of the Prophet. The legitimacy of Ali's claim was enhanced by his marriage to Fatima, the Prophet's daughter. After a turbulent period, Ali briefly held the Caliphate, but after his murder in 661, it passed to the family of his rival, Mu'awiya, who held it for the next century. Supporters of Ali were known as Shi'atu Ali (the party of Ali), which eventually became the Shi'a. Over time, a central quality of Shi'ite practice has been to recognise the right to succession of the descendants of Ali and Fatima, emphasising the notion of direct descent from the Prophet for its religious leaders, the Imams.

Whilst, in origin, the Shi'a branch of Islam differed over succession, and the legitimacy of family relationships with the Prophet, in time Shi'a religious practice became more fundamental, desiring a return to the religious and social practices described in the Qur'an and resisting the introduction of heretical practices, especially those of the West. Associated with this was a desire to see the creation of an Islamic State embodying the principles of Islam. In this Islamic State, the distinction between the religious and secular would not exist; thus, the notion of law outside of its religious context, for example, would have little meaning. Any distinction between politics and religion would also be meaningless. Therefore, the Western concept of democracy in such a State would be irrelevant. Islam is a 'social religion', in that it prescribes appropriateness of behaviour; so even the intimate details of relationship become part of the social structure of the State. This is particularly the case with respect to the relationships between men and women; the Qur'an devotes more to this issue than to any other area of life. Iran, as conceived after the defeat of the Shah in 1979, is such a State, and it is in that context that we must seek to understand the Islamic terrorists.

There is a further feature of Shi'ite history to which we must draw attention in order that we can develop some understanding of the suicide bomber. In 680, Hussein, the son of Ali and his wife Fatima (the daughter of the Prophet), was killed at a place called Karbala in what is now Iraq, in an attempt to overthrow the Caliphate. Both he, and his forces, were ruthlessly killed, and only a sick boy survived. Shi'ites regard Hussein's death as a martyrdom, which is given added significance by the Shi'ite stress on legitimacy of descent of religious leadership from The Prophet. This martyrdom of the kin of the Prophet remains an important feature of religious life for the Shi'ite, and more particularly, supports and sustains the notion of sacrifice and martyrdom as a feature of Shi'ite religious practice. This is evident in many walks of life, and can be seen in, for example, in the Arous ad-Damm, the Brides of Blood, which is a group of women who are dedicated to avenge the death of Hussein through their own martyrdom. It is from the ranks of organisations such as this that the suicide bombers are drawn.

Suicide is not condoned by Islam. Hussein when he was killed at Karbala is not regarded as necessarily having sought martyrdom, but rather that he was chosen for martyrdom by Allah because of his 'special merit'. Thus, members of groups such as the Arous ad-Damm indicate their willingness to become martyrs, but their choice 'for merit' depends upon the representatives of Allah on earth. In Iran, this is regarded to be the Ayatollah Khomeini, who is also Head of State. Through his representatives, the mullahs, those to be honoured by martyrdom are chosen. Thus we can see that there is an intimate link between the practice of martyrdom in Islam (through, for example, suicide bombing) and the 'official' structure of the faith. Given that no distinction is made in contemporary Iran between religion and the State, we can see how what amounts to a form of religious devotion can become an instrument of State policy. In a sense, therefore, we see in Shi'ite suicide attacks, a form of State Terrorism. We might add that actions of this kind belong in a broader context of the use of violence as a means of propagating State objectives.

Many volunteers for martyrdom exist and are trained in Iran. They seek righteousness through suffering, a common enough religious motif. Seeing these acts as a form of religious devotion, yielding religious merit, allows us to place into perspective the apparently bizarre acts of suicide that we have discussed above. It also enables us to make sense of what, to many Westerners, seem to be the bizarre features of the actions of these volunteers. For example, the driver of the truck which devastated the American Embassy in October, 1983, smiled at the Marine Guard of the Embassy Gate on his way into the compound. This was the *bassamat al-farah*, the 'smile of joy'[26] which is worn by martyrs at their time of martyrdom. Martyrdom, because of its promise of merit hereafter, is an act of joy, symbolised by this smile.

The notion of joy in martyrdom can also be seen in the videotape left behind after San'ah Muheidli, a seventeen-year-old girl, exploded a car she was driving in Southern Lebanon amongst an Israeli military convoy on the 9th April, 1985. She killed two soldiers, wounded two more, and killed herself. Before becoming a martyr, she completed, as is required, a will. This, in her case, took the form of the videotape. She entreats her mother to '. . . be merry, to let your joy explode as if it were my wedding day'[27]. Themes like these permeate many of the suicide attacks, and enable us to understand a little of the religious context to what to us seem to be essentially political acts. Indeed, in its context, it is not particularly inappropriate, for in so far as, in an Islamic context, death of this form can yield benefits in the afterlife, then it might be seen as being of positive benefit! These acts properly belong to the category of terrorist, and they do indeed seem close to a concept of the fanatical, but we should note that they are far from irrational once we understand the assumptions on which they are based.

The scale of death resulting from the use of 'human wave' tactics by the Iranian Revolutionary Guards against the Iraqis in the present Gulf war has been enormous. These tactics have not only involved adults, but unarmed teen-age boys, who have been used to force pathways through minefields. The suicide bombers who have captured our attention are the merest tip of an iceberg, a fraction both of those who have died and of those who have volunteered for martyrdom. Given its context, it would be naive to assume that attacks of this form will not be used more often if Iran's interests are threatened. From time to time, reports emerge from Iran of camps which exist for training martyrs in the use of more sophisticated instruments such as aircraft for the delivery of suicide attacks.

The Kamikaze

The Shi'ites are not alone in the systematic use of suicide to further political ends within a facilitating social context, although for the moment, they may be unique in the contemporary world. The Japanese have a long tradition of socially approved suicide in a range of circumstances, including warfare. To the West, the most infamous examples occurred during the Second World War, and of those examples, the Kamikaze pilots probably remain the best known. Indeed, we now use the term 'kamikaze' as something synonymous with suicide attacks. The Kamikaze (or Divine Wind) pilots flew specially modified aircraft which were in effect flying bombs. The pilot guided his aircraft to its target, crashing into it at great speed. Both Shi'ite and Japanese suicides of this kind reflect a different view of self-destruction than the prevailing Judeo-Christian perspective of the West. Morris[28] examines Japanese notions in this context in some detail, and considerable areas of similarity between Shi'ite and traditional Japanese views on 'service' and death are apparent.

Within traditional Japanese cultural contexts, suicide related to achieving some socially or personally defined end has a long and honourable history. Maintenance of reputation, the necessity to keep the etiquette of proper station, the removal of a slur or insult to a name, can all lead to acts of suicide. There is a long list of school principals, for example, who have committed suicide because accidental fire in their school threatened to destroy the picture of the Emperor. Even in the mid-twentieth century, a man who inadvertently gave his child the same name as the Emperor killed both himself and the child, for the given name of the Emperor should never be spoken in Japan. Within its cultural setting, such suicides are purposeful and honourable acts, serving to 'clear the name' and 'reinstate memory'.

Within this context, it becomes possible to understand the actions of the Japanese Kamikaze fighters in the Second World War. Popular images of the Kamikaze from film and television give the image of the fanatic, acting as the tool of the equally fanatical High Command. Interestingly, the decision to use suicide bombings by the Japanese Airforce seems to have been made at a meeting held, not by the High Command, but between Vice Admiral Onishi and a group of young airforce pilots on the 19th October, 1944, where the idea was enthusiastically welcomed. But as Morris[29] notes, '. . . the decision to adopt organized suicide tactics had been made in a matter of minutes, though the psychological groundwork had been laid during many centuries'. Whilst the adoption of such tactics was in the context of the realisation by the Japanese High Command of almost inevitable defeat, the individual pilots who undertook such missions were far from defeatist. Every member of the 201st Airgroup in the Philippines, for example, volunteered for the Kamikaze Units when they were first announced, and recruitment to the Units remained buoyant, indeed fervent, throughout. The Kamikaze pilots were only one element, albeit the most famous, of an array of suicide attack groups used by the Japanese armed forces.

There seems to have been no sense of coercion amongst the Kamikaze volunteers, (as with the Shi'ite volunteers), at least in its initial stages. Later, as the course of the war continued to deteriorate for the Japanese, the process of volunteering became more problematic. Even so, after a brief period of adjustment, the new volunteers achieved what was described as acquiescent 'spiritual calm'. When selected for an actual mission, they reacted with pride, whereas those not selected reacted with bitter, and sometimes hysterical, disappointment. On the night before the mission, those chosen typically slept peacefully and, on awakening, prepared for their mission in an orderly and dignified way. After a brief departure ceremony, involving the pouring of ceremonial cups of sake for each pilot by the Commanding Officer, and a brief farewell speech, the pilots took off for their ultimate destination. After the sortie, the dead pilots would be recommended for promotion in rank, as a form of posthumous honour.

In spite of the heroism and self-sacrifice of the Kamikaze pilots, they were relatively ineffective, in tactical terms, and contributed little to the Japanese war effort; this seems to have been known and understood by the pilots themselves. This is important to note, for the importance of the Kamikaze (and others) lies not in a last ditch attempt at recovery. Contrary to the assertions of some commentators[30], the existence of the Kamikaze does not appear to be a function of the Japanese High Command's inability to assess the progress of the war.

The Shi'ite terrorist, like the Kamikaze, belongs in a social, historical, religious and mystical context that legitimises and sustains such behaviour. Such activity in one sense clearly cannot be regarded as 'normal'. On the other hand, given its context, the participants do not appear to be markedly different from others. We know relatively little of the Shi'ite terrorist, but there is some information available about the typical Kamikaze pilot, which serves to emphasise his 'normal' qualities. He tended to be a University student who had suffered interruption in his education because of the war. They were, in the main, from humanities and law backgrounds rather than science or engineering, and significantly, they tended not to have any form of previous military background. From letters and contemporary comment, they appear to have been quiet, serious, even bookish people, 'above average in both culture and sensibility'. They seem to have been far removed from the 'fierce, superstitious, jingoistic fanatics'[31] of popular image.

The basis of this behaviour, as expressed in letters and other surviving written material appears to have been a 'keen sense of obligation to repay the favours bestowed on them'[32]. The focus of this gratitude seem to have been primarily to the Emperor, and to the notion of Japanese heritage. This is expressed in the final letter written by Lieutenant Yamaguchi Teruro to his father before embarking on his suicide mission:

> . . . The Japanese way of life is indeed beautiful, and I am proud of it, as I am of Japanese history and mythology which reflects the purity of our ancestors and their belief in the

past . . . That way of life is the product of all the best things which our ancestors have handed down to us. And the living embodiment of all wonderful things out of our past is the Imperial Family which, too, is the crystallisation of the splendour and beauty of Japan and its people. It is an honour to be able to give my life in defence of these beautiful and lofty things.

Allied to these sentiments was a sense of the sacrificial act, having no effect on the war as such, but having an intense personal spiritual significance. This can be seen in the following:

> If only we might fall
> Like cherry blossom in the wind—
> So pure and radiant!

This Haiku was written by a twenty-two-year-old Kamikaze pilot. The following, from his diary expresses the same sentiments:

. . . We shall serve the nation gladly in its present painful struggle. We shall plunge into enemy ships cherishing the conviction that Japan has been and will be a place where only lovely homes, brave women and beautiful friendships are allowed to exist . . .

It is not difficult for a Westerner to understand these sentiments, in the sense of patriotism, especially when we look at the form that patriotism has taken in the past (as expressed by Kipling, for example, with respect to the British Empire). It is more difficult for the contemporary Westerner to understand, however, the willing suicide of the Kamikaze pilot, especially in the knowledge that his actions will have little effect on the war. Similarly, the logic of the death of the Shi'ite bomber in a Jihad or Holy War again seems difficult for the Westerner to understand. However, before assigning both to the bizarre and inexplicable, we should consider whether their actions differ that much, at least in psychological terms, from the willing sacrifices that have characterised the United Kingdom and United States servicemen in the First and Second World Wars, who from time to time have embarked on combat in the knowledge of a very low probability of survival.

For the purposes of this discussion, parallels between the Shi'ite suicide bomber and the Kamikaze are clear. It might be argued that these extreme forms of behaviour more properly belong within the context of pre-nineteenth-century terrorism, of the form referred to by Rapoport[33] as 'sacred terror', or 'holy terror'[34]. As we have noted, the social, cultural, or religious context in which they occur is perhaps the critical element in understanding them. The religious context in which pre-nineteenth-century terrorism seems to have existed does indeed seem to have more in common with the Kamikaze than with the Provisional IRA or the Baader-Meinhof group. Martyrdom like that of the contemporary Shi'ite was not unknown amongst the Assassins, and may well share common religious origins[35]. That those religious origins also impinge on the politics of the contemporary world (the perspective from which we tend to view these acts) also has historical precedents.

It is necessary to introduce an element of caution in this discussion, however. We should note that the basis of the Kamikaze's actions was not necessarily religious, at least in the Western sense of the term. Shinto notions of the afterlife differ from Christian or Muslim views, and there seems to be little or no evidence to support the notion that the consequence of death for the Kamikaze pilot, for example, could be expressed in terms familiar to the religious or ethical beliefs of the Westerner.

The Hunger Strike

Suicide to attain a collective political goal is not confined to the Middle or Far East. Politically motivated suicide can be seen in the West within a form of Christian context, demonstrating further that perhaps the critical element is not necessarily membership of a particular religious sect, such as Shi'ites, but perhaps related to more general phenomena. Suicide, through self-induced starvation, as a form of political protest (the hunger strike) has a long history in Europe, and notably in Ireland. In the recent past, it has been a characteristic form of protest primarily used by the Irish Nationalist community, who are predominantly Roman Catholic, and it has been used explicitly to attempt to influence the political situation. Events in 1980 and 1981 focused attention on the hunger strikes of the Provisional IRA and the INLA. However, prior to this, the hunger strike was used by the German terrorist group, the Baader-Meinhof Group. Indeed, many of the tactics adopted by the Irish hunger strikers of 1980 and 81 were foreshadowed by the Baader-Meinhof Group, especially the focus on prison conditions, and the escalation of public impact through staggered deaths.

In the late 1960s, West German radical groups became involved in a 'war' against 'capitalism and imperialism', which resulted in a number of bombings and deaths. A small group of sympathisers coalesced around Andreas Baader, an ex-student, and Ulrike Meinhof, a radical journalist. The Baader-Meinhof group were responsible for a number of bombings and arson attacks against Western military installations and forces, and businesses. A Baader-Meinhof bomb near a Frankfurt shopping centre in 1972, for example, killed a United States Army Lieutenant-Colonel and injured thirteen people. Two weeks later, the group penetrated the United States Army-Europe Headquarters in Heidelberg, and placed a bomb that killed three soldiers.

Baader and Meinhof, and others of the group, were eventually captured, and sentenced to life imprisonment. Whilst in prison, they orchestrated an elaborate campaign to continue what, in their terms, they saw as the challenge to the German State, through accusations of torture and, eventually, hunger strike. In a sense, they terrorised themselves to recreate and continue the process they had initiated in their bombing campaigns.

Horst Mahler, one of the terrorists, said of the hunger strike that it was used '. . . as a whip against the Left to mobilise them . . .'.

The hunger strikes arose out of failures to intimidate the authorities into releasing the convicted terrorists through kidnapping, hostages, bombings and protest. Gudrun Ensslin captures the essence of this, when she described the hunger strikers as using their bodies '. . . as our ultimate weapon'. This threat of death failed to move the German Authorities and, in using their bodies as the ultimate weapon, Andreas Baader, Gudrun Ensslin and Jan-Carle Raspe committed suicide. The circumstances in which this occurred were intended to suggest that they had in fact been murdered by the Prison Authorities; this was not, however, the case.

There are parallels to be drawn here between the examples of political suicide already discussed. All aspire to influence events in some way through suicide. The hunger strike has more in common with self-immolation, however, as opposed to the suicide bombing attack, in that the only victim is the individual who commits suicide.

The hunger strike has been used extensively in Ireland as a form of political protest. It is almost an institutional form of protest, which draws legitimacy from a long history. A politically important suicide by hunger strike which is relevant to the contemporary problems in Northern Ireland occurred in 1920. The Lord Mayor of Cork, Terence MacSwiney, was arrested by the British authorities, courtmartialled, and sentenced to two years imprisonment. He was then transferred from Ireland to Brixton Prison, London, where, in protest, he embarked on a hunger strike which resulted in his death seventy-three days later. This suicide by hunger strike is probably the first occasion where the media played a critical part in achieving the suicide's political ends. These events may well seem to the contemporary observer an excessive reaction to the sentence and its circumstances, but in political terms, the consequences of this death were at the time considerable, serving to mobilise public opinion and increase awareness and tension.

The actuality of hunger strike has been combined with the potential of the hunger strike in the Irish political process. More dramatically than MacSwiney, but much less fatally, after the foundation of the Irish State in 1922 and the subsequent civil war, the mass hunger strike became a form of political protest in the new Republic. On October 14, 1923, 400 prisoners in Mountjoy Prison, Dublin, went on hunger strike 'as a protest against the intolerable conditions obtaining in the prison'. The strike spread to other places of internment in the country and, by 25 October, the Republican Publicity Bureau claimed 8200 prisoners were on strike; an Irish Government statement of around the same time gave the figure as 7750! This extraordinary hunger strike did not last very long, however. By November 6, some 570 remained on hunger strike, with the numbers tailing away during November. This rather bizarre episode serves to illustrate the role of the hunger strike as a form of almost institutionalised political protest in Ireland and helps make some sense of the later instances of it.

The more dramatic recent examples of this form of politically motivated suicide can be seen in the series of hunger strikes held by Republican prisoners during 1980 and 1981 which resulted eventually in the deaths of ten hunger strikers. The political consequences of these hunger strikes were considerable, serving to politicise the Nationalist community in Northern Ireland in an unprecedented way. They became a focus for protest, a process enhanced by the way in which the hunger strikes were stage-managed to result in a regular series of deaths. Indeed, the extreme degree of organisation behind these hunger strikes, and the level of control exercised seem to have served, paradoxically, to diminish their long-term effects. Whilst the name of the first hunger striker to die, Bobby Sands, is well remembered, relatively few people outside of the Nationalist community in Ireland know or remember the names of those who died later. As far as is known, there is no obvious evidence of psychopathology amongst that group of hunger strikers and it would seem inappropriate to seek explanations of their actions in terms of mental illness.

In contrast to the Shi'ite and Japanese examples, it is less easy in these Irish cases to understand the religious context of these suicides. Within the Roman Catholic religion, suicide is not condoned, nor is there any 'official' link between such suicides and ultimate benefit, (as there is in a sense in both Japanese and Shi'ite views on religion). On the other hand, Christianity does have a long history of veneration of martyrs, and given the distinctive qualities of Irish Roman Catholicism, and its links with Irish nationalism, it is possible to see at least some similarities between the Irish Catholic's view on such suicides, and the Shi'ite and Japanese views. It is, however, easier to see a supportive context in Irish history and the romantic imagery of Irish rebellion[36].

It may be that the religious context to such issues rather obscures analysis; the critical factor may not be religion as such, but an environmental context that *both* allows *and* supports it. A characteristic of terrorists like the Baader-Meinhof group and the Provisional IRA is the extent to which they can exercise control over their members. During the period prior to, and during, the hunger strikes, in both groups the prisoners were able to communicate between themselves and outside. The individuals involved were under enormous pressure to conform, and subject to actual, or fear of, intimidation if they failed to do so. It is known, for example, that one member of the Baader-Meinhof group in fear of intimidation asked prison officials to place her on the 'danger list', although she was not participating in the hunger strike. Similar intimidation appeared to be evident amongst the Northern Irish hunger strikes.

The power of group pressures on conformity should not be under-estimated nor should we assume that this does not extend to suicide.

Indeed, in other contexts, we have evidence of the extent to which such pressure can result in suicide. In recent times, the most notable example of suicide on a large scale which appeared to be the result of extreme pressure to conform is the mass suicide of the followers of the Reverend Jim Jones in Jonestown, Guyana, in 1978.

Jones founded a religious cult, called the Peoples Temple, in California, and moved to Guyana in 1977 where he and about 1000 followers lived. The cult was subject to accusations of 'brainwashing' and coercion against its members which were investigated by a United States Congressman, Representative Leo Ryan, who undertook a fact-finding mission to Jonestown. Ryan, three journalists and a Peoples Temple defector were shot to death on an airstrip as they were leaving the area, accompanied by some eighteen members of the Temple who had approached him and said they wanted to leave. A former Peoples Temple member was subsequently convicted of conspiracy in this murder, which appeared to be an attempt by Jones to prevent knowledge of conditions in Jonestown spreading to the outside world. Hours after the murder of Congressman Ryan, Jones and 912 of his followers, men, women and children, committed suicide by either gunfire or poisoning. Parents killed their families, and then themselves.

It is difficult to understand the particular circumstances that resulted in this mass suicide. What can be certain is that, whilst no doubt there was some coercion involved, the majority of Jones's followers voluntarily killed themselves and their families. The explanation of this behaviour is usually presented in terms of conformity—the collective pressure causing the individual members of the cult to kill themselves. Given evidence like this of the power of pressures to conformity, suicide either through hunger strike or in some other way, becomes less difficult to understand. The tight world of the prison, its isolation, inherent abnormality, and the pervasive necessary antagonism between prison officers and prisoners, could only serve to enhance the pressure to conform. Analyses of the Jonestown suicide would emphasise similar features.

In the case of both the Irish and German hunger strikers, the suicides were preceded by periods of confrontation and 'surrogate' torture that would further have enhanced the pressures prisoners were subjected to. Accusations of torture were made by the Baader-Meinhof group against the prison authorities that subsequently were admitted to be false. The Irish hunger strikes were preceded by the 'dirty protest', an extraordinary period of self-inflicted degradation by prisoners who refused to wear clothes, and deliberately fouled their cells. The critical political element in both of these cases is the extent to which the media were involved in these protests, both as the principal audience, and as the mechanism for its transmission to the community outside. Well-orchestrated support movements could then make use of it as a focus around which political protest could be developed. However, these periods of surrogate torture also provided the critical psychological context for the prisoners in which the hunger strikes could be undertaken.

Both the Shi'ite and Japanese suicides were rather different, in the sense that the individuals concerned were not confined. On the other hand, both contemporary Shi'ite society, and Japanese society of the time, show many attributes of intense control, with restrictions on extra-societal influences. In many respects they are as 'psychologically' closed as the prisons which sustained both the Baader-Meinhof and the IRA suicides.

Suicide and Terrorism

As with terrorism, the hunger strikers were incidental victims in political protest. They differ from the victims of a terrorist bombing, for example, by being compliant, and indeed instrumental in the violence. In this respect, therefore, this form of suicide certainly appears to be if not a form of terrorism, closely related (the term 'Pseudo-terrorism'[37] has been used to refer to it). As political suicide, it is unique, in that the other forms of political suicide discussed here lack the organisational and media capacity to capitalise on the event. The closest parallel to it is self-immolation. However, as far as can be judged, the known examples of political self-immolation were essentially personal acts, and lacked the group dimension (either coercive or supportive) of the hunger strikes.

The Kamikaze and Shi'ite suicide attacks address a related, but different forum. In these cases, the individual appears to be truly incidental, in that his death is an inevitable but incidental consequence of a successful mission. Whilst we might find such deaths horrific, the focus of the action is not in terms of the media use of the individual death, but in terms of other violent attributes of terrorist action.

Fanaticism and Terrorism

We can see that the notion of fanaticism is complex. Commonly held assumptions about the relationship between fanaticism and mental illness, for example, seem to be inappropriate. Some clues as to the nature of the cognitive processes underlying the fanatic can be discerned from the analysis of prejudice and authoritarianism, but these alone still seem unsatisfactory. It is clear that our analysis needs to take the social and cultural context, as well as personal factors into account, to understand properly the nature of the concept. Indeed, perhaps the most significant feature of the discussion above is a recognition of the role of the cultural context when judging the nature of fanaticism.

This discussion does have a bearing on the analysis of terrorism. We can see that other kinds of act of an extreme nature can occur which might have attributes in common with terrorism. We can also see that it may well be that the term Fanatical can be applied to some terrorists. It also introduces into the classes of things that might be termed terrorism, the politically motivated suicide, or threat of suicide. Politically purposeful self-destruction may be relatively rare in our society, although not unknown as can be seen above. But in societies (or self-defined social systems) which legitimise such activity, it seems inappropriate to regard such behaviour as evidence of mental illness, nor, given its particular broader social context, of fanaticism, in any pejorative sense.

Our discussion of the fanatic, therefore, leaves us with rather uncertain conclusions. We use the term to refer to extreme behaviour, which in the main we disapprove of. Our particular perspective may well lead us to label the terrorist as fanatic, in that terrorism involves the use of extranormal violence. It may indeed, therefore, be part of the cluster of attributes of the terrorist. We might especially feel this is an appropriate term to use where his actions lead to self destruction, and given the religious and social context noted above, the term fanatic seems particularly appropriate. But even in these extreme circumstances, the particular cultural context to which the individual belongs may well alter our view of it. The ascription of the term fanatic is a process of labelling, rather than a description of the inherent qualities of individuals. It does not refer to psychological qualities of the individual, and may not in the end particularly progress our understanding of the concept of Terrorism. The Fanatic and the Terrorist may have related psychological qualities but, once more, neither are necessarily unique in this respect.

CHAPTER 6

Terrorists

Psychological accounts of terrorism are few, and those that exist have, in the main, attempted to address what motivates the terrorist, or to describe his personal characteristics. Both of these approaches seem to assume that those who commit terrorist acts can be identified by such attributes. Research in this area has rarely gone beyond this assumption.

Indeed there has been an ambivalence on the part of many psychologists to become involved in research in this area at all. This may lie in part in the nature of the discipline. Although psychologists are interested in the social context of behaviour, they are primarily interested in the personal qualities of that context, in contrast, for example, to sociological or political approaches which might be expected to have much more interest in terrorism as a social movement. This quality of social movement (in terms of the political aspirations of terrorism) we have already noted to be an important attribute of terrorism and this, to some extent, leaves the psychologist with his individual orientation in a quandary.

In spite of this, the relative lack of systematic social and psychological research in this area may at first sight seem rather odd and unexpected, given the extent of contemporary public concern about terrorism. This lack of research becomes a little less surprising, however, when the problems of working in this area are examined. One substantial difficulty for workers to face is that the issue of terrorism impinges on many areas of concern to government. This has resulted in much research in this area being government or security force related and funded, and not therefore neces-sarily available to the general public, or other researchers. The reasons for this are not always obvious, and the area is bedevilled by secrecy, which makes objective analysis very difficult. It reflects a concern that the fruits of research may be of value to the terrorist, by alerting dissident groups to tactics or thinking that might jeopardise police or security force action, or perhaps by alerting terrorist groups to areas of interest and weakness. Where research may have direct operational relevance, this, of course, is understandable; but much of the work that needs doing in this area would not necessarily make much direct impact on operational areas. Analyses of crime are not discouraged because criminals might learn from them; why should we regard terrorism in any different way? Furthermore, excessive secrecy means that such research is not exposed to the criticism of peers, an important element in the research process. One consequence of this is that research conducted under these conditions can suffer from relatively limited conceptual development. Indeed, when research of this nature does eventually emerge, such criticism often seems very appropriate[1].

Another practical reason for the limited quantity and quality of much published research, and perhaps of greater significance, lies in the very nature of terrorist action and its association with violence and illegality. Kellen[2] noted that there is a dearth of primary source material, and this is related to essential features of the process of terrorism. The only terrorist available to the researcher for interview or investigation is one who has been caught and imprisoned, and/or reformed. Clearly, attempts to generalise on the basis of such samples must be of limited value. Any evidence derived from such sources must be viewed with some suspicion.

The researcher must also be alert to the potential for the abuse of the research process through false accounts, planted by one or other set of protagonists. In particular, primary source material in the form of news reports or comment on terrorist incidents, or details of incidents, which lack verification must be treated with great caution. Objective analysis of the kind undertaken by impartial investigators may well not be welcomed by terrorist groups, or their political enemies. The reasons for this may well lie in the exposure of excesses, but it may also reflect on more general features of terrorism. Research is a form of communication, and if we remember the role of communication in the direction of terrorist activity, we can see that it may be in the interests of one or other set of protagonists either to influence or control the dissemination of research information.

It might be expected that psychological, as distinct from sociological investigations of terrorism would in particular be characterised by the use of experimental, or at least empirical, methodologies. Such work is in fact significantly absent from the literature. Work of this kind is difficult in the extreme to conduct. Such investigations would require access to terrorist groups for example, *and* involvement in their acts — clearly an impossibility for most researchers. To a lesser extent, the same difficulty applies to systematic observational studies.

Another problem for research concerns the general lack of conceptual clarity in the analysis of terrorism or the terrorist. The discussion in earlier chapters has identified some of these problems. Given conceptual confusion and the lack of agreed attributes, it is not surprising that psychologically-based investigations are lacking. This, coupled with the often implicit assumptions underpinning notions of terrorism (about mental illness, for example), only adds to the problems of the research process. Strangely enough, lack of definitional clarity may not be such a problem for other disciplines, who might have more concern with the broader processes of terrorism. But for the psychologist, who must focus on *particular* behaviour, the lack of agreed attributes represents a quite fundamental difficulty. What is taken as the subject matter for investigation, if we are unsure as to the descriptive qualities of the behaviour?

Attempts at psychological explanations of terrorism using terms drawn from other disciplines may underlie many of these conceptual issues. An example of this can be seen in the attempt to identify special qualities of violence as qualities of the terrorist. Many circumstances involve the use of instrumental violence, but not all those circumstances are properly described as terrorist incidents. The political aspiration of terrorism defines it as a political act, but this does not mean that there is any necessary psychological reality distinguishing terrorist violence from other forms of violence. The political context of the terrorist act which is so important is not something that can be readily expressed at the same level of analysis as violent behaviour; one is an observable behaviour (an act of violence), the other is a concept (political context). Furthermore, that context does not refer to *psychological* attributes.

Descriptions of Terrorists: Terrorists in General

Notwithstanding, one approach to the social and psychological analysis of the terrorist is to attempt to identify and describe some generalisations about them. This will inevitably be a risky kind of activity, given the definitional problems referred to above. On the other hand, we do make generalisations about people, and certainly from a psychological perspective, there is value in classifying people with respect to psychological and social attributes. In doing this, one approach is to try to establish generalisations about the terrorist from what might be known about large numbers sharing some common attribute (nationality, gender, etc.). Because of the nature of the evidence used, this approach tends to focus on relatively simplistic social and psychological variables or concepts. It is an approach characterised by attempts at generalisations based on median or 'average' attributes of people.

Russell and Miller[3] compiled evidence on what they regarded as eighteen primary revolutionary movements, including Middle Eastern, Latin American, West European and Japanese groups, using data derived from news reports of the period 1966–76. The groups on which their analysis was based were somewhat mixed in terms of their geographical and social contexts. It includes groups such as the Popular Front for the Liberation of Palestine, the Black September Organisation, the Provisional IRA and the Basque group ETA which have a predominantly nationalistic aim, and the Japanese Red Army, the Baader-Meinhof Group, and the Italian Red Brigade, which might be thought to be more generalist in focus, seeing their aspirations in broader left wing political terms. Arguably, these kinds of differences in focus might be of some significance, in that perhaps different kinds of aspiration might well attract rather different kinds of participant. This issue remains unclear.

A number of consistencies can be identified between the various groups, although these are largely in terms of contextual social factors (such as age) rather than in terms of psychological variables. Nevertheless information of this kind is of considerable value, and serves to set the scene for more focused studies. The usual age for terrorist group membership was remarkably consistent at from twenty-two to twenty-five, based on evidence from arrested group members, and known participants; only in Japanese, Palestinian and West German groups was the likely age of membership over twenty-five. For the Baader-Meinhof Group, and the 2nd June Movement, over 100 members reflected an average age of 31.3, whereas for the PLO and the Japanese Red Army, the average was in the late twenties. It is not easy to explain this discrepancy in age, but one variable may be the extent to which the groups recruit their support from university students (who are predominantly in the eighteen to twenty-three range) or whether they recruit from other occupational classes.

The age of the leadership of terrorist groups, as distinct from their ordinary membership, is however higher. Mario Santucho, the founder and leader of the Revolutionary Army of the People (*Ejercito Revolucionario del Pueblo*) was forty at the time of his death in July, 1976, and his principal lieutenants were of a similar age. Ulrike Meinhof was forty-two when she committed suicide in 1976, and most of the leaders of the West German terrorist movement at that time were in their thirties or forties. Carlos Marighella, often regarded as one of the major contributors to the theoretical development of terrorism, was fifty-eight at the time of his death in November, 1969.

Active membership of the groups studied by Russell and Miller was predominantly male—over eighty percent of significant terrorist operations were directed, led and executed by males. The Uruguayan Tupamaros groups made most use of females amongst Latin American groups, but the most notable role for females in this study seems to be in subsidiary or support activities, like intelligence collection, couriers and nurses. From time to time however, women have occupied important, and very often leading, operational roles in terrorist groups. Indeed, where women have been active, it has tended to be as leader. Leila Khalid, for example, had an important role in the Popular Front for the Liberation of Palestine, Fusako Shigenobu was a leader of the Japanese Red Army and Norma Ester Arostito co-founded and provided substantial theoretical and ideological support for the Argentine Monteneros. More typically, however, women seem to have occupied support and service roles within terrorist groups. This seems to be as much a pragmatic decision based on perceived strengths, rather than for any chauvinistic reason. Women living together, for example, rarely attract the kind of comment that a group of men may, and therefore they can more easily establish safe houses. Women may also have greater freedom of movement than men, raising less suspicion in the eyes of the security services, and therefore well suited to movement of weapons and materials. Finally, women may well have a role in areas such as intelligence gathering, for similar reasons, and by virtue of their sexual attraction and favours.

An exception to this role for women can be seen in the Baader-Meinhof Group, and the 2nd June Movement. In the Baader-Meinhof Group, women contributed in the region of one third of the operational membership and played an active part in the group's violent activities. There seems to be no evidence to suggest that there was any form of role restriction practised by either the Baader-Meinhof or the Red Army Faktion, and women freely undertook all the range of activities of the groups. The same seems to have been the case for the 2nd June Movement. An example of this can be seen in Ilse Jandt, a terrorist associated with the 2nd June Movement, who both planned and carried out the murder of an informant, Ulrich Schmuecker, in June, 1974.

Most terrorists appear to be unmarried. This seems to apply to some seventy-five to eighty percent of European, Middle Eastern and Asian terrorists. Where a participant is married, they tend to sever family ties on embarking on a terrorist career. Only the Tupamaros in Uruguay seem to have had an appreciable number of married members, a fact that seems to have caused some operational difficulties for them. Depending on whether the groups operate in rural or urban environments, so the terrorists tend to have their origins in appropriate rural or urban backgrounds. In particular, membership of most groups that impinge on the European nations and the United States are predominantly urban. The focus of their activities, not surprisingly, is therefore mainly upon urban centres. The predominance of urban backgrounds also extends to the Palestinian movements, whose members have often spent time in urban environments, even if they were born into a rural family.

The socio-economic status of terrorists is worthy of attention, given the expressed espousal of many groups of left wing radical views. In statistical terms, most terrorists have mainly middle class, well-educated backgrounds. Often their parents are professionals (doctors or lawyers for example), or government employees. The backgrounds of the Baader-Meinhof group illustrate this clearly; Baader was the son of an historian, Meinhof the daughter of an art historian, Horst Mahler the son of a dentist, Holger Meins the son of a business executive, and Gudrun Ensslin the daughter of a clergyman. However, this is not the case for all groups, notably the paramilitary groups in Northern Ireland. There, both protestant groups (such as the Ulster Volunteer Force and the Red Hand

Commando) and the catholic groups (such as the Provisional IRA, the Official IRA and the Irish National Liberation Army [INLA]) are drawn predominantly from working class backgrounds. This may well be a reflection of the nature of the conflict in Northern Ireland, when compared to the activities of other terrorist arenas.

Russell and Miller identify some two-thirds of terrorist group members as having some form of university training. Approximately eighty percent of the Baader-Meinhof group, for example, had university experience. Even ETA, the Basque separatist and nationalist group, has a sizeable minority membership with university backgrounds. Given this apparently important role for students in terrorist activity, Russell and Miller have identified universities as the major recruiting ground for terrorists. It may, on the other hand, be argued that the experience of university itself gives rise to the questioning of society's values, and that this, rather than presence at a university, is the critical issue in determining recruitment to terrorist organisations. For whatever reason, universities certainly have proved to be ideological training grounds for many terrorists.

Thus in statistical terms, Russell and Miller draw the following composite of the typical terrorist. The individual is likely to be single, male, aged between twenty-two and twenty-four with some university experience, probably in the humanities. He is likely to come from a middle- or upper-class family, and was probably recruited to terrorism at university, where he was first exposed to Marxist or other revolutionary ideas. Some confirmation to these views has been provided by Schmidten[4] in analyses of German terrorist groups. Universities, particularly in Berlin, Heidelberg, Hamburg and Frankfurt, provided a large fraction of group membership. Students in general were also recruited in other environments.

How useful is this composite picture? Its utility depends largely upon assumptions of uniformity amongst terrorist groups, and the acceptance of uniform characteristics in the data base from which the summaries are drawn. We know already, however, that not all terrorist groups conform to the above composite picture. Certainly, the Irish Terrorist Groups do not appear to share the class nor educational background outlined above. On the other hand, this form of essentially 'survey' material serves to flesh out the rather shady individual that we tend to see as the terrorist. We are left with the picture of a rather ordinary individual, lacking obvious signs of social deprivation or disadvantage.

Another contribution to the same approach can be seen in Cooper[5], who presents a study which in some respects is similar to Russell and Miller. It offers an overview of terrorist behaviour from perhaps a more explicitly psychological perspective, although taking a relatively sympathetic view of the terrorist. Whilst it is expressed at a rather general level, and is on occasions not particularly explicit in citing evidence for the points made, nevertheless it does raise a number of issues relevant to this discussion. He notes that terrorism is rarely a full-time occupation, which might serve to distinguish the terrorist from the mercenary or soldier of fortune. This analogy is sometimes made with respect to the international dimension of terrorism, and is an important point to note.

He also notes that there may well be an aspiration, at least for some terrorists, to more legitimate political expression; terrorism (in their case) being a step (albeit unconventional) on the route to political power. It is difficult to evaluate this assertion, although it is of course frequently noted that a number of contemporary political leaders may have their origins in some terrorist group associated with a struggle for independence. It may well be, however, a form of *post hoc* generalisation, rather than a motivating condition evident in the young terrorist. The acquisition of power may well be a consequence of a successful terrorist campaign, and thus the terrorist might be thrust into the position of political figure. He himself may well not necessarily welcome this change of role, or perform it effectively.

The famous Latin American revolutionary, Che Guevara, seems to be an example of this. During the two years of revolution in Cuba, Guevara distinguished himself as a dedicated, courageous and effective revolutionary[6]. His background however seemed to ill prepare him for this role. As an adolescent, he demonstrated an interest in the treatment of leprosy, which he sustained when he left his home country of Argentina to travel to other South American States, working, for example, as a male nurse in a leprosarium in San Pablo in Peru. He seems to have redirected his enthusiasm and energy away from tropical medicine when he saw the role of the CIA in Guatemala in overthrowing a reformist regime. The rewards of his eventual revolutionary success in Cuba included the Directorship of the Cuban National Bank, and subsequently Minister of Industries. But he seems to have been ill suited for these roles, and he himself appeared to derive little pleasure from them. He left them, in fact, and, after a period in the Congo training guerillas, he went to Bolivia, where he met his death. Guevara seems to have been a successful revolutionary who had political power thrust upon him, rather than it being a goal to which he worked.

A further point which Cooper[7] makes is that '. . . the terrorist has to work very hard, psychologically and practically, at what he aspires to become'. We should perhaps take this to refer not to the physical requirements of terrorism, but to the effort required to remain a terrorist (although circumstances facilitate this). The terrorist rarely has military training before embarking on his terrorist career, and often comes from a family background which would ill prepare him for a life of privation. Cooper's point also extends to the nature of the terrorist act, however. He emphasises the ordinariness of the terrorist, and the fact, therefore, that he has to learn to kill, or at least to distance himself from the consequences of the acts he initiates. In this respect, he appears to be like the soldier, who also has to learn to kill or otherwise involve himself in violence. It is also worth noting that, in general, whilst the terrorist may well be responsible for some quite terrible and ruthless acts of violence, he is rarely barbaric in the sense that the Mafia, for example, might mutilate or deliberately maim its victims. Clearly, this is not necessarily the case, as can be seen by the kinds of atrocity committed by the Mau Mau in Kenya, for example, or by the Provisional IRA in Northern Ireland.

Barbarianism in killing or injury is, Cooper suggests, more typical of 'repressive terrorism' used to coerce and control. This may, of course, characterise the response of the state (as in Argentina during its last period of military rule, for example), but it can also be seen in the efforts of terrorist groups to maintain control over their own members (the characteristic punishment shootings, knee cappings and savage beatings of the Irish terrorist groups, for example). By stressing the 'humanity' of the terrorist, (although we should remember that we are using the term 'humanity' in a restricted sense), Cooper serves to remind us of an alternative perspective to terrorism from that which emphasises abnormality or psychopathology. This analysis is clearly consistent with that developed in earlier chapters, in its emphasis on the normal, rather than abnormal.

In the same context, Jenkins[8] draws attention to the relatively limited scale of most terrorist activity, and especially fatalities. Given the potential for mass slaughter, few incidents (less than one percent of all terrorist activity in the last decade) has involved the death of large numbers of victims in a single incident. It might therefore be more appropriate to think of scale in a symbolic, rather than numerical, context. It is all very well to discuss this at a conceptual level, however, but we must not lose sight of the fact that the victim of the terrorist remains a victim. To dismiss him as an incidental casualty does not remove the fact that he is a casualty who may well have no links whatsoever with the terrorists aims or grievances.

Perhaps the most important characteristic Cooper[9] draws attention to is the loneliness and isolation of the terrorist from the society which, para-doxically, he may well profess to defend. This essential loneliness, he argues, inevitably focuses the terrorist within a political context and confirms his marginal states in society, imposing a natural limit and constraint on the scope of terrorist action. Whether such isolation precedes involvement in terrorist activity, or is a result of it, is difficult to assess. Certainly, the operational terrorist *by definition* is acting outside of the law and must, if he wishes to avoid detection, resort to secrecy and inevitable isolation. Such isolation may well constitute an important psychological variable, impinging on both the individual and the nature of the group to which the terrorist belongs.

At a general level, Cooper's observations are of value and certainly help to inform our analysis of terrorism. At the more individual level, however, they all seem to suffer from some of the problems associated with Russell and Miller's approach. The kinds of generalisation made in attempting to identify broad characteristics must inevitably gloss over important detailed individual issues. If we assume 'terrorists' to be some form of homogeneous category, then clearly these approaches have something to contribute. But even within the terms set by, for example, Russell and Miller, there are clearly important differences between groups, that may well have a profound bearing on our understanding of them. The discussions in the earlier chapters have made the complexities of the notion of terrorism apparent. In the light of this, it seems unlikely that attempts at identifying uniformity of attributes will be successful.

Female Terrorists

We can explore consistencies between terrorists from a different kind of perspective, however. We can attempt to develop accounts and descriptions of particular groups of terrorists, making relatively specific generalisations more possible. One important attempt has been published by Galvin[10] for female terrorists. The role of women in terrorist movements has attracted considerable interest, for a number of reasons. The woman terrorist seems to offer a challenge to the contemporary stereotype of the woman as caregiver and protector and the notion of the violent woman seems to give rise to both horror and fantasy for Western man. It also seems to offer an unusual reflection on the notion of 'equality' of opportunity, and clearly reflects upon our most deep seated prejudices about gender appropriate behaviour, especially with respect to fighting and aggression. The female terrorist also has another unusual feature which has attracted attention. In numerical terms, the extent of involvement of females in terrorism greatly exceeds the extent of involvement of females in crime.

Galvin makes the important initial point that the role of the female terrorist is conditioned by both her membership of a terrorist group *and* her femininity. Thus, whilst those attributes of femininity regarded as characteristic, such as softness, delicacy and showing less restraint than males, do not preclude or even seem to be relevant in terrorist membership or action, nevertheless, female characteristics may well be important in affecting the dynamics of the terrorist group, or be reflected in the process of group membership.

In particular, unlike men, women in most contemporary Western societies do not, in the nature of things, acquire skills with weapons or gain experience of combat (or surrogate combat) through membership of youth groups and army service. At a simple level, we tend not to expect female children to play with guns as we do male children — the process of sex-role stereotyping. Thus, whilst for many men, it might be argued that terrorism might reflect a progressive development (in some sense) of either natural or encouraged aggression, this is more difficult to argue for women. In the light of this, it may be suggested, therefore, that terrorist membership is a more active process for women than for men.

A common route of entry into terrorism for female terrorists, Galvin notes, is through political involvement, and belief in a political cause. There appears to be some evidence that women are more idealistic than men and therefore it might be argued that failure to achieve change, or the experience of death or injury to a loved one, may well give rise to extreme frustration and desire for revenge, impelling at least some women towards extra-normal activities. Galvin also argues that the female terrorist enters into terrorism with different motivations and expectations than the male terrorist. In contrast to men who Galvin characterises as being tuned into terrorism by the promise of 'power and glory', females embark on terrorism '. . . attracted by promises of a better life for their children and the desire to meet people's needs that are not being met by an intractable establishment'. This, combined with the frustrated idealism referred to above, might be helpful in explaining why the female terrorist seems to be more persistent than her male colleagues.

Another significant feature which Galvin feels may characterise the involvement of the female terrorist is the 'male or female lover/female accomplice . . . scenario'. The lover, a member of the terrorist group, serves to introduce the female into the group. This may represent a form of 'secondary' terrorism, where the individual is not required necessarily to undertake actual terrorist action, but rather to serve in a support role, of the form noted by Russell and Miller[11]. Aiding and comforting may characterise this form of terrorist membership, and it should of course be noted that this role serves a very important purpose, in providing and defining a substance and context to the terrorist group, materially contributing to the dynamics of group membership. Implicit in this route of membership is a form of subservience and subordination to the group member, however, and such female secondary terrorists might well be subjected to some form of exploitation, either sexual or operational, in the sense of being used as decoys.

Women in themselves can have value in a terrorist organisation however, as Galvin notes. Attack by women can be rather less expected than by men, a factor which may have operational significance for the terrorist group. Pregnancy and care of children, may well be significant in giving security forces a false sense of ease in, for example, an ambush or attempt at bomb planting. 'A woman, trading on the impression of being a mother, non-violent, fragile, even victim like, can more easily pass scrutiny by security forces . . .'[12].

The actions of Nezar Hindawi, an arab terrorist referred to in Chapter 5, and his exploitation of his Irish girl friend, illustrates both the way in which females can be sexually exploited by terrorists, and the value of the female (or at least some attributes of the female) in an operational sense.

Hindawi deliberately used his pregnant girlfriend as a walking bomb in an attempt to blow up an El Al airplane in April, 1986. The girl had previously been abandoned by Hindawi when he knew she was pregnant, but he re-established the relationship and promised to marry her (all within a period of a few days). The marriage was to take place in Israel, however, and the girl was to travel there alone, meeting Hindawi in Tel Aviv where they would marry. The unfortunate girl was stopped at Heathrow airport during a baggage check when attempting to board the flight, carrying sufficient explosives in her hand baggage to destroy the plane (and the passengers, herself and her unborn child). There can be no doubt that Hindawi deliberately engineered this; he even drove the girl to the airport and saw her off. Such cynicism and disregard for life (of even his own child) is beyond belief; as an example of sexual exploitation, it probably is without rival.

We make judgements on the basis of non-verbal features of individuals[13]. Thus, what we wear, the way in which we deal with people, even the extent to which we maintain eye-contact, are all cues on which we form impressions and make judgements. The stereotypes (sexual or otherwise) which we bring to this process are also very important in influencing our judgements. The security forces are no less subject to this than others. Use of these factors may well constitute one of the most operationally important attributes of the female terrorist. The mother pushing her child in a pram seems to convey all the cues of passivity possible—caring, presence of children and loving behaviour. Such a situation also, of course, constitutes for the terrorist an almost perfect opportunity to move materials and weapons around in the pram. This is because the non-verbal cues in this situation make it very unlikely that the security forces will search a pram—as innocent an object, you might think, as you could get. A pram also offers an excellent example of a moving bomb, which can be wheeled into some either sensitive, or populous area (carrying a baby as well as explosives) and left (without the baby) to subsequently explode. Using the same principles, Hindawi might well have judged that his pregnant girl friend was unlikely to attract attention. In this instance, he fortunately was wrong although we should note that she appeared to have been detected by a routine search, rather than arousal of suspicion. As she appeared not to know of the presence of the bomb, she would of course have no reason to act suspiciously. As a general principle, therefore, non-verbal cues are an important source of information in impression formation, and an element of that is gender; even more so, it might be argued, is pregnancy. The operational value of this for the terrorist is clear.

Women have also been used as sexual 'bait', both drawing men into the terrorist group, and also of course, drawing targeted individuals into ambushes. Female sexuality can be argued, for example, as a significant factor in the recruitment of Michael Baumman into terrorism, and similarly Joe Remiro into the Symbianese Liberation Army (SLA). The availability of sexual favours certainly seems to play a role in sustaining membership of the terrorist group, and it might be argued that, in some cases, sex itself seems to unify and consolidate group membership. Thus with respect to the SLA Pattie Hearst says 'Free sex was one of the principles of the cell. It was obvious . . . that revolutionaries operating underground could not go out on the street and find sex in the usual way. Therefore, everyone in the cell had to take care of the needs of others. No one was *forced* to have sex in the cell. But if one comrade asked another, it was "comradely" to say yes.'[14]. In this context, the female terrorist can be seen to occupy a quite pivotal role. We should note, however, that this does not necessarily eliminate sexual exploitation of the female terrorist group member.

As a means of understanding better the role of women as an element in the dynamics of terrorist groups, the kind of approach developed by Galvin has obvious utility. Because it addresses a major element of the whole, it is possible to develop more specific descriptions and analyses than the kind of statistical summary offered by Russell and Miller[15]. It is perhaps unreasonable to expect a general survey to offer insights into the particular reasons for group membership, but by drawing our attention to the inappropriateness of many of the stereotypes of the female in the context of terrorism, Galvin serves a useful purpose in further refining our notion of the terrorist. The female terrorist challenges our stereotyped views on the 'naturalness' of aggression and, in particular, makes us re-evaluate the relationship between presumed male attributes and the process of violent political change. Indeed, for some women, the attraction of terrorism might well be that challenge to stereotyped roles, a challenge they may well be unable to make in any other way. It is tempting to speculate on the role of the feminist movement in this respect.

Weinberg and Eubank[16] have presented a complimentary view of the woman terrorist to that of Galvin, focusing on a particular group of Italian woman terrorists. They surveyed biographical information on 451 female terrorists active between 1970 and 1984. By taking a broader biographical perspective, they are somewhat similar in approach to Russell and Miller, but because they address a more limited and homogeneous range of terrorists, they are able to relate their findings to the social and political context of women in Italy. Thus, unlike those studies reviewed so far, they address the context of the development of the female terrorist, as well as describing her characteristics.

In social terms, Italy has changed considerably since the Second World War, and these changes are particularly apparent in the role of women in society. Major social changes affecting the status of women include the approval of civil divorce in 1974 and the endorsement by referendum of abortion in 1981. There was a significant rise in the number of women attending university (thirty-six percent increase from 1973 to 1982), and many more women than formerly entered the work force. Associated with these changes has been a reduction in the power of the Catholic Church, and a change in political allegiance of women.

This changed social context seems to have provided the backdrop to the increased female involvement in terrorism in Italy. The biographical data base used by Weinberg and Eubank contained data on 2512 individuals, of whom eighteen percent were female. Contrary to the conventional stereotypes, not all Italian terrorists are left wing. The typical European terrorist group that captures the headlines (such as Baader-Meinhof, for example) is of the left, but of Italian women involved in terrorism, some ten percent of the total were associated with neo-fascist groups.

In contrast to the relatively passive role adopted by women in other terrorist groups, Italian women terrorists seem to have had a much more active role; of the sample studied by Weinberg and Eubank, seventy-three percent were classified as having either an active or a leadership role. This is substantially greater than the kind of involvement of female terrorists referred to earlier. As a group, Italian female terrorists come overwhelmingly from an urban background, often married to other terrorists, but with a significant minority (28%) the siblings of other terrorists. The typical age range on arrest is 20-29 (68%). In terms of occupation, they are likely to be students (35%), clerks, secretaries, nurses or technicians (23%) or teachers (20%). These figures would suggest that as a group, they are relatively well educated.

Perhaps the most striking feature revealed by this analysis is the role of family relationships in the development of the female terrorist. The nature of the data used by Weinberg and Eubank (newspaper reports) makes detailed analysis difficult, but a highly significant relationship between female terrorists and their relationships to other terrorists was found when males and females were compared. It is not possible from this evidence to discover whether that high degree of family relationship was the result of being introduced to terrorism through the family (especially husband), or the result of some other factor. On the other hand, given that the female terrorists seemed to have little political involvement prior to association with a terrorist group, and that they tended to join the terrorist groups later than men, this lends some weight to the notion that immediate family relationships were critical determinants in terrorist involvement for women.

Along with the work of Galvin[17], Weinberg and Eubank certainly support the view that the female terrorist differs from the male. The emphasis given to this difference may well be conditioned by social factors. The Italian female seems somewhat different from other female terrorists, and this may well be related to the changing role of women in modern Italian society. On the other hand, the significance of the divergence of such terrorists from the stereotyped female role, highlighted by Galvin, should not be underestimated.

A Terrorist Organisation

Another approach to the description of individual kinds of terrorists has been taken by Clark[18] in his analysis of the Basque separatist group, ETA (*Euzkadi ta Askatasuna*). Clark identifies as his target population a nationally defined group, in contrast to the sexually and politically defined group identified by Galvin. In doing this, it would be reasonable to expect a greater cohesion around a particular cause than in the case of the female terrorist. Clark undertook a detailed study of the ETA organisation and membership, based largely on secondary studies, newspaper accounts and officially released information, as well as detailed case histories of 48 ETA members, and more limited data on 447 other members. Within the context of studies of this kind, it represents probably one of the most adequate and comprehensive analyses. It is useful to contrast this study, in fact, with the kind of more journalistic analysis of terrorist groups. McNight[19], for example, whilst appearing to undertake a psychologically oriented approach to such an analysis, in practice produces little more than a superficial sensationalised discussion.

Like Russell and Miller, Clark reveals that the age of entry into ETA is around the mid to late 20s; its membership is predominantly male typically from a working class or lower middle class background. The data presented on socio-economic background is limited, but it would appear that relatively few members were unemployed, or living on unemployment compensation (given the relatively high levels of Basque unemployment in general, this is unusual). Very few seem to have upper class backgrounds and relatively few come from the middle classes. It is also a matter of interest to note that Clark found in his sample no ETA member with farming occupations or from farming backgrounds.

Although ETA is commonly associated with a distinctive ethnic and nationalistic perspective, Clark found only four or five out of ten members were the offspring of two Basque parents (which is below the average for the Basque population as a whole), with a considerably higher percentage of ETA members having only one Basque parent than the Basque overall population (eighty percent as opposed to sixty percent for the Basque population as a whole). He also notes that the families of ETA members were not necessarily nationalistic (although many were). Nor had the families of Clark's sample been subjected to particular oppression. This seems to suggest that the family, in this context, is not necessarily the focus for nationalistic expression and that, at least in some cases, extra-family influences may be important. ETA does, however, tend to recruit from Basque speaking areas, and in particular, from small cities, rather than metropolitan areas. These may well form the necessary focus for nationalist aspirations.

Actual recruitment to ETA seems a gradual process. Once joined, members tend to live relatively conventional lives, punctuated by bursts of terrorist activity. In this respect, therefore, the life of an ETA member differs from the communal living that seems to have characterised some of the European or American terrorist groups (the SLA for example). Presumably, two factors in this are the relatively large size of ETA and the relationship between the national aspirations of the organisation and its geographical location. Recruitment to any clandestine organisation is of course likely to be a gradual process, given the need to guard against infiltration by police informants. Testing the new recruit, in terms of his commitment, is not simply a matter of ensuring operational competence.

Within ETA, as Clark notes however, ambiguity of membership can extend to the kind of role occupied by the individual in the organisation. In any complex terrorist movement, there are various vital support roles that need to be filled. The individuals who actually carry a gun and undertake operations will be limited in number. The weapons used in an attack, for example, are unlikely to be carried to the location by the terrorist undertaking the assassination. Certainly, he is unlikely to retain the weapon after a shooting for example, both to safeguard himself from incriminating evidence and to protect the weapon in the event of him being caught. So, other members of the organisation will play a role in perhaps hiding weapons (or parts of weapons) and in moving the weapons away from the scene. This is of course in stark contrast to the small terrorist cell which operates without wider logistical support, or to the terrorist incursion into, say, another country.

The organisational complexity of a large terrorist group can be illustrated by reference to an organisational table of ETA (militar) published by Clark[20] and reproduced below in Fig. 6.1.

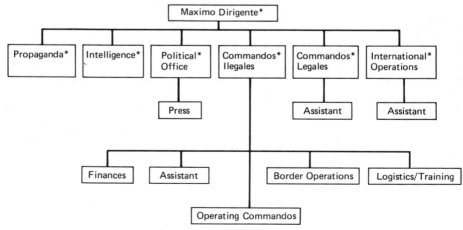

Fig. 6.1. Organisation Table of ETA (*militar*) as at February 1981.
*Members of Executive Committee (after Clark).

The most striking feature of this table is its similarity with the functional organisational chart you would expect to see of a large business undertaking. The various function of the organisation are represented within a command hierarchy and functional heads constitute an executive committee, who decide on organisational and operational policy.

Clark[21] notes that the operational unit of ETA is the 'Operating Commando', which may consist of four or five individuals who actually carry out operations. The operations of these units are controlled by the Executive Council. At the level of the commando, there are several different roles that can be identified. The 'ilegales' are people with known police records, who undertake the more dangerous and violent missions, such as assassinations, bank robberies, etc. These are the people we most commonly refer to as terrorists. Given their known records, these members receive some form of payment from ETA, enabling them to live more covert and unconstrained lives. In contrast, the 'legal' member is not known to the police, and they can continue to work in their job, and live in their community. These members provide much of the intelligence to the organisation (identifying targets, noting the movements of individuals targeted for assassination, etc.). They might also be involved in communication between members, acting as couriers, etc. A third category of 'commando' member is the '*apoyo*', the supporter. These people would not actually take part in operations, but may supply logistical support during an operation, by offering a safe house, food, etc.; or they may own property that has hiding places for weapons or people within them. It is likely that the active, but non-operational membership of ETA greatly exceeds its actual active operational membership.

The command structure of ETA is quite sophisticated, with aspects of the organisation such as intelligence, propaganda, press liaison, finance, etc. under direct executive control. Whilst the physical location of this command structure is somewhat unclear, it depends to some extent on using French territory as a relatively safe base. Parallels in terms of structure between ETA and another relatively large nationalist orientated terrorist organisation, the Provisional IRA, are very clear. The latter too has an elaborate hierarchical command structure, with clear differentiation of function. It too derives some 'safe' logistical support from within the Irish Republic. Indeed, this kind of structure may be an inevitable feature of any large terrorist organisation, and is probably more related to the needs of managing complex resources, rather than anything to do with the qualities of terrorism as such.

The issue of membership of a terrorist organisation is a very important one in determining our concept of the terrorist. In focusing on the individual who actually commits the terrorist act, it is very easy to forget that, in some cases, such as ETA and the Provisional IRA, there may well be a sophisticated support structure behind him. Such support individuals are terrorists by association, who presumably also share guilt by association. We have discussed in Chapter 3 the enormous costs of running terrorist movements, and the consequent logistical and financial problems. This must inevitably lead to some specialisation of function in groups with large cash flows (such as the Provisional IRA) if only at a general accounting level. In attempting to make psychological generalisations about terrorists, a failure to recognise this complexity of organisation may well invalidate our efforts.

For many members of ETA, language, or the problems associated with the propagation of the Basque language (Euskera) served as their introduction to the politics of Basque nationalism. Actual membership of ETA is described by Clark as following a 'searching' phase: 'During their teen-age years, they wandered restlessly . . . in a search for solutions to the crises that afflicted them as individuals and their culture as a group.' He argues that this searching process may (almost randomly) lead to some form of negative interaction with authority, thus confirming the rebel into the revolutionary—a rigid and inflexible (and perhaps prejudiced) police force would contribute to this process. Thus we see a process of movement away from society, which is to some extent, self-sustaining. Unlike the other European terrorists however, ETA is a relatively large and organised group, and membership acquires more formal properties than that of the essentially ad hoc revolutionary cell (as is also the case in the Provisional IRA). Thus Clark describes membership in terms of approaching the recruit by existing members, with a gradual introduction to the organisation (perhaps lasting for several months), and with a related gradual escalation in involvement. It is interesting to note that a number of Clark's sample themselves resisted initial membership approaches, some times for as long as eighteen months to two years. Clark failed to find evidence of single 'catalytic' incidents that were associated with conversion and membership.

Membership of ETA seems to affect the family and social life of its members. Normal social and family life often seemed to suffer, but associated with this was a rather paradoxical increase in the importance of Basque culture and context, presumably to support the activities of the member. Clark does not describe the family, however, as the principal support for the ETA member; rather other ETA members seem to provide that supportive context. There seems to be little evidence of female companionship, or involvement in their lives. However, given the above, active membership of ETA seems to be relatively shortlived. Clark estimates that active membership is generally less than three years.

Clark's account demonstrates the virtues of relatively simple in-depth descriptive studies of specific terrorist groups. Clearly, the dynamics of ETA membership are conditioned by its context and the focus and development of the individual member of ETA will reflect that context.

Although such a study is inevitably limited, it reveals aspects in common with those accounts already noted; but it also reveals interesting differences in emphasis which are significant. Comparative studies addressing social and psychological issues of similar terrorist organisations clearly need to be undertaken and an obvious area of comparison would be between ETA and the Provisional IRA.

Concluding Comments

The features that immediately strike the reader from this series of composite pictures of the terrorist is their heterogeneity. Whilst it is a predominantly youthful occupation, both sexes are involved in a variety of roles. This is to some degree conditioned by the social context in which the group operates, and men tend to predominate in leadership roles. Neither social background, educational opportunity or attainment seem to be particularly associated with terrorism. Nor is there any particular political focus for the terrorist, although they tend to be predominantly (but not necessarily) of the left.

We would find it difficult to identify predictors of potential terrorists from this picture. Very many people share the kinds of attribute that can be identified. The reasons for this may be that there are, perhaps, *no* special causes of terrorism, in the sense of a common class of explanations, as there probably are no 'special' causes for many complex forms of behaviour. Rather a complex set of circumstances, dependent upon the chance occurrence of events within facilitating contexts, represents the *individual's* causal story; each individual, perhaps, having a different and unique one. Whilst the reasons for any kind of psychological development (say in terms of the choice of a particular job, for example) are special to the individual, we do not assume a special class of explanation appropriate for each kind of possible job choice. If we regard terrorism in this light, it would seem to be consistent with the kinds of explanations we adopt for other complex behaviour. We will develop this theme further, in the following chapter which explores some individual accounts of the development of the terrorist.

CHAPTER 7

The Individual Psychology of the Terrorist

The specifically psychological literature on terrorism suffers from many of the conceptual difficulties we have noted earlier. Nevertheless, there have been a number of attempts to develop psychological analyses of the terrorist, and the conditions which give rise to terrorism. These have generally taken the form of interviews, where the interview data has either been presented in terms of case histories, or where attempts at generalisations have been made based on collections of interviews. This evidence has sometimes been supplemented by psychometric assessment, or more general types of psycho-sociological analysis.

The Psychodynamics of Terrorism

We have already discussed the difficulties associated with assumptions of mental illness in the analysis of terrorism in Chapter 4. Nevertheless, this approach has exerted a strong influence on psychological thinking and represents one of the principal avenues along which investigations have developed. It has been expressed in psychological accounts mainly from a psychodynamic perspective. These accounts draw their theoretical support from the writings of Freud and other members of the psychoanalytical movement. Its principal feature is an emphasis on unconscious motivating states, which have their origins in some form of childhood pathology.

We will see in the following chapters a number of attempts to explain terrorism in psychodynamic terms. It is rather surprising that the limited literature of terrorism should have taken this direction. Psychodynamic explanations have a waning role in psychology, and generally speaking, have been supplanted by more empirically-orientated approaches. That psychoanalytic approaches should persist in this area is some indication, in fact, of its relative neglect. Another reason may also be the implicit assumptions of abnormality which many psychodynamic approaches make.

The dominant psychoanalytical interpretation of terrorism in the literature is presented in terms of processes related to the Oedipus complex, a reaction of sons against fathers. The Oedipus complex is a central feature of the psychoanalytic portrait of both normal *and* abnormal individuals. In origin, the term refers to the legendary Greek King Oedipus, who accidentally killed his father and married his mother. It refers to the male child's striving to seek his mother's love, which results in unconscious wishes to eliminate (in fantasy) rivals for that love, which may include other siblings, and the father. Associated with this is an unconscious fear of retribution from those they seek to replace. According to psychoanalytic theory, the unconscious resolution of this complex results in a conversion of the fear of retribution into more acceptable equivalents which permit expression in conscious form. Freud accorded this great significance in the development of male children. A parallel female state, the Electra complex, can be identified in terms of the girl's unconscious love for her father, but is regarded as having much less significance.

Most children work through these feelings, working out the conflicts in their everyday life without expression in any form of pathological behaviour state. Nevertheless, Freud thought the residues of this experience persisted, and influenced the adolescent's and adult's attitudes to gender and sexuality. Whilst Freud saw the origins of this in terms of psychosexual development, the role of the father also embodies notions of authority. The Oedipus complex extends beyond sexual envy, to include authority as the symbol for the father. By this view therefore, the terrorist seeks to resolve his underlying Oedipal complex by acting against authority, and so, by extension, the State, which symbolically substitutes for the father. Authority figures are identified with the father, against whom the terrorist is 'really' (and unconsciously) acting.

This kind of account lays emphasis on the pathology of childhood, and therefore it might be expected that investigations of the early childhood of terrorists would be revealing. These are in some degree considered later in this chapter, but a major difficulty with this approach is the relative lack of information on the childhood processes that have operated in known terrorists. To anticipate that discussion, there seems to be little consistent evidence supporting the notion of abnormal childhood experiences in the terrorist. On the other hand, what constitutes abnormality by this perspective may well be relatively subtle, and only accessible after prolonged psychoanalysis, a process to which few, if any, terrorists have been exposed!

However, a not unreasonable assumption related to this may be that the way in which the child resolves his Oedipal complex is related to the kind of environment in which he lives. If that environment is violent, it may well predispose the child to the use of violence in later life. This kind of explanation has an obvious appeal in the analysis of terrorism.

A study which may have some bearing on this, and which seeks to describe the origins of terrorist behaviour in terms of violent childhood pathology is Fields[1]. Fields suggests that early exposure to terrorism can lead to the development of terrorism in the adult. Thus, the child living in an environment where terrorists are active, as in some parts of Northern Ireland, is more likely to develop into an adult terrorist than the child brought up elsewhere. This can be related to the kind of psychodynamic interpretation offered above, and seems to lend it some support.

On the other hand, this clearly cannot be the only factor in the development of terrorism for it is the case that relatively few people who grow up in parts of West Belfast, for example, actually become terrorists. Fields does not particularly develop the psychoanalytic notions outlined above and is more concerned with evaluating the effects of 'British repression', rather than the analysis of the terrorist. She argues that where an indigenous culture has imposed on it a legal system and institutions from an alien group (presumably the British, or Northern Ireland non-nationalists in this case), children growing up in that environment suffer serious disruption in moral judgement. Implicit in this view seems to be the notion that the child, as a victim, reacts to his upbringing by espousing terrorism.

Fields' work is based on a psychometric assessment of children in Northern Ireland, rather than of actual adult terrorists, and the work suffers accordingly from a lack of validation with adults. It also suffers from problems common to many accounts of this form of investigation; a failure to distinguish between correlation and causation. Whilst the correlational evidence of large-scale psychometric assessment might indicate avenues for further exploration, it clearly does not offer sufficient grounds for causal inference. Significantly, Fields also fails to offer explanations of the mechanisms whereby such childhood influences become apparent—are we dealing with imitation, defective motivation, or what? Explanations of this form can be seen to have limited utility. Analyses of such issues in Northern Ireland are difficult, and only limited evidence is available to evaluate the complex nature of the social conditions there. Social deprivation and prolonged exposure to violence may well seem likely predisposing states to social unrest and psychological harm, especially to children. On balance, the evidence available seems to suggest otherwise[2]; this probably extends to other societies that share these problems.

A number of other authors have attempted to develop psychoanalytically orientated accounts of terrorist motivation. These have focused on the violence of terrorism and drawn on concepts such as 'regressive hope' derived from the mother complex[3], repressed hate related to parental abuse[4] and blockage of functional empathy[5]. Other analytically orientated authors have proposed related explanations in social terms; the brutality exhibited by terrorists mirroring the subtle and covert brutality in everyday life[6], for example. The utility of such *post hoc* analysis is difficult to evaluate.

The violence of terrorism, as we have noted, is one of its most disturbing attributes, and the terrorists' attitudes to violence have attracted a number of investigators. Research in this area often again draws upon psychodynamic theories. Knutson[7] presents a typical view of this kind of approach in terms of social pathology. She suggests that terrorist acts stem from feelings of rage and helplessness engendered by the belief that society permits no other access to information dissemination and policy creation other than through terrorism and its associated violence. In psychological terms, therefore, the violence of terrorism results from what is essentially a form of frustration, a kind of more general explanation of violent behaviour already encountered. This analysis was based on interviews with terrorists in American prisons. Her interviews revealed an ambivalent attitude to the use of violence by the terrorist prisoners, with a strong theme of 'we had no choice' recurring in many. The ambivalent attitude to violence does not necessarily characterise all terrorists, however. Morf[8], for example, noted an explicit involvement of violence amongst members of the FLQ (*Front de Libération de Québec*) from before their membership for the terrorist organisation. These terrorists also showed no ambivalence towards the use of violence.

Knutson's approach is addressed from an essentially political perspective, rather than psychological, and the explanation offered is consistent with the notion that political ideologies can be represented as motivating states. Whether political aspirations are equivalent to psychological states is a matter for debate. We must also note that in interviews of the kind used by Knutson it is difficult to distinguish occasions when terrorists are actually describing some motivating state from those occasions when a convenient rationalisation is being offered. In summary, apart from the reference to frustration and its links with aggression, an issue we have already discussed in Chapter 2, we are left with little useful additional information as to why the terrorist becomes violent (as opposed to many others who experience political frustration without recourse to violence).

A more explicit psychodynamic account of the terrorist's attitude to violence, and the constraints on violence, is offered by Slochower[9], who proposes that terrorist action provides feelings of self-destruction and individualism, which in turn affect the terrorist's feelings of insecurity. It might be argued that feelings of insecurity weaken the restraining forces which in more secure individuals control and limit the expression of violence. Terrorist violence becomes evident in individuals lacking those restraining forces. A similar kind of approach was proposed by Kelman[10] who drew attention to other forces that might reduce the potency of those restraining forces: authoritisation, routinisation, and dehumanisation.

Social Pathology

Other authors have offered explanations of terrorism within a framework emphasising social pathology. Kampf[11], for example, discusses the attraction of extremism to 'affluent youth'. He suggests that problems have arisen because of people's failure to adjust to the expansion of material wealth and knowledge. Permissiveness, the erosion of traditional values and the breakdown of family life represent to Kampf the context in which extremism and terrorism might develop. The process offered is one focusing on frustration, and resultant aggression. It is an account orientated to one section of the community (the relatively young affluent) and makes assumptions about some stable form of society in the past against which permissiveness and modernity represent a maladaptive reaction.

Hassel[12] similarly focuses on the relatively young affluent sections of the community and on an explanation again emphasising the effects of contemporary societal change. Once more, the violence of terrorism is linked to frustration, on this occasion the frustration of achieving peaceful societal change. He extends the analysis somewhat, however, by locating the psychological foundations of terrorism in sadism, masochism and necrophilia. Furthermore, according to Hassel, the goal of attaining societal change through violence becomes lost with the substitution of the means of change (violence) as the goal.

Another related approach to this analysis, but developing it within a somewhat more psychological conceptual account is offered by Watzlawick[13], who highlights the notion of utopianism as an underlying element in terrorism. Rather like Hassel, Watzlawick contrasts the desire to achieve political change with reality, and postulates this discrepancy as a mechanism which might provide the context to terrorism. This again is a view closely related to the frustration-aggression hypothesis we have encountered before. However, he supplements this by drawing attention to other attributes of perfectionism, notably its tendency to become the justification for atrocity and its links with fanaticism. In particular he draws attention to a sequence of states that might characterise terrorism and fanaticism: simplification, the desire to change the world based upon having found 'the truth', belief in destroying the existing order, belief that the ends justify the means, and selective compliance.

Watzlawick's account has a number of interesting attributes for a psychological analysis. It locates its explanation firmly within the social context of the individual, but it also offers mechanisms by which at least some of the activity of terrorism might be interpreted and which, whilst not necessarily expressed in psychological terms, might nevertheless be amenable to more explicit psychological specification. This account also has much in common with Rapoport[14] referred to earlier in Chapter 3. However, by linking the notion of terrorism with fanaticism, there may be an implied assumption of some form of psychopathology, which as we have already noted, is not necessarily warranted.

The Terrorist Personality

A tempting approach to the analysis of terrorists is to seek explanation for their actions in terms of their personality dynamics. Personality can be defined as the characteristic patterns of behaviour and modes of thought that determine a person's adjustment to the environment. Studies of personality typically seek to establish broad patterns of personality attributes, or traits, that can be used to predict individuals' responses in particular situations. This approach has parallels with the analysis of terrorism in terms of abnormality, which was discussed in Chapter 4. It differs in seeking explanation in terms of 'normal' personality structures, rather than deviant qualities.

We have, in fact, already encountered a version of this kind of approach in Lanceley's analysis of the hostage taker as antisocial personality[15] in Chapter 4. He uses the attributes of the antisocial personality to predict potential outcomes in the hostage situation. Other authors have emphasised different personality structures. Sullwold[16] refers to two broad classes of personality traits held by the terrorist, based on work with the various West German terrorists. One is the extrovert; people possessing such attributes are unstable, uninhibited, inconsiderate, self-interested and unemotional. The lack of emotional responsiveness in such people limits their capacity to react to the consequences of their actions. Psychopathy and sociopathy share similar attributes, and might be distinguished in terms of the extent and severity of the lack of emotional responsiveness. Such people seek stimulation, which leads them to embark on dangerous and exciting activities to compensate for their lack of emotional feeling. Terrorism is a potent activity for this individual. The other personality trait emphasised by Sullwood is neurotic hostility. This individual rejects criticism, and is intolerant, suspicious, aggressive and defensive. He or she is extremely sensitive to external hostility, which results in the expression of aggression and further hostility.

Problems

Many of the different kinds of psychological explanation that we have encountered are little more than commonsense accounts. They make reference to broad concepts (social or political frustration, societal context of childhood, psychoanalytic accounts of childhood pathology) which, on examination, are not readily translatable into more detailed psychological concepts. They suffer, accordingly, from a lack of specificity and a failure to address what may be the most important problem from their essentially political perspective — why it is that so few people exposed to the presumed generating conditions of terrorism actually become terrorists.

The studies also suffer from problems of focusing on particular populations, and attempting to generalise what are essentially rather specific accounts, to broader populations. The scale and extent of contemporary terrorism makes this kind of approach unlikely to succeed. If we examine known bombing incidents, for example, from 1977 to 1983, over 2000 are thought to have occurred. In some sixty-eight percent of those cases the ethnic identity of the perpetrators can be identified[17]. Armenians, Palestinians, Lebanese, Turkish, Italian, Northern Irish and West Germans are the most numerous ethnic groups. No information is available as to the socio-economic class, income or age of participants, but whilst it might reasonably be assumed to be a youthful pursuit, the diverse ethnic and cultural backgrounds of the likely participants clearly present enormous difficulties in attempting to make generalisations about common precipitating states. We cannot assume terrorists to be an homogeneous population.

Accounts of terrorism of this kind very easily commit what is known as the 'fallacy of composition'[18]. If we can identify some common characteristics shared by a particular group, then it may seem a deceptively reasonable assumption that these characteristics are in some way involved in the development of the attributes of the whole of that group. In the case of Fields[19], for example, she identifies early exposure to terrorism as a significant feature in the subsequent development of terrorists. This is presumably on the grounds that it is an attribute shared by many of the population of terrorists. But it is also an attribute shared in some sense by most of the population of Northern Ireland, (and arguably the rest of the television viewing world). The number of people involved in terrorism, even in Northern Ireland, are known to be few. Therefore, it follows that early exposure alone simply cannot be a feature of the development of terrorism, otherwise why are there so few? Clearly the situation is more complex than this. Whilst it may be that early exposure of the form referred to by Fields is a factor, its effects, if any, are presumably only apparent in the context of a broad array of other influences. The fallacy of composition refers to inappropriate generalisations from the particular attributes identified, which fail to take into account the incidence of those attributes in the general population. Field's use of her data illustrates this problem.

A complicating characteristic of many of the attempts to offer psychological generalisations about terrorist motivation which we have already noted is often reference, sometimes explicitly, but more often implicitly, to assumptions about abnormality or deviance. The discussion in Chapter 4 suggested that this is not necessarily a useful orientation, and the same cautions apply when considering explanations in terms of presumed personality traits and pathogenic childhood environment. The fundamental problem seems to arise from attempts to force psychological meaning out of the concept of terrorism. As a concept, it makes no necessary reference to psychological states and suffers from such uncertainty and ambiguity that it inevitably limits generalisation.

It is worth noting briefly that not all authors have adopted assumptions about psychopathology. In contrast, some have taken assumptions of rationality as a starting point. The concept of rationality in psychological terms is as unclear as the concept of abnormality, but at least these approaches do not draw on assumptions of psychopathology and therefore specialness. Seeing the terrorist from this perspective might also encourage us to look for those things which we know affect the behaviour of non-terrorists.

Hilke and Kaiser[20], for example, are sceptical of accounts of special characteristics of terrorist motivation and suggest that terrorist violence is rational in the sense of being a means to an end and in psychological terms, not necessarily abnormal. Margolin[21] offers a similar kind of account, emphasising not so much the normality of terrorist behaviour (which it clearly is not), but its susceptibility to the *normal* rules controlling behaviour. This is an important point, and in conceptual terms represents a considerable advance on those views already discussed. We might be able to see this more clearly by looking at such accounts that are available of individual terrorist histories. This area is fraught with difficulties, but these latter approaches might offer us helpful insights into the nature of our problem. We will consider these issues further in Chapter 8.

Individual Accounts

Terrorists seem to be a very heterogeneous group, and because of this, attempts to identify general attributes seem likely to fail. However, we can turn to analyses of *individual* terrorists to further our discussion. These accounts might be expected to highlight the unique features of development in particular terrorists, which may be a much more profitable approach than trying to identify general features. We must note one caution, however, before proceeding. Such individual accounts that are available have come either from interviews, often with journalists, or from autobiographical sources. There is no way in which these can be checked for accuracy, nor is it necessarily easy to separate fantasy and rationalisations from actual causal circumstances.

Information sufficient to give a reasonably detailed and accurate account of individual backgrounds and development is available from Kellen for four terrorists[22]: Michael Baumman, founder of the West German '2nd of June Movement', Hans-Joachin Klein, a member of an offshoot of the Baader-Meinhof group, Zvenko Busic, a Croatian nationalist, and Kozo Okamato, a member of the *Rote Armee Faktion*, and participant in the Lod Airport massacre. Accounts of this kind are closer to case histories, rather than empirical investigations, but they do offer the opportunity for describing and identifying psychological and social characteristics of the people concerned, in a way not possible in the other literature reviewed. Approaches like this, given their methodological limitations, clearly have some utility.

We can approach the accounts of the four terrorists from a broadly developmental perspective, beginning with the context and process which led to their embarking on a terrorist career. There are in a sense two decisions to make for the potential terrorist in embarking on terrorism[23] — the decision to break with society in some sense, and the decision to join a subversive or terrorist group. Our society has a long tradition of having groups of people who reject its values — nuns and monks represent an extreme, institutionally approved, form — and many people in some sense or another become distant from or marginal to society. However, few take the further step of joining a subversive group. It might be argued that there is in fact a further step in this process. This is the involvement in violence, which need not necessarily be a feature of association with a subversive group.

It is interesting to note that no particular pattern of childhood experience characterises the four terrorists we will consider. Baumann describes himself as a 'normal person', from a working class family. He was born in 1947, in East Germany, moving to West Berlin when he was twelve. He lived in a rather featureless and undistinguished working class housing estate, and worked as an apprentice in the building trade. He left this job because, by his own account, he could not face the monotony of it. 'I did all sorts of shit jobs until around 1965 when my story began to be not so conformist anymore. Actually, with me it all began with rock music and long hair'. There then followed what seems to be an increased moving away from society, and an increased exposure to the political ideologies of that time, an exciting and embracing period. The symbolic importance of growing his hair long cannot be overemphasised. At that time, men with long hair were the subject of great social disapproval, which was probably more evident in Germany than elsewhere. It was a visible sign of rebellion and rejection of social values.

Around that time in Germany many young people began to question the values of contemporary society and Baumann appears no different from many of his contemporaries. He describes, however, an increasing drift towards political radicalism and eventually violent terrorism. This drift was associated with the development of a circle of friends who were also marginalised from society '. . . you start building contacts with a few people like yourself, other dropouts . . .' It is very difficult to judge whether this drift reflected something within Baumman (insecurity, for example, in the way that Sluchower[24] describes), or whether the society in which he mixed 'drew him along' by virtue of its attractions. These attractions would undoubtedly include the membership of a small tight group, but also a distinctive and, for many, highly attractive life style. The visible signs of social rejection like long hair simply confirmed and enhanced the movement away from accepted social values, with its evident rewards '. . . If you had long hair, there were always an incredible number of chicks hanging onto you, all these factory girls. They thought it was great, a guy like that . . .'

Unlike Baumann, Hans-Joachin Klein, did not come from a normal working class background. His father was a low-ranking police officer. Klein himself, however, describes himself as a worker. He, unlike Baumman, did have an unhappy childhood, and in particular describes considerable and enduring friction with his father. His mother, who was Jewish, died in Ravensbruck Concentration Camp, and he never knew anything of her. Physically, Klein was a poorly developed and weak child. He was brought up initially in an orphanage and then with foster-parents, until he was nine or ten. He then went to live with his father. His father seems to have been a particularly unpleasant man (by Klein's account) who is described as domineering and demanding. Klein's home life seems to have been unusual, to say the least; he was sent to bed at eight o'clock when he was eighteen, which he did '. . . without batting an eyelid'. Frequent beatings, which persisted into his late teens, seem to have been a major feature of his life with his father.

A landmark in this relationship occurred when he was twenty, as a result of his father attempting to take away from him a gift from his first girl friend. His father tore a chain bracelet from his wrist because he thought it looked effeminate. '. . . At that moment, I hit him for the first time, a good wallop. From that moment on, he no longer had the courage to touch me'.

Klein's childhood, as described, was clearly unpleasant. He experienced many of the events which might well be associated with subsequent problems in adult life. It clearly lends itself to interpretation in terms of childhood pathology contributing to his eventual terrorist violence. However, in this respect, Klein is not unique, and others who have not developed as terrorists also experience unfortunate upbringings. This simple point remains a critical issue for developmental accounts.

Like Baumman, Klein describes a gradual drift towards terrorism, starting with separation from society and contact with politically active groups. It may well be that a period in the army (as part of his National Service) contributed to his marginalisation from society. Klein gained initial employment as an engineering apprentice. He had little success at this, however, and worked as a telegraph messenger for a year or two. He became a member of a gang, where '. . . we pinched motors and went joy-riding until the tank was empty. Somebody grassed and I ended up in the nick with the others'. On his release, he was helped by a prisoner's association to find a job in a restaurant in the student area of Frankfurt.

This seemed to mark the first point of contact between Klein and the world of political dissent and student protest; hitherto he had clearly become somewhat marginalised from society, but lacked any apparent political dimension.

The third terrorist we will consider, Kozo Okamato, does not seem to have had a disturbed or unusual childhood. He was the youngest of six children, the son of a retired schoolmaster married to a social worker. His mother died, and his father re-married without any apparent adverse effect on his son. He had, as far as can be seen, a normal and happy childhood.

Unlike Baumman or Klein, he had academic opportunities and he was moderately successful in both school and university. He was not known to be particularly politically active in extremist groups whilst at university, although he was a member of a radical student movement. His contact with, and introduction to, terrorism appears to have come through his brother, Takeshi. Takeshi was a member of the *Rote Armee Faktion*. Later, with others, he hijacked a plane and forced it to land in Korea. It was he who introduced Okamato to terrorism through the *Rote Armee Faktion*. The fact that his brother was so intimately involved with extremist politics may suggest a degree of family exposure to such political ideas, but there is no evidence of the gradual marginalisation from society that seems to have characterised both Baumman and Klein. In this case, it would presumably be argued that the most important influence was family membership and family influences, rather than the kinds of personal experience which might lead to rejection of society.

Whilst Klein, Baumman and Okamato were all members of what might be described as essentially left wing terrorist groups, espousing in some way or another a form of internationalism, Zvenko Busic, the fourth terrorist we will consider was a Croat, an ethnic group oppressed and suppressed (according to his own account) by the Yugoslav Government. In a sense, Busik's childhood might be characterised as being set apart from society, in so far as he describes his own great interest in, and commitment to, Croatian nationalism. Given the lack of sympathy with views like this by the Yugoslav authorities, anyone holding them would inevitably be marginalised from society to a degree. Neither his father or mother are described as being particularly nationalistic however, although they are seen as religious. None the less, there clearly emerges from his own account a sense of support for his nationalism from within the family.

Busik attended university in Yugoslavia in the 1960s, and then moved to the University of Vienna, critical of anti-Croatian experiences in Yugoslavia. He was unable to support himself in Vienna, however, and went to the United States, where he gained manual work. Even at this point, he was clearly unusual, in that he had developed the habit of carrying a gun 'for self defence', which led to some trouble with the police. He returned to the University of Vienna, but was subsequently expelled, by his account, from both the University and Austria in 1971. This resulted, it appears, from involvement in anti-Yugoslav demonstrations and actions. Clearly, therefore, at this point, Busic had become politically involved in Croatian Nationalist activities. He subsequently describes contact with other terrorist groups in Berlin and Ireland.

For these four individuals, there is no particularly obvious series of common childhood experiences or parental relationships that can be used to account for their involvement in terrorism. A process of movement away from society can be seen, however, and similarly a gradual increased contact with extremist groups, once that context had been created. This might be argued to be the case for Okamato as well as the others, although for him it might be a process that, in some sense, took place within the family. In terms of the discussion of the influence of early childhood pathology earlier in this chapter, these accounts fail to support consistently any particular view.

Klein, Baumman and Okamato all identify points at which a particular incident seems to have finalised a process of movement away from society to espousal of violent political protest. For Baumman, that point occurred in 1967 during a visit of the Shah of Iran to Berlin, when a student friend named Bruno Ohnesary, was killed by a policeman. That incident had a profound effect on the German left, and Baumman in particular, and seems to have had an important effect in confirming his radicalisation. 'That gave me a tremendous flash, one cannot really describe it. It really shook me to the bones'.

Klein identifies a series of critical points that seem to enhance and confirm his progress to terrorism. The first has already been noted, when at the age of twenty he struck his father. The second was the sight of the police beating a young girl during a riot. He describes himself flying into an uncontrollable rage and assaulting the police officer, for which he himself was beaten up. It may be tempting to speculate on the significance of his father's occupation as a policeman as a contributing factor to this incident. Klein describes his father's account of police work in terms of 'defenders of the weak' (a surprising view in the light of his aggressiveness towards Klein). When he saw the police beating the girl '. . . two images collided, my image of women, and my image of cops . . . from that moment on I began to think'[25].

This incident for Klein only becomes meaningful when seen in the social context in which Klein lived. His growing commitment to violent protest was undoubtedly helped by the kinds of friend with whom he began to spend time. He describes them as 'anti-authoritarians'; one was a student, others were people who had dropped out of work, an apprentice printer and a young factory worker. Initially, they weren't a part of any group, but Klein describes a gradual process of politicisation, drinking and socialising in the centres of political activity in Frankfurt. By becoming more radicalised, Klein came to be more and more involved as a political activist, with a growing involvement in violent protest. The Vietnam war provided a focus for his radical activity. 'What would have been the point of demonstrating peacefully against genocide? Each time, there were groups looking for confrontation. I was always in one of those'[26]. The escalation from paving stones to petrol bombs came about 'through force of habit', a gradual spiral of increasingly violent protest, each requiring an escalation in violence to gain media attention.

The third, and apparently decisive step on Klein's way to terrorism was the death in prison of Holger Meins as a result of hunger strike. Meins was a member of the *Rote Armee Faktion*, and had been arrested with Andreas Baader on June 1, 1972. He died in prison on November 9, 1974, having gone on hunger strike during September of that year. 'I put that first pistol of mine into my pocket the night I heard Holgar Meins had died in prison.' At this time, Klein was already a member of the Revolutionary Cells. He had been introduced into this group by Karl-Heinz Boese, the leader of the Revolutionary Cells at that time. (Boese had contacts with the Palestinian terrorist organisations, and was eventually killed at Entebbe, Uganda, during the Israeli commando operation to release hostages from a hijacked aircraft).

In the case of Okamato, the decisive influence of his brother's introduction of him to the *Rote Armee Faktion* seems to have been a similar critical incident introducing him to the terrorist world. This differs from the experience of the others noted, however, in that his subsequent involvement in terrorist action, the Lod Airport massacre, seems to have resulted from his acceptance of the authority and leadersip of the *Rote Armee Faktion*. Whilst it would be wrong to describe Okamato as a reluctant terrorist, his actual involvement and initiation into terrorist action was unusual and unplanned. Indeed, it had elements of the comic about it. He received in Japan a letter from the *Rote Armee Faktion* telling him that if he wanted to see his brother (who had already completed a successful hijacking) he should go to Beirut where his brother was. His family confirm that it was a genuine desire to see his brother that led him to go, although there was also an offer of terrorist training made in the same letter. He left for Beirut, but en route, he was given an assignment to fly from New York to Paris in an El Al 747 to reconnoitre its interior arrangements. He selected the wrong type of aircraft, however. He checked in for a flight on a 707, realised his mistake and aroused suspicion when he tried to change to a 747, and eventually left New York on a 707. This seems an unlikely beginning for an international terrorist!

No critical incident can be identified for Busic's involvement in terrorist violence. On the other hand, we should note that whilst he was responsible for the death of a New York policeman in 1976, resulting from the explosion of a bomb which he had planted, he did not appear to intend to kill or injure, but rather to gain publicity through hijacking a TWA plane and distributing leaflets. Busic did, in fact, take steps to minimise the danger of his bomb, without success. This contrasts with the other three terrorists we have considered who were personally involved in violent encounters with the security forces: Okamato, for example, was the only survivor of a group of three who killed twenty-six people ruthlessly and injured eighty at Lod Airport, Israel, in 1972.

A number of features characterise these particular individuals' involvement in terrorism:

a. a decision actively to fight society with violence inside a like-minded group;
b. disillusionment with ordinary life;
c. perhaps the possession of special skills. Klein, for example, had acquired skills with explosives whilst in the army. Andreas Baader had a considerable interest, and more particularly skills, with weapons (after Kellen[27]).

A critical element which emerges from these case histories is the provision of opportunity to join the terrorist group. Whilst it must be accepted that such groups in some sense have an origin, and may well coalesce around a leader, most terrorists become members of existing groups, or found their own after membership of another group. A vital element, therefore, is the existence and accessibility of a group within the individual's social context. Furthermore, that group must also both offer membership, and in turn accept the individual into membership[28].

Once a member, other forces familiar to investigators of group processes become important. In an otherwise disordered life, membership can provide support, entertainment, friendship, purpose and sex. The very nature of the terrorist group emphasises closeness and control over action, all of which both bind and confirm the member. Given a rejection of 'bourgeois' life, the life of a terrorist group can provide the almost opposite lifestyle, a living through of ideals. Whilst the stresses of terrorist action may be considerable, the pleasures of the life should not be discounted, especially when contrasted with unemployment, poor housing, or demands which the individual cannot or will not fulfil. Baumann makes the relevant point that during his involvement with terrorism, he had '. . . an exceptionally good time . . .'[29].

Accounts of this kind represent a fruitful way of approaching the analysis of terrorism. As a series of what are essentially case histories, their most useful attribute is a concern with the individual and the analysis in relative detail of his actions. We must be cautious however not to overextend any generalisations that we might draw from this kind of evidence. Other authors have used the same or similar evidence to make generalisations which do not bear detailed examination, especially with respect to the effects of early childhood experiences. Ulrike Meinhof's parents died, leaving her to be brought up by a politically active woman; Andreas Baader was brought up in an otherwise all female household; Bernward Vesper grew up in tyrannical surroundings, the son of a well-known Nazi apologist[30]. This has led some authors to speculate on such childhood pathology as a critical variable in the development of the terrorist. Whilst such evidence is undoubtedly suggestive, it does not seem to be, however, conclusive evidence that such events are necessarily pathogenic. Other terrorists do not seem to share such backgrounds (e.g. Baumman, Okamato), and of course many people who do not have any connection with terrorism have similar, or even worse, backgrounds. Whilst it is not possible to dismiss it as a contributing factor, assertions about predispositions based on notions of childhood pathology must be treated with scepticism.

Psychological Profiling

More systematic approaches to individual analyses have looked at the 'psychological profiling' of terrorists. This technique has its origins in the American FBI's work in forensic psychology. Its use in criminal investigations is based on extensive scene of crime analyses of the victim, the crime and its environmental context. It seems to be of most value in investigations dealing with bizarre crimes, or unusual serial crimes, such as multiple murders[31]. In these areas it has had considerable success, particularly where there are signs of psychological dysfunction at the scene of the crime[32] in terms of ritualistic positioning of objects, mutilation of corpses and so on. In evaluating the utility of this approach, the discussion on the relationship between mental health and terrorism in Chapter 4 is clearly relevant. The contexts in which psychological profiling has been most successful seem to refer to the actions of abnormal individuals, who express their pathology in some way in the crime.

These techniques have been used in the context of the analyses of both terrorist incidents and terrorists. One area of great operational utility lies in the analysis of the hostage taker[33]. The profiling of the hostage taker can assist the negotiating team in the management of the hostage situation, through providing information about the content, emphasis and timing of negotiating strategies. A number of sophisticated psychological profiles relevant to particular classes of action such as hostage situations have been constructed. The United States Federal Aviation Administration's hijackers profile programme is an example[34], which appears to be successful. Whether this procedure will be useful in other kinds of terrorist situations is less clear. These tend not to involve interpersonal communication and are frequently characterised by choice of targets which are innocuous and difficult to predict. The hostage situation might be a special class of activity rather set aside from other forms of terrorist action.

Another use for psychological profiling has been reported by Heyman[35]. He was approached to undertake psychometric assessment of a captured member of the Italian terrorist group, the Red Brigade. Based on this assessment, Heyman and his colleagues were able to identify features of the terrorist which were of value to the Italian authorities in their subsequent interrogation. He was described as '. . . an intelligent and determined person who was now highly discouraged and disillusioned'. This resulted in his turning against society, and against himself, giving rise to '. . . a strong quality of masochism: a desire for punishment or even self-destruction.'

Psychological profiling can use as its subject matter apparently unlikely aspects of terrorist activity such as their writings. The intention is again to identify from the analysis of terrorist writings useful individual qualities. Heyman[36] illustrates the technique by showing how such analyses of written material may have significance, in determining how the terrorist group might be managed in operational settings. He and his colleagues analysed communications from two separate terrorist groups. Neither of the groups are named, but the reader may be able to identify which groups they are from their attributes!

One group was composed of 'natural born losers', people who were unable to manage their social lives and job-related activities. They were people who 'thought with their guts', and then found arguments to justify what they felt in everyday life: 'rejection, jealousy, resentment, vindictiveness, hostility and bitterness.' They 'act tough and belligerent; but this is a brittle front that covers a lot of insecurity and inferiority.' They were thought to be highly vulnerable to stress and fatigue.

The other group they studied was quite different. Its members were 'clever, insightful, sophisticated, intellectually bright and well disciplined'. They showed a strong humanitarian sense, transmitting this in their communications.

Heyman uses these examples to illustrate the operational potential of psychological profiling of this kind. The tactics that might be adopted to deal with them *should* differ, and reflect their underlying psychological make-up. In the former group, for example, in a hostage situation, stress induced by delaying tactics may well cause them serious disorientation and disruption. This would be unlikely in the latter case.

These techniques can help to identify the vulnerabilities of the terrorist group, and can therefore be of direct help in setting operational priorities. The analysis of the writings of terrorist groups can, however, yield valuable insights into more detailed qualities of terrorist rationale, and cognitive processes. Miron and Douglas[37], for example, describe the analysis of threat messages in hostage situations as an aid to their management. Cues related to aggression may well have special significance for the well being of the hostage.

A more extensive development of this approach can be seen in Miller[38], who gives one of the most sophisticated psycholinguistic accounts of the analysis of the writings of terrorists. He notes that the analysis of texts can indicate both political and psychological 'signatures' or messages. He confines himself largely to the analysis of the German terrorist movements (principally Baader-Meinhof and the *Rote Armee Faktion*) and he analyses the various terrorist communications as propaganda, and also as avenues to explore terrorist 'thinking'. Whilst the authorship (single or multiple) of the texts are largely unknown, given the problematic nature of any investigation in this area, Miller's work represents an approach to laying the foundation of a 'cognitive-psychological' investigation of terrorist movements. Steinke[39] describes further uses of this technique within a German context.

Work in this area may be of considerable practical importance. We have already noted that Dror[40] draws our attention to the relatively limited array of operational strategies used by most terrorist groups, as opposed to the range of possible strategies available. He suggests one of the reasons for this may lie in both the cognitive and group characteristics of the terrorist and the group he belongs to. Analyses of terrorist communications may obviously assist in better understanding this notion. We should note, however, a discussion of future trends in terrorism by Jenkins[41], who notes the same 'conservatism' of terrorist tactics, but attributes it to the success of present tactics in achieving terrorist aims.

Such linguistic analyses can yield provocative insights into the dynamics of terrorist action. Lichter[42] notes that some authors have drawn parallels, based on linguistic analyses, between contemporary German terrorist groups and early Nazi activity in the 1920s, especially in the context of the authoritarian nature of the movements. Merckl[43], for example, undertook a content analysis of autobiographical statements of a large number of early Nazis. He notes several parallels between the self description of early Nazis and the 'new left' terrorist groups, including 'antimaterialist self-righteous idealism, a sense of being special or different, a rejection of bourgeois origins in favour of lower class sociality, and finding strength in the role of the social and political outcast'[44].

Such accounts clearly draw on notions of authoritarianism introduced and developed by Adorno *et al.*[45], but represent an interesting extension of the notion to left wing groups, as opposed to the essentially right wing fascist context of Adorno's writings. Lichter[46] reports a study which offers some empirical support to this view, in terms of analyses of various projective tests. Whether or not these views extend beyond the German terrorist groups of the 1960s and 1970s remains to be seen.

Concluding Comments

The psychological approaches to terrorism described above have largely failed in their aspiration to characterise the terrorist in general. Perhaps that is because all such characteristics are present in the general population. On the other hand, the kinds of more individualised accounts we have looked at do yield insights into both the nature of terrorist life, and the forces that might shape it. They also enable us to speculate on the sorts of circumstances that might facilitate entry into the terrorist world. These studies might not help us to predict in advance, but they do help us to understand.

CHAPTER 8

Processes of Terrorism

There is no singular psychological attribute to describe the terrorist. If, then, they are not 'made' in this sense, how do they become terrorists? Can we identify either individual or social forces that lead to terrorism? We can examine this by looking at the effects of factors which we know might operate at these levels, and see if they help us to understand better how an individual might become a terrorist. We will do this through a discussion of two psychological phenomena that have been used in the explanation of terrorism—identity and the effects of the terrorist group.

Identification

The process of identification enjoys some currency in contemporary accounts of terrorism. Both Schmid[1] and Crenshaw[2] have proposed this concept as a factor in the development of the terrorist. Identification has been proposed as an important developmental feature in many behaviour states. It is a term that has its origins in psychodynamic theories of the nature of personality and social development and refers to the unconscious process by which an individual takes on characteristics of another person. These characteristics may be in terms of attitudes, patterns of behaviour or emotions. We might note, however, that given the overall lack of use of psychodynamic concepts in contemporary psychology, it is rather surprising that identification should have attracted such interest.

We can see the suggested process most clearly in children. As the child develops, it acquires many of the attitudes and attributes of its parents. This is often strikingly apparent in the young child, who might use phrases and gestures which closely parallel those of its parents. Later, children can be seen to reproduce the attributes of other significant individuals they encounter (notably teachers). It can be seen as a way for the child to acquire behavioural repertoires without necessarily having experienced all the circumstances that might produce them. The child identifying with the parent is thought to respond as if he or she were the parent, feeling sad, for example, when the mother is upset.

If identification takes place, not all the behaviour of the 'role model' (the person who is identified *with*) is subject to this process. Identification seems to be selective; some aspects of the role model's behaviour result in identification, and other aspects do not. The teenager, for example, might identify with his pop idol, and wear clothes, use gestures, talk in particular ways, that might characterise the idol. The idol's moral habits or religious views, however, might not be identified with.

Identification is regarded as particularly important in the process we know as 'sex typing'. A young child quickly acquires culturally appropriate sex-specific behaviour. All cultures define in some way appropriate kinds of male and female activities. Children rapidly learn these social 'rules' of behaviour appropriate to masculinity or femininity through the process of identification, initially with the gender appropriate parent, later with other significant individuals. This process of identification in childhood is relatively well understood, and seems to have fairly lawful properties.

The process of identification has also been proposed to extend into late childhood and early adult life, as a factor influencing development in adolescence. A major characteristic of adolescence in Western societies is the search for identity[3]. Many young people begin around this time to question their own, and their parents' values in a wide range of areas. This results in the questioning of the roles of childhood (like dependency, for example), as part of the adjustment to adult life. The adolescent's sense of identity seems to develop out of childhood identification, and a significant contributor to the change is the peer group to which the individual belongs. Indeed it is thought to gradually usurp the role of family and school as the most potent source of role models.

Proponents of this view suggest that an analogous process might apply in the development of terrorism. The protester against society, or the terrorist, might be thought to act as a role model in the development of terrorism. We know that the typical age of joining terrorist movements is the late teens or early twenties. The potential terrorist is therefore an adolescent or young adult, subjected in these terms to the strains of searching for identity, and vulnerable to the pressures of identification. Peer groups are an important feature of adolescence (the gang, for example) and where that peer group is already marginalised from society, and may already include violent individuals, we see a possible route into terrorism. Evidence for the existence of processes like this can be seen in Klein's account[4] of his own development into terrorism, where he talks of the role of his peer group in enhancing his marginalisation from society, and making him politically aware.

There is further evidence that might be used to support this view. In the discussion of the development of individual terrorists in Chapter 7, qualities that might be interpreted in terms of identification can be discerned. The German terrorist Baumman, for example, draws attention to the importance of the attempt on the life of the student activist, Rudi Dutschke, as an important impetus to his development as a terrorist: '. . . The bullet might just as well have been for me . . . I now felt I had been shot at for the first time. So it became clear to me . . . we must now fight without mercy . . .'.

Shaw[5] describes a process similar to identification in the development of the terrorist, which he terms the 'personal pathway model'. This draws on concepts like socialisation to account for its development. In support of this view, he uses the account of the early childhood of Vladimir Illich Sanchez, the notorious terrorist 'Carlos'. His father was an influential member of the Venezuelan Communist party and he seems actively to have promoted his son's entry into terrorism. He sent him to a KGB-run Cuban training base when he was sixteen, and subsequently sent him to Moscow for his university education, which was thought also to have involved some training in terrorist techniques. This can be interpreted in terms of identification, where his father initially, and subsequently his various teachers, occupied positions as role models for the young Carlos, facilitating and condoning the use of violence in a political context.

The extent to which family ties are important in the development of terrorism might well be one of the major arguments which supports the role of identification as a factor. The family is a potent focus for identification, and we would expect to see some influence on the child growing up in families condoning terrorist approaches to politics. Weinberg and Eubank[6] make reference to the role of the family in the context of the Italian female terrorist as we noted in Chapter 7, and we have already seen in Chapter 6 that family may, on occasions, play a role in the development of some individual terrorist. Processes of identification may be an especially powerful force in families which have a history of civil dissent characterised by violence. Histories of previous family involvement in the Republican movement in Northern Ireland, for example, are a feature of many contemporary IRA terrorists and their political leaders and it is difficult to resist speculation about identification in these circumstances.

Gerry Adams, the present president of Sinn Fein, the political wing of the Provisional IRA, is a good example of a family commitment to terrorism, expressed over several generations. His father was shot and wounded by the Royal Ulster Constabulary in an incident in the 1940s. His uncle was one of the IRA engineers during a bombing campaign in Britain during the late 1930s and 1940s, who married one of the bomb couriers. Another uncle was an officer commanding IRA prisoners in a jail break in the 1940s. His brother, Dominic Adams, was sentenced to fourteen years imprisonment in 1986 after being caught redhanded during an IRA operation in Belfast[7]. In an environment that is supportive of this kind of behaviour, and where it may actually confer status on the family, identification may well be an attractive explanatory concept to use.

However, evidence relating the role of the family to terrorism is not confined either to Italy or Northern Ireland. There is evidence of a large number of couples and brothers and sisters participating in terrorism in Germany, suggesting that both family and personal connections play an important role[8]. This is also the case with many of the Middle-Eastern terrorist groups. Whether we are dealing with the process of identification, or the effects of a supportive environment (without reference to identification), or both, remains obscure.

Identification in this context may also have elements in common with revenge as a causal factor in terrorism. Revenge often figures prominently in the rhetoric of terrorism. In the example given above of Baumman's feelings when he heard of the death of Rudi Dutschke, revenge might be seen to augment identification. Trotsky[9] draws attention to the importance of revenge as a precondition for the development of terrorism '. . . Before it is elevated to the level of a method of political struggle, terrorism makes its appearance in the form of individual acts of revenge . . . The most important psychological source of terrorism is always the feeling of revenge in search of an outlet'[10].

Where the terrorist might be said to identify with the victims of inequality, or injustice, then revenge certainly may be apparent in the rhetoric of terrorism. Whether it represents a valid psychological explanation, however, remains uncertain. The idea of revenge as a psychological force seems to have most in common with notions of frustration. Perhaps the links between revenge and violence are similar to the presumed links between frustration and aggression discussed in Chapter 2. By suggesting a link between frustration and aggression, this kind of explanation would offer a mechanism for the development of violent aggressive acts. Revenge might also contribute as an element in the process of identification.

We are left unclear in this account why the social protester turns to violence. It might be accounted for by reference to the violent attributes of the role model, but whilst violent individuals might well become role models for large sections of the community, relatively few of those who might be influenced in this way seem to move on to become terrorists. This is one of the fundamental problems in understanding the development of the terrorist. Does the concept of identity contribute anything additional to our knowledge of the processes involved in the development of terrorism? We can evaluate the question in two ways, first by reference to identification as a unique psychological process, and secondly in terms of more general social explanations of the terrorist.

The concept of identity is of uncertain status in psychology. It certainly refers to and describes identifiable behavioural changes that occur in early childhood. The concept of identity, however, also refers to the process whereby those changes occur, and at this level, it is not clear that this is the only explanation for what we see. A much simpler explanation of the same events can be developed in terms of imitation learning, for example, without making reference to complex, and essentially inaccessible, unconscious forces. Bandura and Walters[11] have developed a very coherent account of imitation learning expressed in terms of the consequences of imitation to the individual. In the case of Carlos, for example, presumably he received great parental and social approval for emulating the terrorist. He seemingly proved to be a good student, but we do not need to seek explanation in terms of inaccessible processes to understand why this happened to him. This is not diminishing the importance of the facilitating context (which might include the family) in the development of the terrorist. It is suggesting, however, that simpler explanations are available to account for the same process ascribed to identification.

When we look at the social context of identification as an explanation of the terrorist, we encounter a more worrying feature. By expressing the development of the terrorist in these terms, we are implicitly making reference to processes that lead to the creation of what has been termed 'the whole person'. This can also be described in terms of an ultimate ideal state for the individual, representing his adjustment to his world. Concepts like 'self actualisation' are sometimes also used in this context. We must be very careful that we do not fall into two traps which await us when expressing the development of the terrorist in these terms.

The first of these traps is to suggest that by not conforming to a culturally 'ideal' state of self development, the terrorist is in some sense lacking. We can see examples of this approach in Shaw[12] where he makes reference to 'narcissistic injury' as a developmental feature of the terrorist. This refers to an event '. . . interpreted by the individual as critically affecting his view of himself or self esteem.'[13]. Disruption of family life may be one source of narcissistic injury, occasioned by, for example, loss of the father. Physical defects, or failures in attainment, might also fall within this category. Unless we are very careful, we will fall into the trap of assuming what amounts to a mental health explanation of terrorism, which we have already seen is not a particularly helpful way of conceptualising the terrorist. We will also run the risk of committing the fallacy of composition. By failing to recognise the incidence of these kind of features in the broader non-terrorist population, we erroneously identify causal factors (see Chapter 6 for a fuller explanation of this fallacy). Few people do not have something which by *post hoc* analysis could be interpreted in Shaw's terms of 'narcissistic injury'. Yet terrorists are rare.

The second trap again lies in the implied notion of self development in the concept of identification. We can be led into thinking that whatever results in self development is psychologically desirable and should therefore be condoned. We can imagine explanations that describe the process of terrorism, like the development of any other form of behaviour, in these terms; the terrorist 'expresses himself' and his social responsibility in terms of his behaviour. This is a covert way of condoning terrorist behaviour, removing it from its horrific context, and presenting it in a sanitised way.

It seems reasonable, therefore, to conclude that the concept of identity has limited value in helping us to understand some of the reasons why individuals become terrorists. The nature of the process remains obscure, and there is no consensus to its explanation. In particular, it is not clear that even if a concept like identity is useful, it can be best explained within a psychodynamic framework, or in the simpler terms of imitation learning. Whilst it draws our attention to the role of family, and the social environment, in the development of the terrorist, it does not particularly progress our understanding.

The Terrorist Group

We all live in groups of some kind or another. They are a pervasive feature of all our lives, and they confer on us many benefits. They provide the opportunity for companionship, entertainment, and development. In groups we can associate with people who share our values, we can find support and groups can even help us to attain our life's goals. The family is a form of group to which most of us have belonged and in which we have spent our earliest days. As we grow older, we join different kinds of group; the local gang, classmates, youth club and so on. In most cases we choose to belong to a group, but sometimes we are placed in groups by others, or by circumstance. People who work in the same location, for example, may be identified as a group where membership is not defined by choice, but in terms of employment. From this perspective, the terrorist group is one more group, and as far as can be seen, it shares the forces and dynamics of other kinds of group.

Groups do not simply confer advantages; they also influence their members to an impressive degree. Membership of a group can often contribute to a change of attitude and behaviour which would be difficult to achieve in other ways. The consequences of belonging to a group can be profound, and can exert a major influence on what group members do. Given that terrorists are members of groups, it follows that an understanding of the process of group dynamics may help our understanding of why terrorists commit the acts they do. This approach might also help us to understand some of the unresolved issues in the earlier discussion about the role of identification, especially with respect to the influence of the family in the development of the terrorist.

We have noted that individual terrorists are very varied in their attributes, but in terms of their structures and organisational features, terrorist groups may be less varied. Merari[14] has proposed four basic types of terrorist group, based on the population from which they draw their support and the nature of their operating environment. A major class of group are the Xenofighters who direct their activities against foreigners in some sense, in contrast to the Homofighters, who direct their activities against their own countrymen. Both of these major classes can then be further sub-divided into whether or not they have a domestic base, or are located in a foreign country; thus domestic based Xenofighters (e.g. EOKA, FLN, Frelimo), foreign based Xenofighters (e.g. PLO, PFLP), domestic-based Homofighters (e.g. Red Brigade, *Rote Armee Faktion*) and foreign-based Homofighters (United Croats of West Germany) can be identified. Using this system, some groups are not so easily classified, however. The IRA, for example, are in a sense domestic based Xenofighters (against what they regard as British occupation forces), but they are also domestic based Homofighters (against Northern Irish Protestants and their Catholic opponents) and foreign based Xenofighters and Homofighters (to the extent that they use bases in the Irish Republic).

The value of this kind of taxonomy lies not in its completeness, however, but in its capacity to delineate and describe differences in aspirations and operational imperatives of the various groups, and therefore to indicate the kinds of attractions to membership for individuals. The nature of the groups, it can be reasonably assumed, determine their priorities and activities. Merari indicates some of the characteristic modes of action of the various types of group, which illustrates this point. He notes, for example, that since Xenofighters are not dependent on their target population for support, they can have less regard to scale of injuries they inflict. The Homofighter, in contrast, because he in some sense is a part of the community in which he operates, must have regard to the immediate, as well as long term, consequences of his actions. These differences can be illustrated by the actions of the Provisional IRA, who inflict indiscriminate damage through bomb attacks on Security Force targets, perhaps located in either protestant or neutral areas, but use much more specific forms of action in contrast to bombs (such as knee capping or murder) against members of the catholic communities.

A somewhat simpler classification scheme, with greater relevance to our discussion, has been described by Post, who has identified two major types of terrorist group[15], each of which may attract different kinds of individual, and exert influences on those members in dissimilar ways. The first kind of group he identifies is what has been termed the *anarchic-idealogue group*. These are often relatively small terrorist groups committed to the overthrow of their own government and society for ideological reasons. Groups such as the Red Army Faktion in Germany, or the Italian group Red Brigade would be examples. The second type of group are the *nationalist-separatist groups*. These are often relatively larger, and are motivated by nationalism or regional aspirations of some kind, often involving independence. The Basque organisation ETA, and the Irish Provisional IRA are examples of this kind of group.

The nature of such groups gives some indications of the features of membership that might be important. Nationalist groups may well command grudging support amongst their community, if not explicit enthusiasm. In that community, for a young person to join a well-established organisation of this kind might be seen, as Post notes, almost as a 'rite of passage' into adult life; an expression of solidarity and commitment to the community in which you were born. Often, there is a folk history on which to draw, and local heroes to emulate, in which parents or families can participate. These features might help us to understand some of the factors we referred to in the role of families in the process of identification.

The anarchic-idealogue group, in contrast, lives in isolation from its community. Unlike the nationalist group, the anarchic-idealogue group draws its strength from political ideals, which provide both the goal to aim for, and the justification for methods to achieve that goal. Membership of the nationalist type of group might almost occur by default as part of growing up; illustrations of this can be seen in our earlier discussion of ETA membership in Chapter 6. In contrast, membership of the anarchic-idealogue group requires an active choice. Sometimes this is expressed as a 'leap' into membership, which once taken, proves difficult to negate. The accounts we have already examined in Chapter 7 of individual involvement with terrorism illustrate this point, for all of these refer to membership of anarchic-idealogue groups. Klein in particular gives us a very good picture of the progress of membership, the final 'point of commitment' that confirms marginalisation from society, and wholehearted commitment to the 'cause', expressed through the group[16].

The Dynamics of Groups

We have already noted that membership of a group of any kind is not a static process; the group can be seen as a dynamic entity that both confers benefits *and* influences the group member. The dynamics of group influences have been the subject of an enormous amount of research over the past decade or so, and are relatively well understood. Of the range of forces which seem to characterise the group, we will primarily focus on two which seem to be particularly relevant in helping our understanding of the terrorist group — the process of deindividuation, and the role of the group leader. Little *direct* work is available and therefore we can only assume that these features operate in terrorist groups as much as they do in others. In fact, however, there are grounds for supposing that these forces might be somewhat exaggerated in terrorist groups. We might also note at this point that the terrorist group may be quite complex in its organisational structure (see Chapter 6), but the effects of group membership would still seem to be relevant to our discussion at whatever point at which the group structure impinges on the individual member.

Membership of a group can lead to a lessening of restraint against impulsive or unusual forms of behaviour. It has been recognised since the last century that crowds behave in ways different from individuals on their own[17]. The political crowd, 'the mob', is a potent force well known to political leaders[18]. This same phenomenon, however, applies equally to small groups, and in small groups the process whereby it occurs is referred to as *deindividuation*.

The essential quality which seems to affect the development of deindividuation is self-awareness[19]. In order to regulate our activity in relation to others, we have to be aware of what we feel, think and do. Under some conditions, which might be characterised as the result of group membership, self-awareness can be blocked. The conditions which give rise to such blockage are anonymity, a high level of arousal, feelings of close group unity and a focus on external events and goals. These conditions are all typified by the terrorist group, of either type. All terrorist groups involve some measure of secrecy, thereby conferring anonymity, and their involvement in illegal acts gives rise to high levels of psychological stress and arousal. Both secrecy and illegality contribute to intense group unity and all terrorist groups, almost by definition, are focused on external events and goals, in terms of the 'armed struggle', the achievement of 'liberation', or whatever other rhetoric expresses their ideology. Indeed, it would be difficult to design group structures that were more facilitating of generating these conditions!

When the conditions described above exist, they give rise to two effects. First, for the individuals concerned, self-awareness is sharply reduced, and secondly, shifts in their perception of experiences occur. When these conditions arise, a *deindividuated* state is said to exist. The consequences of this are quite profound. The restraints on otherwise prohibited behaviour are weakened, and the individual concerned is able to do things (like acts of violence) which under normal circumstances he would not engage in. Along with that occurs a decrease in the individual's capacity to monitor or regulate his own acts, an interference in ability to engage in rational thought or long term planning, and a reduction in concern with how others regard his behaviour.

We can illustrate and summarise this process more clearly through a diagram. We can see in the process of deindividuation a very powerful force operating in the effects of the group on the individual. Recent developments of this approach have emphasised the importance of deindividuation on *private* self-awareness, as opposed to public self-awareness[21]. This refers to the effects of deindividuation on the loosening of internal standards and the influence of existing social norms.

The process of deindividuation has received empirical confirmation and support and seems to refer to an important quality of *all* groups. Evidence of it can even be seen, for example, in relatively innocuous groupings that

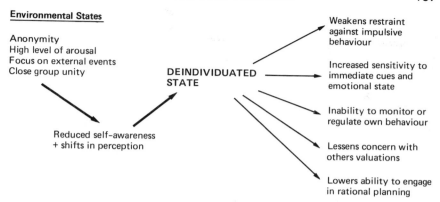

FIG. 8.1. The Process of Deindividuation (after Baron and Byrne[20]).

young children might make. We might expect it to be more evident, however, in circumstances involving intense stress, and indeed, many war time accounts, notably recent contemporary accounts of the experiences of soldiers in Vietnam, make reference to effects of this kind. For our purposes, it refers to a process of enormous importance in helping us to understand why terrorists appear to be relatively normal people on the one hand, and on the other, capable of such horrific acts of violence. Furthermore, the process of deindividuation offers a means of explaining that paradox in terms that have currency in circumstances outside of the terrorist group.

It can also offer us a way of understanding another paradoxical feature of terrorist groups. In the main, the rhetoric of terrorism refers to 'liberty', 'freedom' and 'lessening of constraints'. By their very nature, terrorist groups are antiauthoritarian, (where authority is expressed in the State), offering a challenge and alternative social system (ideological or national) to the one that now exists. In addition, the attractions of the terrorist lifestyle might be thought to apply to the liberated youth, breaking free from the shackles of his society. The female terrorist might well be thought to be associated with the women's liberation movement, or at least to share common values. Yet in operation, most terrorist groups that survive any length of time require an extreme degree of conformity of their members. This has been referred to by Post as 'the paradox of conforming anti-authoritarians'[22]. Opposition to social authority outside the group, is matched by fervent conformity within the group. Dissent is rarely tolerated, and expressions of loyalty to the group become of paramount importance. Failure to give that loyalty can result in disproportionate hostility and anger by members of the group. This can be very clearly seen in the vicious punishment of transgressing group members by the Provisional IRA. We can resolve this paradox however when we consider the effects of distortion in perception and loss of self-awareness produced by deindividuation. 'Group think' is a term sometimes used to describe this kind of effect. Work on the German terrorists largely confirms the importance of group pressures in the maintenance of the terrorist group[23].

We can also identify a feature of decision making that may be relevant to the above discussion, and which may enhance the effects of deindividuation. The social psychological process of *entrapment*[24] refers to 'a decision making process whereby individuals escalate their commitment to a previously chosen, though failing, course of action in order to justify or "make good on" prior investment'[25]. This notion may have relevance to the process which contributes to the development and sustenance of cohesion in the terrorist group, especially in the context of deindividuation. The terrorist group sets the scene for intense pressures, often involving decision making by the individual. The direction of decision making is specified by the group (and possibly its leader). Entrapment characterises the spiralling of commitment so frequently seen in members of terrorist groups.

In a sense, most groups have qualities of psychological traps, but the terrorist group seems to enhance these qualities. Psychological traps have been identified by Rubin as having three critical qualities[26]. They have an ability to lure or distract the trap's victim into behaviour which ultimately is quite costly to him, either in psychological or social terms. Secondly, they are constructed in such a way as to permit decisions that only allow greater movement into the trap. Finally, efforts to escape serve to increase the trap's bite.

When we look at the accounts of ex-terrorists describing the group of which they were members, these qualities become very evident. The lure of the terrorist group is something we can well understand. Klein's comments on its sexual opportunities, for example, illustrate one kind of lure; companionship and belonging are probably more important qualities, and describe forces we have all been exposed to in some sense or other. Once a member of the terrorist group, decision making by the individual is forced more and more towards meeting the group's ends. The pressure towards conformity that the group can exert is a powerful force in this respect, and the process of deindividuation allows the expression of violence that terrorist activity requires. Once the process begins, it is very difficult to stop it. Again, to quote Klein 'If you're long enough in the underground, you sooner or later pitch everything overboard. From humanity to your political ideals. You sink deeper and deeper into the shit. Once you've taken this path, all that's left is a straight road. You can't turn around'. Escape routes from the group become reduced as violence escalates[27]. The terrorist becomes the target of the security forces by his actions as a terrorist, but if he tries to leave, he also becomes the target of the group of which he is a member. The ex-terrorist is a danger to the group because of his knowledge and also because he has rejected group values, making him a traitor 'to the cause'. Clark[28] notes that one force which discourages ETA members from leaving is the fear of reprisal. Former members of ETA are often subjected to attacks, sometimes by the security forces seeking, perhaps, to pay off old scores when the protection of ETA membership is no longer there, but also by ETA itself.

Group forces of the kind described may exert power, and may facilitate the expression of behaviour that under different circumstances would be inhibited. The *direction* that behaviour takes, however, is the result of other kinds of issues, notably the nature of group decision making, and the role of the group leader. When considering this in the context of the terrorist group, we have to take a further issue into account — the structure of the group, and its relationship with either its broader organisation, or other related groups.

Small groups that coalesce around a particular ideology, or are a response to particular circumstances probably do not belong to any overall structure; they operate on their own, set their own agenda, and also make their own decisions. Groups of this kind are sometimes referred to as 'autonomous cells'. There may be similar groups, perhaps embracing similar ideological positions which constitute a broad coalition, but decision making will be confined to the autonomous group. This kind of structure is not necessarily solely a characteristic of the single issue group, or the small group. Some larger movements such as the 2nd June Movement deliberately created this structure, delegating to its individual cells much of the decision making.

The other kind of organisational structure that can be identified is the hierarchy. A characteristic of large terrorist organisations, like the Provisional IRA, ETA and the Red Army Faction, is a structure very like that adopted by any large business (see discussion in Chapter 6). Decision making is centralised and information passed down to smaller active units. Very little autonomy is left within the active group and they have little effect on the decision-making process. Structures of this kind are often authoritarian, and indeed, it is within this kind of organisation that we see most clearly the 'conforming authoritarian' paradox referred to above. In practice, in an organisation like the Provisional IRA, for example, the individual active terrorist will have little or no idea of the kinds of target selected, or of the overall strategy being followed by the organisation. He will be expected to follow the orders given to him without question. The local group may identify potential targets in their area and pass that information up the hierarchy for approval. After approval, the individual identified to undertake the action will be detailed for a task shortly before it is to take place. He may not even know the location or the target until he is actually at the scene. Weapons, and any other requirements, will be provided for him, and taken away afterwards. The co-ordination of such activities places massive demands on the terrorist organisation, and a complex administrative and support structure is necessary to make it work. Because of this, it is worth noting that naive headcounting of *active* terrorists in groups like this is largely meaningless, given the extent of the necessary support system.

In terms of directing operations, the loose democratic structure of the anarchic-idealogue group can prove problematic. Divisions over leadership can easily emerge; whilst the groups may be highly democratic, to have many voices expressing different views does not tend to encourage decision making. Such groups are also inherently less secure, in that the decision making is spread widely across the group, with all members knowing the content and direction of debate. Small decision-making groups of this kind are also subject to a psychological phenomenon termed 'risky shift'[29]. Contrary to commonsense expectations of conservative decision making, discussion in small groups can result in more risky decisions being made after group discussion. Well-established empirical evidence supports this view. This is probably better characterised as a shift towards polarisation, in which group discussion can lead some members to become more extreme in views already held than when they started the discussion. In other words, where individuals before a discussion may feel somewhat inclined towards a particular action, after discussion they become much more decisive in undertaking that action. In terms of the kinds of issue a terrorist group might discuss, this represents a very worrying effect, and in it we can see a force towards enhancement of expression of extremity through violence.

These kinds of issues can characterise decision making in hierarchical organisational structures, but the nature of the filtering process, in rising through the hierarchy, can to some extent control the individual qualities that contribute to it. The hierarchy, in fact, has a number of advantages over the looser structure for the terrorist. It is more secure, in that individual members cannot compromise decision making, because they are not aware of it. Indeed, if this structure also enforces a small cellular structure, in which individual members of the cells do not know members of other cells and have limited knowledge of members of the hierarchy (perhaps communicating through one person) they become very difficult to compromise through penetration or the use of informants. A negative feature of this, however, is that the group becomes relatively insensitive to the environment in which it operates. For a nationalist organisation, as opposed to an ideologically based organisation, this may be a major problem. Wolf[30] discusses the utility in this context of various forms of terrorist group organisational structures.

The overall structure of the group affects decision making in the ways outlined above. It can also affect the capacity of the individual to exert a leadership role. Clearly, in the loose organisation, a leadership function can become more apparent and, as we have noted above, challenges for leadership, based on conflicts over decision making, are much more possible than in the hierarchical organisation. Because of this, the loosely structured groups are less cohesive, and tend to fragment much more readily. Disputes over leadership, of course, occur in hierarchical groups, but the structure mitigates against fragmentation, and in circumstances where the group works within a supportive community (as might a nationalist group), that community lends added force to sustain group cohesion. That this is not always strong enough can be seen in the splintering of ETA referred to earlier, and in the split in the Irish Terrorist groups into the Provisional IRA, the Official IRA and the INLA.

A complementary approach to this analysis of terrorist organisations has been developed by Strentz[31]. He discusses, in some detail, the possible dynamics of group organisation in the terrorist group and draws particular attention to the relationship between the leader and others. This work is based largely, but not exclusively, on experience of the Symbianese Liberation Army (SLA). He identifies, and draws a distinction between three kinds of participant in terrorist groups: leaders, activist/operators and idealists. The mixture of, and relationships between these kinds of individual determine the nature of the group and its dynamics. The leader, for example, is characterised by total dedication, and is often a trained theoretician with what Strentz describes as a 'strong' personality. The activist/operator is, according to Strentz, an opportunist, perhaps with a criminal record, and a deviant personality in some sense. The idealist, in contrast, is often the university drop-out, whose life is characterised by a search for 'truth'; he (or she) is often the minor functionary.

Within the Symbianese Liberation Army (SLA), made notorious by its kidnapping of Pattie Hearst, Nancy Ling Perry was the archetypal leader in Strentz's terms. She was an intelligent woman, a graduate in English Literature from the University of California. She had the conviction of her own certainty, a certainty which she transmitted to her group. She was intolerant of the views of others, and demonstrated a rigidity of belief that seems close to obsession. An example of the activist/opportunist from the SLA was Donald DeFreeze. He was a college dropout, leaving school at sixteen. By the age of seventeen, he had fifteen felony arrests; he failed to complete his last prison sentence, absconding from the California Correctional Training facility at Soledad in March, 1973. He next reappeared as a member of the SLA in February, 1974. DeFreeze appears to have been the typical 'heavy', showing little appreciation of the political context in which he was placed by Nancy Ling Perry. His value to the SLA lay, not in his ability to conceptualise, but in his capacity to undertake *action* in order to propagate their ideas. To complete the analysis, Angela Atwood was one of the idealists within the SLA. She had a history of political involvement before becoming involved with the SLA, but was a former school teacher and waitress.

More extensive comparative studies are necessary before the essentially limited analyses typified by Strentz can be evaluated. However, he suggests that the form of group organisation he describes can be identified in other terrorist groups, ranging from the Provisional IRA to the Japanese Red Army. If this analysis is correct, then clearly it can offer some insights into the decision-making context of the groups, and may be of value in predicting operationally relevant features, such as the likely effect of pressure on decision making, or under interrogation, for example. We really need more information, however, to judge this issue.

In media accounts of terrorism, the 'charismatic' leader often figures as an important unifying and directing force. This may be the case in some groups, but certainly there is no evidence that the *overt* leader must necessarily be dominant. 'Carlos' as a figure achieved notoriety as an important terrorist, and was often given media prominence. One of the most famous incidents in which he was involved was the attack on the OPEC ministers in Vienna in 1975. In operational terms, Carlos seems to have 'led' the group who undertook the attack[32], but they were an essentially *ad hoc* grouping, derived from a number of different terrorist organisations. The man behind the operation, and who might be said to have initiated both its planning and execution, was Wadi Haddad, one of the founders of the Popular Front for the Liberation of Palestine. In this example, leadership functions are far from clear, but Haddad might well be thought to be the force behind the attack, in terms of the forward logistical and operational planning, rather than the more public figure of Carlos. Given the nature of large hierarchical terrorist organisations, or the kind of transnational grouping described here, the notion of 'leadership roles' might be quite problematic.

Indeed, this raises another issue. The capacity for Palestinian Terrorist groups, for example, to draw on activists from other organisations implies a high degree of co-ordination. Increasingly, terrorist actions are rarely self-contained, and nor are the different groups wholly isolated from one another. There is, in fact, good evidence of the linking and sharing of resources between different groups. Terrorists need safe bases from time to time and they need money and weapons. These seem to be readily available on a scale that suggests some form of background involvement from a State source.

Organisational features of terrorist groups may be of importance to the security forces in operational terms, as indicators and constraints on a terrorist group's decision-making strategies and capacities. Dror[33] has drawn our attention to the organisational qualities of terrorist groups that facilitate or modify change in operational practice. He suggests that the terrorist group is subject to the kind of organisational pressures encountered in other organisations, with a tendency towards conservatism in choice of strategy, or kinds of targets.

The mechanisms of change, the process of decision making, the relationship between organisational structure and its conservatism may be subject to analysis from perspectives in organisational psychology. Flow of information between elements of the group may be a critical aspect of this. Structures developed to maintain security (the cell system for example) place constraints on information flow. This, whilst desirable from the point of view of security, also constrains the structure for efficient decision making, and may lead the terrorist leadership to misperceive its effectiveness, or the value of particular strategies. Contemporary concerns with unconventional terrorism make this kind of approach particularly important.

Conceptualising the terrorist group in this way, if it is an accurate account, offers some very important advantages. It gives us a structure in which to locate terrorist decision making which is relatively well understood, and enables us to extend our analysis and address important practical issues such as the relationship between terrorist activity and innovation of terrorist tactics and methods. This problem must be of concern to security forces and governments subject to the threat of terrorism, and answers to it presumably would play an important part in operational planning. Dror[34] makes reference to the inherent factors of organisational conservatism and routinisation as limiting conditions on the development of innovative terrorist action. These factors are also evident of course in the security forces, however, who can be subject to the same kind of organisational analysis.

Indeed, a reciprocal relationship might be said to exist between terrorist action and organisational change, and security force action and organisational change. Where security force activity is proactive, rather than reactive, the operational initiative may lie with the security services, giving them an advantage over the terrorist group. On the other hand, such reactivity may stimulate innovation in the terrorist organisation as a response to improved effectiveness. Enhanced and innovative security force activity might paradoxically, therefore, stimulate the development of unconventional and novel terrorist tactics! Solutions to this problem will have great operational significance.

The above is closely related to the principles of reciprocity in warfare described by Clausewitz[35]. The above might be regarded as little more than a restatement of his 'third reciprocal action', where he refers to the 'mutual enhancement' which results from improvements on one side being replicated by the adversary. Indeed, to paraphrase Clausewitz, we might say that dealing with terrorism is like war, 'a constant state of reciprocal action, the effects of which are mutual'[36].

However, this raises a very important issue, illustrating a sense in which dealing with terrorism is not like warfare. Because, at least in the West, the terrorist operates in an environment that is, in some respects, normal (or at least not overtly mobilised for war), holding the initiative in terms of armaments, personnel, and the like does not give the ascendancy that would be expected to follow in conventional warfare. The environmental constraints on security force activity effectively negate the value of material advantage, thereby paradoxically conferring the initiative on the terrorists. Although, as we have noted above, there can be reciprocal developments in terrorist activity, resulting from improvements in security force tactics and other factors, the security services are, in the main, inevitably on the other side of the reciprocal relationship. Effectively, they are placed in the position of catching up operationally on the developments of the terrorist group. An emphasis on physical force solutions to terrorism will inevitably fall into this position. Because of this, it may be that armies, with their emphasis on extensive and extreme force, are inappropriate vehicles for the management of terrorism.

The context in which terrorism takes place is all important in this respect. Both anarchic-idealogue and nationalist-separatist groups operate within communities that, whilst they may be supportive, are in the main not directly involved in the terrorist actions and, more particularly, are not usually involved in open insurrection or revolution. Unless this is recognised, the 'overflow' in the use of physical force in response to terrorism can impinge on, and effectively radicalise, an otherwise ambivalent community. The government then '. . . has no alternative except to intensify repression' (Marighella[37]).

A further issue to which it is worth drawing attention is the consequence of innovation for the security services, as opposed to the terrorist group. In general, terrorism is a low financial cost activity; conversely, managing terrorism has become a high cost activity, in terms of both manpower and technology. Furthermore, the large bureaucratic structures that are necessary to control modern police forces and armies are very unwieldy and inherently resistant to change. Because of these factors, innovation in tactics by the security services can be difficult and costly, perhaps needing complex retraining of men. This is rarely a problem for the terrorist organisation.

A further complexity in the analysis of the response of the security services lies in the nature of the work of the security organisations, especially the police. As far as they are concerned, the management of terrorism may be a high priority in their activities, but in democratic societies it is not the only activity they undertake. Indeed, even in such areas as West Belfast, for example, police activity bears a striking similarity to police work in other less hostile environments. The management of terrorism may be a dramatic, but not necessarily full time activity for the individual member of the security services on the ground[38]. Conflicting demands on the time and priorities of the security services severely limit their capacity to react to change, enhancing the pressures towards conservatism. It can also lead to the kind of 'routinisation' of activity referred to by Dror[39], which may well represent one of the major problems for the security services working in such areas.

Much of the evidence on which to base discussion of group forces is inevitably sketchy and more related to conjecture rather than hard fact. Evidence of relevant group activity derived from other sources, however, may well assist our analysis. A useful article by Wright and Wright[40] reviews the related notion to the terrorist group of 'violent groups' which is of value to our discussion. Drawing on evidence from a range of sources (cults and religious groups, but not necessarily terrorist groups) they draw attention to the kinds of psychological processes involved in the creation of group 'identity' and 'norms' as elements in the development of group control over the individual. Perhaps the most dramatic example of the force of such pressures is the 1978 mass suicide of the religious community led by the Rev. Jim Jones in Guyana, referred to in Chapter 5. The importance of the leader in this context is obvious.

It is not clear whether the terrorist group embodies forces other than those evident in other forms of group; evidence of this is limited, but it seems unlikely that there are such special forces (as opposed to activities). On the other hand, whilst it is possible to make generalisations about group forces, and the way in which these might become evident, the critical issue may well be the manner and extent to which they interact with the terrorist organisational structure. We have already noted that the organisational structures of terrorist groups vary; not all, for example, live in the form of a clandestine commune. Members of the Red Zora, for example, the women's grouping of the German Revolutionary Cells, live as normal citizens, working within small independent groups[41]. Presumably, the kinds of pressure to which such structures are subjected will be rather different from the truly separate 'underground' movement. In large terrorist groups, like the Provisional IRA and the Basque ETA, different members of the group will live under different kinds of pressure. Those members of the group actually involved in shootings or bombings, the so-called Active Service Units, for example, are subjected, presumably, to different sorts of group forces than those individuals involved in support operations. Similarly, living within a community that is broadly supportive, (or at least not openly hostile), as members of the Provisional IRA might live in West Belfast will result in different experiences of group pressure than those to which members of the Provisional IRA undertaking operations in mainland Britain are subjected.

In examining the power of the group to maintain behaviour, we can also begin to understand some of the reasons why terrorism can appear to become detached from the circumstances in which it operates. The Provisional IRA, for example, seems to have self-perpetuating qualities. It has little role in the political processes of Northern Ireland and does not appear to be gaining support, precipitating revolution or producing social change. Indeed, the performance in elections, in both the Irish Republic and Northern Ireland, of its political wing, Sinn Fein, suggests little change in its minority appeal. Yet it continues to function. One reason for this might lie in the power of the group to sustain itself—a self-perpetuating cycle—which, given the historical context of nationalist-separatist groups, and the support of a committed (albeit relatively isolated) minority of the community, may represent a very powerful force.

Concluding Comments

The above does not offer an adequate embracing explanation of one of the fundamental problems of terrorism; why some individuals in a given context and with relatively common experiences become, or do not become, terrorists. The concept of identification which has been offered as an explanation seems to add little to our knowledge. The important issue relates to the use of violence, for as we have seen, the critical quality in analyses of terrorism is the relationship between political activity and violence. Many people are politically committed and active; few commit terrorist acts. This remains the major challenge facing analyses of the terrorist, and as yet, there is little empirical evidence available to answer the question.

This is, of course, not a problem unique to the analysis of terrorism. It would be difficult to describe comprehensively the forces that lead to any major life choice. Why some people become police officers, social workers, academics or psychologists is wholly obscure, and we can only, and then in a very general sense, tentatively identify the kinds of factor that might be important. Perhaps this relates back to our earlier discussion of the attempt to find a 'specialness' in terrorism. Our surprise at our inability to identify the forces that give rise to terrorism reflects just such an assumption, which we might not make for other kinds of life choices.

On the other hand, the above analysis may well offer some help in conceptualising some of the forces that might contribute to that process. The notion of the group, and the pressure and forces embedded in the group do offer a means of analysing the problem within a psychologically valid framework. There may be no particular route to terrorism that can be separated from the social and political circumstances operative on the individual. But there may be common processes to which that individual is subjected once those contextual circumstances facilitate involvement with terrorism.

CHAPTER 9

Terrorist Behaviour

[*Whether rational or irrational, he (the terrorist) is governed as we all are by the same laws of behaviour*[1].]

Attempts to identify different rules which might explain terrorist behaviour have, in the main, proved ineffective. Earlier chapters have reviewed some of the problems in this, and indicated the difficulties they might lead us into. A major problem in analysis has been identified as the assumptions we bring to the issue, many of which emphasise notions of the 'specialness' of terrorism and the terrorist. This has influenced both conceptual discussion and research. We can see it in a number of ways, ranging from attempts to describe the personal attributes of the terrorist, to attempts to identify common pathogenic developmental characteristics. In general, these approaches have had little utility.

The overriding concern of any analysis of terrorism is to try to answer the question 'What causes it? Why does it occur?'. From a psychological perspective, we need to rephrase that question to 'What causes *him* (or her) to do it?'. We can consider this issue in two ways, neither of which is necessarily mutually exclusive, but which may lead to differences in approach. The first is to adopt a broader political and cultural framework, and from this, try to explain causative forces at an individual level. This involves the expression in psychological terms of the kinds of economic, political and sociological forces which seem to be factors in the development of political terrorism. To embark on this is to seek one view of 'the causes' of terrorism, and the utility of the approach would be demonstrated by success in identification of such 'causes', and presumably thereby help our understanding. This raises all sorts of difficulties, however, about the relationship between individual action, and the broader social context; it also expresses the essentially psychological activity of analysis of individual causes of behaviour in terms derived from other disciplines. An inevitable problem for this at the moment is that we lack conceptual structures to achieve this essentially cross disciplinary task effectively.

Notwithstanding the above, most of the available literature which we have reviewed falls within this approach in some sense, and in general we can conclude that it fails to fulfil its promise. There are exceptions to this,

however. Merari[2], for example, describes an essentially descriptive classification system for terrorist groups (referred to earlier in Chapter 8) which
emphasises function, based on target population and base of operation.
This has the value of drawing attention to the context in which the terrorist
organisation operates, and thereby emphasising the effect of that context
on its mode of action, functions and the consequences of its activities on its
audience and membership.

The second approach is to take a more focused view, which encompasses
much more limited objectives. Rather than seeking to identify some
socially determined generic basis of terrorism, or the terrorist, the focus
might alternatively be centred on objectives related to understanding the
processes of terrorism, and in so doing attempting to understand, control,
and perhaps predict, events at the level of the individual. Such an approach
has to have regard to the broader social context of terrorism, but would be
both orientated to, and judged, not in terms of explanations derived from
other contexts (other disciplines, for example), but in terms of behavioural
objectives. In achieving this essentially 'psychological explanation', it
would also fulfil the kinds of objectives for the development of a 'forensic
psychology' described by Kaplan[3], in terms of having operational or
practical relevance as a primary orientation. Merari[4] in some measure
approaches this objective, by emphasising function, but his classification
system remains expressed at a relatively general level.

A Structure for Analysing Terrorism

What would developing this second approach mean in the analysis of
terrorism? Would it serve any practical value? One obvious reorientation
that would follow from this essentially practical way of approaching the
problem would be in terms of the kinds of solution adopted to deal with
terrorism. At the moment, security forces tend to rely on physical
technological solutions[5] which, as we have noted in Chapter 8, will always
ultimately be limited in their potential. The reciprocal relationship
between the security services and the terrorist which we have noted
inevitably results in a spiral of threat and counterthreat. Regardless of
success, the escalating costs of technological solutions to terrorist innovation alone represent a major challenge that Governments have to manage
in increasingly harsh economic climates. This is, of course, an important
additional point of pressure for a terrorist organisation, and one which is
readily exploitable.

There is a pressing need to develop non-technologically orientated
methods of addressing the problems of terrorism. On the other hand, we
have seen that many conventional psychologically non-technological
approaches fail to offer promise; in those cases where promise has been
fulfilled, the area addressed has been relatively limited. The contribution

of psychology and the behavioural sciences to such incidents as hostage negotiation, for example, are well known and developed. However systematic, empirical and operationally orientated psychological analyses of terrorist activity outside of the hostage situation are relatively scarce. This is the direction that would be indicated by following the second line of approach discussed above, and it may well have great utility.

The application to terrorism of knowledge about the nature of groups derived from sources other than the analysis of terrorist groups, has been shown in Chapter 8 to be one approach of potential value. It helps us to understand the nature of the terrorist organisation, and how that organisation exerts its influence on the individual terrorist. Organisational structure clearly affects the dynamics of terrorist membership and decision making.

We should remind ourselves however that we know of these processes, not from analyses of terrorists, but from *basic* research on small groups and other organisations. Following this approach, and given our limited empirical knowledge of terrorism, it might be possible to develop from *other* aspects of psychological inquiry ways of furthering our conceptualisation of terrorism. Whilst terrorism is not a particularly new phenomenon, systematic study of it is. The progress of that study, however, bears a resemblance to that of other examples of troublesome behaviours, such as crime. It may be useful, therefore, to examine the development of thinking on crime as something which will offer useful analogies for the analysis of terrorism.

Analogies with Crime

Until relatively recently, psychological thinking about crime was dominated by attempts to identify particular personal attributes of individuals that might be associated with a propensity to commit crime. Thus, the notion of the criminal personality became prevalent and, in further exploring these notions, efforts were made to identify generic qualities of criminals[6]. The parallels with the analyses of terrorism we have encountered are of course striking. Both seek some form of particular and essential attributes to distinguish the terrorist or criminal from other categories of people.

The greatest difficulty with this approach to crime, however, is the repeated failure of such analyses to identify unique pathologies of the criminal condition that do not occur in the general non-criminal public. The failure to identify generic properties of criminals inevitably calls into question the utility of this approach. The discussion in the early part of this book drew similar conclusions with respect to the analysis of terrorism.

In practical terms, approaches to crime emphasising criminal attributes have proved to have little utility in terms of crime control. Crime prevention techniques have tended to develop along the lines of increased hardware sophistication, in part on the assumption that because the criminal has criminal tendencies, he must be deterred, rather than prevented. This follows, if we see criminal attributes as part of the personality structure; they become inaccessible to immediate change. This is a very negative approach to the problem, but there is another, and more fundamental difficulty, with this view. Even if attributes of the potential criminal were known and identifiable, it is difficult to see what might be done with such knowledge, at least in terms of crime control. The potential (or even high probability) to commit an offence does not constitute sufficient grounds under our present legal systems for arrest or other direct preventative action. What else can we do to prevent crime? We are thrown on to deterrence, and technological solutions to crime prevention.

Within the personal attribute approach to crime, the only way of addressing prevention is in terms of what happens to the offender when he is caught. Knowledge of the determinants of criminal behaviour might then be thought to have a role in the development of effective strategies for rehabilitation of convicted offenders on committal to prison, or other facilities. Thus crime prevention, if it is to occur, must be focused on the offender when he is convicted. He can then be 'treated'. The parallels with the analysis of terrorism we have already encountered in earlier chapters are obvious and striking!

Increasingly, however, the view that prison has any role in controlling crime through the regime offenders are exposed to has been called into question. Authors such as Brody[7] and Martinson[8] began a process of challenge to this general approach by demonstrating in empirical terms the inadequacy of rehabilitative strategies to change subsequent criminal behaviour. This challenge has resulted in a major re-appraisal of such approaches. As part of this re-appraisal, there has been growing interest in what is termed the 'situational' approach to crime prevention[9]. This approach does not have the understanding of the broader concept of crime and the criminal as its focus, (although the analysis may contribute to that), but rather seeks solutions to the problems of crime by better understanding of the immediate environmental context in which crime is committed.

An example of how this kind of analysis might proceed can be seen in Bennet and Wright's analysis of residential burglary[10]. Instead of attempting to describe generic attributes of criminals, they focus on the problems associated with a particular crime (residential burglary). They used convicted burglars as subjects in a series of investigations of relationships between particular kinds of environmental cues or cue clusters (lights in houses, car in drive, availability of cover, and similar factors) and the decision to commit burglary at a particular property. A burglar's behaviour is closely related to the presence of cues of this kind and he seems to use them in his decision to offend to predict both risk and reward. These environmental accounts of crimes like burglary are also consistent with the more general kind of analysis of policing offered by Sykes and Brent[11] and lend empirical and conceptual support to other situational crime control notions, such as neighbourhood watch, as a technique of crime control.

The assumption underlying this view is that the criminal is 'broadly rational in nature'[12]; this view has received coherent expression by Cornish and Clarke[13]. The basic assumption they make is that the offender benefits from his criminal choices, and that *this* benefit is the determining factor in his commission of crime. What benefit might mean in this context is a matter for analysis. In the example given above a number of benefits can be identified, some more obvious than others. Money or goods from a successful burglary would be one kind of reward, but the burglar also gains excitement from his activity, status amongst his peer group and confirms his membership of that marginalised group.

Support for this view comes from approaches to the analysis of crime based on other disciplines. Becker[14] proposed the 'rational-actor' model of criminal behaviour, which used the techniques of economic analysis to describe criminal behaviour in terms of the utility of the choices available to the criminal. There are clear parallels here, in that the emphasis on 'benefit' described above, and the economic concept of 'utility' are clearly closely related.

Like terrorism, crime is varied, committed under a range of circumstances, and is sometimes purposive. It often results in victims that may well have little knowledge of, or contact with, the criminal. Without necessarily making assumptions about the *criminal nature* of terrorism, it seems possible to draw analogies between the processes of crime and the processes of terrorism. It is not necessary to assume that they may be aspects of the same essence to see that there may be utility in thinking about them in the same way. Of course burglary, as in the example above, or other crime for that matter, tends not to be committed in the same kinds of circumstances as terrorist actions are. Apart from the violence of terrorism (which, of course, can characterise some crimes anyway), a notably different feature is the intense group qualities of terrorism. These qualities might be present for the criminal, but they are nowhere near as potent or important. On the basis of the discussion in Chapter 8, we might assume that such group forces might be of great significance for the terrorist, constituting perhaps the major controlling consequence for the context to his acts.

Extending this analysis of crime to terrorism has attractions. Cornish and Clarke[15] make a fundamental distinction between criminal involvement and criminal events, which we can usefully extend to the analysis of terrorism. In their terms, 'involvement' refers to those processes which lead to choices for a criminal about becoming involved in crime, remaining in crime, and leaving a criminal career. The determinants of 'events' can be seen as quite separate. In making decisions about events, the criminal utilises different categories of information. These different factors influencing the criminal career of an individual may overlap, but can be conceptualised as quite different processes.

When this conceptual structure is applied to terrorism, it enables us to make sense of some of the confusion we have encountered in the literature. In the main, the analyses of terrorism which we have considered have been concerned with 'involvement' decisions, although they have not always been expressed in these terms, and indeed may have been addressed at a level of generality that does not allow of meaningful analysis. Much of the work on the social attributes of the terrorist falls generally into this category. However, much clearer 'involvement' forces have been identified in the analysis of group pressures on the individual, in terms of initial attraction to the terrorist world, and the conditions that maintain and polarise the individual once a member of it.

The 'event' factors in terrorism have received little investigation, and are a major area for conceptual and empirical development. The same group forces that we have discussed above might constitute one potent event factor for the terrorist, in that they provide the principal personal audience and consequences for his actions. Group approval we know to be an important element in the terrorist's own accounts of his actions and other factors can similarly be identified from the discussion in Chapter 8. What we are lacking however is any analysis of the *other* situational factors that lead to terrorist decision making; the parallel to the investigations of burglary, for example, described above. This should constitute one major priority for research.

The distinctions we have outlined above are not solely of conceptual value; they may be of operational consequence as well. For the police officer or others who have to deal with the problems of both crime and terrorism, the lack of agreed conceptual definitions, which we have identified in earlier chapters, need not necessarily hinder the development of methods of management. To follow the analogy with crime further, whilst situational accounts of crime do not address questions about the social meaning of crime, they do help us to understand the environmental factors that contribute to the commission of *particular* crimes. The management of terrorism from the perspective of the security services can be thought of in one sense as addressing both the 'involvement' and 'event' qualities of terrorist behaviour. The day-to-day problems faced in terrorism, as distinct from longer term political and security policy issues, are however, essentially 'event' problems, and lend themselves to analysis in these terms.

In placing the analysis of crime within the context of other non-criminal behaviours, and by seeking answers to the determinants of particular criminal acts not in some special inaccessible world of criminal social meaning, but in terms of the kinds of explanations of behaviour we would seek in other contexts, we make the problem of criminal behaviour more accessible to solution. A similar approach applied to terrorism would provide a structure for both operational *and* conceptual analysis, and in doing that, offers an opportunity for the integration of terrorist theory with operational practice. This must be a major priority for any practical research.

This general approach lends itself to expression in behavioural terms[16]. The factors contributing to both the 'involvement' and the 'event' processes can be conceptualised in environmental terms as various psychological stimuli that either 'set the occasion' for the terrorist act or terminate it. Analyses of residential burglary have also been expressed in this way[17]. In more technical terms, we would refer to these factors as discriminative stimuli or reinforcing stimuli[18]. A behavioural approach is a useful one to take in this context. Given that the terrorist is under the control of such stimuli, recognition by the security services that an event constitutes a discriminative stimulus for the terrorist, for example, offers them a means of effecting some control over him. They can do this by changing the discriminative stimuli which are either a part of, or evident in, the situation. Addressing the problem in this way enables an existing well developed conceptual system for analysis and action to be drawn on. It would also, incidentally, serve to complement and extend the 'physical technology' orientation of much of the contemporary approach to terrorism[19] by developing a 'parallel' behavioural technology.

The approach described here is no panacea. It does not immediately offer solutions. Certainly, at first sight, it does not necessarily inform at all what seems to be the principal research focus of terrorism expressed in socially based analyses. On the other hand, in the same way that analogous approaches to crime control may well contribute to the conceptual analyses of crime, so might the approach to terrorism proposed here contribute to the conceptual social analysis of terrorism. But this is not its major strength. This lies in placing the argument and analysis within a systematic empirical framework of known utility. What is now needed to enable this approach to be evaluated is a series of investigations into the environmental 'event' determinants of terrorist behaviour. Investigations of this kind are lacking in the public literature. We can, however, identify clear links between this analysis and analyses of the physical deterrence of terrorist-related intrusion in nuclear facilities described by Karber and Mengel[20]. Combining that approach with the behavioural analysis described above offers an exciting opportunity to progress discussion beyond physical vulnerabilities.

An analysis which is related to the above has been proposed by Sandler[21]. Based on Becker's economic analysis of crime, it applies the 'rational-actor' model to terrorism, developing models of terrorist activity based on the concept of utility. Its assumptions (of behaviour related to its context, rather than the individual's aspirations) are clearly related to the analysis proposed here. At the moment, Sandler's work seems, however, most appropriate to understanding the broader issues of bargaining and resource allocation, in contrast to the incident focus proposed here.

Contribution

In the light of the above, in what particular way might a behavioural approach contribute to the analysis of problems? As we have noted, perhaps its principal contribution would be to locate the analysis within an empirical context, establishing a base not only for descriptive accounts, but also enabling systematic analysis through experiment and modeling. This may well in fact contribute to the kind of conceptual analysis called for by Schmid[22]. He notes that the concept of terrorism has been '. . . subjected to a double standard based on definition power and in-group—out-group distinction', the result of factors such as its derogatory power, its emotive nature, and (although he doesn't explicitly refer to it) the attempt at specialness. A functional analysis of terrorist behaviour would enable us to focus on, for example, the use *and* consequence of violent acts, which may offer utility in understanding more clearly the instrumental character of terrorist violence. An extension of this analysis to encompass media coverage of terrorism, for example, might have great utility.

As we have noted, there is evidence to suggest that terrorist violence is far from random in intent, if not execution. Such victim analyses that have been undertaken suggest explicit choice. Both Lyons and Harbinson[23] and Pockrass[24] have indicated the extent of selective victimisation by the Provisional IRA, and similarly Clark[25] has noted a similar selective victimisation by ETA. We need to know more about this aspect of terrorist action. Particularly fruitful comparisons might be made between different kinds of terrorist groups; but at least by focusing on the consequences of terrorist choices, and the circumstances surrounding them, we may be better able to understand terrorist behaviour.

Given the above, a wide range of directions for further investigation become possible. One direction may be to focus on the role of cues like those discussed by Bennet and Wright[26]. In this respect, what we identify as cues might range from the geographical features of a location, particular individual qualities, to the immediate social environment. Their essential qualities are, however, objective identification and the capacity for them to vary or change.

We can envisage a complex relationship between discriminative environmental properties and terrorist activity. In one sense, we can think of the terrorist as being under the control of discriminative stimuli in, for example, the choices he makes in identifying targets. A better understanding of the determinants of such choices, and the extent to which such choices can be modified by environmental change, would constitute an important area of investigation for preventative measures. Such an analysis could extend beyond the relatively limited immediate environmental context, as discussed above.

On the other hand, on analysing the same situation from the perspective of the policeman, or member of the security service, he can also be thought of as being under a form of environmental control in his recognition of cues that indicate potential terrorist threat (the suspicious vehicle, recognition of environmental incongruity, and so on). An analysis of the role such cues might have in the discriminative control of the police officer would offer clear utility in terms of risk analysis and prediction, as well as providing a systematic basis for training initiatives.

Indeed, a better understanding of the process underlying such discriminative control may well assist in our analysis of the concept of terrorism itself, by providing an empirical base for taxonomic discussions. By placing the analysis of terrorist behaviour within the same general framework used to analyse other behaviour, it may be possible to develop a rationale for control and management of terrorism, without denying the extra-normal qualities of terrorist violence and action.

We might also see another kind of benefit from this approach. At the moment, the principal response to terrorism is essentially technological, often with a heavy reliance on intelligence and the collection of covert information. A change of emphasis may help in reducing an over-reliance on activities which may themselves ultimately represent steps on the road to what we have described as State Terrorism. An often quoted comment about the State's response to the challenge of terrorism is that 'we must fight terrorism with terrorism'. In this comment, we can hear echoes of the slogan painted at the Argentinian Prison, the Villa Joyosa — 'We will carry on killing until people understand' (see Chapter 3). We have already noted that a reciprocal relationship between terrorist activity and security force activity can be described. Whether recognised or not, such reciprocity cannot be allowed to extend to methods and justification on the part of the States response. Claims to legitimacy are not qualities that can affect this judgement.

Adopting a different emphasis might, however, address the problem of that reciprocal relationship in another more positive sense. An emphasis on intelligence and covert activity as a means of addressing the problems of terrorism certainly itself results in reciprocal responses from the terrorist groups to limit 'leakage', through the intimidation and murder of informants, adoption of more secure organisational structures (as discussed in Chapter 8), etc., and similarly to match tactics. Changing attention to situational determinants and consequences may help to break out of a potentially dangerous and essentially unrewarding reciprocal spiral, offering perhaps more hope in the management of the problem.

Retrospect

One of the initial objectives set for this book was to promote reflection on the nature of terrorism and the terrorist from a psychological perspective. A critical assumption we can identify which seems to permeate our thinking and to diminish our capacity to analyse the problem, is the assumption of 'specialness'. The qualities of terrorism which worry us (its violence, its victimisation of innocents) seem to lead us to assume some kind of different explanation from those of other kinds of worrying activities. The very term 'terrorism', with its implied consequences, effectively misleads us into assuming relationships which seem inappropriate and the promiscuous use of the term yet further complicates our analysis. In Chapter 2, we discussed these consequences from a psychological perspective, reviewing what the term might mean with respect to its victims, the public in general, and the political process. By examining the nature of violence, we begin to see that terrorist violence may differ little in psychological terms from other forms of violence.

When we examine the nature of Terrorism in Chapter 3, we see that there are senses in which States, just as much as secret societies, may be involved in terrorism. By extending this analysis further, we see that there are a number of different kinds of terrorist actions that can be identified, and that our concept must extend beyond the direct political arena, to such areas as criminal fund raising and social control. For terrorist actions to be effective, however, we must know about them, and we can identify as a critical element the media, the communicators and mediators of terrorist action to the public.

When we turn our attention to the individual terrorist, we again encounter assumptions about his nature which may complicate our analysis. Chapter 4 discusses some of these assumptions with respect to mental health, and Chapter 5 with respect to Fanaticism. The critical point to emerge is that whilst some terrorists may be mentally ill, and some may indeed be fanatical, they need not necessarily be so. Terrorism may indeed provide the vehicle for the expression of mental illness, or fanaticism, but when we examine what little we know about these issues, we find a much more complex situation emerging, where context, rather than personal attributes, seems to be all important. Describing the terrorist in terms either of abnormality or fanaticism offers little to our analysis, and simply obscures the terrorist further from view.

The general theme of the importance of context also emerges out of the discussion in Chapter 6 of the Terrorist. There is little by way of useful generalisations that we can make about the terrorist that would lead us to suggest predictive explanations of behaviour in terms of personal attributes. This view is reinforced in Chapter 7, where a discussion of the individual psychology of the terrorist again suggests little utility in this kind of approach. A more fruitful perspective emerges, however, when we examine the processes of terrorism in Chapter 8 where we see how the pressures of group membership might shape and direct initiation into terrorism and the development of terrorist action. Finally, in this chapter, Chapter 9, we review and discuss an alternative model which might lend itself to the analysis of the problem.

It is probably naive to imagine that terrorism is a problem with a solution. It is, however, very clearly a problem for many governments, the political process and for some people. A psychological approach will no more solve that 'problem' than any other approach; but it might encourage us to analyse it both systematically and rationally. What such an approach might contribute above all is a more sophisticated view of the individual who undertakes terrorism.

Both sociological and political analyses of terrorism emphasise the difference in the kinds of aspirations of terrorist groups—ideological and nationalistic emphases are one relatively simple way of categorising them. If, as is argued in this book, concepts such as the 'terrorist personality' or other structures that attempt to seek common attributes are of little value in the analysis of the terrorist, are we then left with no psychological qualities to the terrorist? In a sense, the answer to this is 'yes', and in another sense the answer is 'no'. It is 'yes' in that there are no common originating psychological conditions that can be identified which might function as 'the attributes of the terrorist'. There are probably as many different life stories as there are terrorists. Whilst we can identify broad factors in very general terms (e.g. family history, a precipitating incident), in themselves, these factors are not enough to provide an explanation. This need not surprise us; it is an analysis that can be applied to attempts to explain many of an individual's life choices.

On the other hand, if the approach suggested earlier in this chapter is of any value, then whilst there may not be a set of 'attributes' that can be identified, nevertheless we can begin to identify the *processes* that might lead to terrorism, and the commission of terrorist acts, in terms of their functions and consequences for the individual. The structures that we might draw on in that analysis are not in themselves unique to accounts of terrorism; they might as readily be applied to the analysis of any life choices. But the *analysis* that might emerge would be specific to terrorism. In this latter sense, therefore, we may be able to identify psychological attributes of terrorism.

How might this latter analysis then relate to social and political analyses? Do we have to fall back on essentially extra-psychological accounts to provide the conceptual structure for psychological analysis? The answer to this is quite clearly 'no'. In the same way that there are no particular attributes of the terrorist, there are likewise no particular personal attributes associated with the political analyses of terrorist movements. The virtue of the approach proposed here is that we do not have to assume commonality amongst terrorist group membership (which there clearly is not), or some relationship between terrorist motivation (using motivation in a political sense) and psychological motivation. It allows us to look at terrorist participants using the same perspective, which might allow eventually behavioural generalisations to emerge. Thus the range of membership of terrorist groups from the Provisional IRA, ETA, the Baader-Meinhof Group, *et al.*, can be examined and analysed from within a coherent common perspective.

Postscript

Familiar things, you might brush against or tread
upon in the daily round, were glistening red
with the slaughter the hero caused, though he had gone.
By proxy his bomb exploded, his valour shone.

(Extract from *From the Irish* by James Simmons[27])

We used a quotation from James Simmons to begin this book, and it is fitting that it is closed with reference to another poem of his. Simmons' poems have the capacity to bring us face to face with the reality of the terrorist's acts. When we are faced with the consequences of terrorist acts, the romance of the terrorist disappears. It is difficult for most of us to imagine someone carefully thinking through and planning a bombing attack, and then actually planting the bomb, with the intention that incidental passers by will be killed or horrifically injured. By his deed his valour does indeed shine through!

But in spite of the horror, we must resist the temptation to withdraw from systematic analysis of his actions. We must avoid the assumptions that can so easily colour our view. Whether we like it or not, terrorism is a feature of modern political activity. It is unlikely that it will diminish and it is naive to imagine that it is something that can be defeated or eliminated. The injustices (perceived or real) and circumstances which give rise to terrorism seem to be endemic qualities of the modern world and, whilst media attention, personal fulfilment and political power continue to be features of it, it will persist.

We might, however, learn better to understand terrorism. This book has attempted to develop one way of progressing that understanding, using a psychological perspective. If we can achieve some understanding *and* translate that understanding into measures to influence the incidence of terrorism, we might at least reduce the role that terrorism might play in the achievement of political change. In the behavioural approach outlined above, a focused model that might progress our understanding has been proposed which lends itself to practical use. The model enables us to begin the integration of theory with practice, a necessary foundation before any progress can be made. The model has not been elaborated on at length, because we really need systematic and detailed behavioural evaluations of situations before we can progress it; but it does at least offer an alternative approach.

Reducing the role that terrorism plays in contemporary political processes is not something which will follow from a psychological approach alone. It requires both a concerted effort from a range of disciplines and the integration of that with practical activity. It is very easy for an academic analyst to approach a problem from his own perspective and to offer solutions optimistically. The practitioner knows that the situation is more complex than any single discipline approach, and he can very easily feel that his needs are not being addressed.

At the outset, we said that this book was not a manual for either the security services or the terrorist. It set out to inform, to identify some issues which complicate our analysis and, perhaps, to offer ways of solving some of the problems. It has adopted a broadly psychological perspective, and the evidence reviewed suggests that this perspective might have value in the way we think about terrorism and the terrorist.

To see a full development of thinking in this area, we must seek a drawing together of different perspectives. Neither psychology, sociology or political science will 'solve' the problem of terrorism; 'solutions' are far too early in the development of our thinking. Before we can devise solutions, (if solutions there be), we must first try to understand. For all our sakes, we must have confidence that this can be achieved.

CHAPTER NOTES

Chapter 1. Introduction

[1] Simmons, J. *Poems 1956–1986*. The Gallery Press, Dublin, 1986.

[2] *Christian Science Monitor*, 1972, 14 Sept. p. 20.

[3] The Provisional Irish Republican Army (Provisional IRA) is a branch of the Republican Movement in Ireland. They should be distinguished from the Official IRA, which, in its turn, should be distinguished from the IRA. The IRA grew out of attempts to fight the British Forces in Ireland in the 1910s. It played a major role in the eventual expulsion of Britain from the Republic of Ireland, but to a large extent became dormant in Northern Ireland until the late 1960s when it re-emerged as an active paramilitary force. In 1969, the IRA split into two wings, the Official IRA, who had a Marxist orientation, and the Provisional IRA who followed a more traditional Irish nationalist orientation. Each has a political wing attached to it. The Provisional IRA is associated with Sinn Fein, the Official IRA with the Workers Party. The origins of Irish nationalism are very complex; a useful review is provided by Kee, R. *Ireland. A History*. (Weidenfeld & Nicolson, London, 1980). An account of recent political developments in Ireland which help to place current violence in perspective can be seen in Kenny, A. *The Road to Hillsborough. The Shaping of the Anglo-Irish Agreement*. (Pergamon Press, Oxford, 1986). An accurate account of the Provisional IRA and its activities can be found in Bishop, P. and Maille, E. *The Provisional IRA*, Heinemann, London, 1987.

[4] Bell, D. H. Comment: The origins of modern terrorism. *Terrorism*, 1987, **9**, 307.

[5] Schmid, A. P. *Political Terrorism*. North Holland Publishing Co., Amsterdam, 1983.

[6] The Ulster Defence Association (UDA) is a protestant paramilitary organisation in Northern Ireland. It is a legal organisation in the Province and is involved in political activity. It has associations with illegal organisations such as the Ulster Volunteer Force (UVF), the Ulster Freedom Fighters (UFF), and other more shadowy groups such as the Red Hand Commando. As is the case for the IRA, the history and context of the UDA is complex. See Kee referred to in note 3, for an account of its origins and the symbolic role of protestant paramilitary organisations in contemporary Northern Ireland.

[7] ETA is a nationalist organisation fighting for the independence of the Basque area of Northern Spain/Southern France. It has been responsible for a consistent campaign of violence. See Chapter 6 for an account of its membership characteristics.

[8] Rapoport, D. C. Fear and trembling: terrorism in three religious traditions. *The American Political Science Review*, 1984, **78**, 658.

[9] Peters, R. S. *The Concept of Motivation*. Routledge & Kegan Paul, London, 1958.

Chapter 2. The Problem of the Identification of Terrorism

[1] Popper, K. R. *Conjectures and Refutations: the Growth of Scientific Knowledge*. Routledge & Kegan Paul, London, 1963.

[2] Fattah, E. Some reflections on the victimology of terrorism. *Terrorism*, 1979, **3**, 81. See also Flynn, E. E., Victims of terrorism: dimensions of the victim experience, and Hatcher, C. A conceptual framework in victimology: The adult and child hostage experience. Both in Wilkinson, P. and Steward, A. M. *Contemporary Research on Terrorism*. Aberdeen University Press, Aberdeen, 1987.

[3] Lyons, H. A. and Harbinson, H. J. A comparison of political and non-political murderers in Northern Ireland, 1974–1984. *Med. Sci. Law*, 1986, **26**, 193.

[4] Pockrass, R. M. Terroristic murder in Northern Ireland: Who is Killed and Why? *Terrorism*, 1987, **9**, 341.

[5] Schmid, A. P. *Political Terrorism*. North Holland Publishing Co., Amsterdam, 1983.

[6] Bassiouni, M. Prolegomenon to terror violence. *Creighton Law Review*, 1979, **12**, 752.

[7] See for example Crenshaw-Hutchinson, M. *Revolutionary Terrorism*. Hoover Institution, Stamford, 1978, and Wilkinson, P. *Terrorism Versus Liberal Democracy: The Problem of Response*. Institute for the Study of Conflict, Conflict Studies No. 76, London, 1976.

[8] Crenshaw-Hutchinson, M. *Revolutionary Terrorism*. Hoover Institution, Stamford, 1978.

[9] Thornton, T. P. Terror as a weapon of political agitation. In Eckstein, H. (Ed.) *Internal war. Problems and Approaches*. Free Press of Glencoe, New York, 1964.

[10] Wilkinson, P. *Terrorism and the Liberal State*. Macmillan, London, 1977.

[11] Freedman, L. Z. Why does terrorism terrorize? In Rapoport, D. C. and Alexander, Y. (Eds.) *The Rationalization of Terrorism*. University Publications of America, Frederick, MD, 1982. See also Berry, N. O. Theories on the efficacy of terrorism. In Wilkinson, P. and Steward, A. M. *Contemporary Research on Terrorism*. Aberdeen University Press, Aberdeen, 1987.

[12] Fields, R. M. Child terror victims and adult terrorists. *J. Psychohistory*, 1979, **7**, 71.

[13] Greisman, H. C. Social meanings of terrorism: reification, violence and social control. *Contemporary Crises*, 1977, **1**, 304.

[14] Symonds, M. Victim responses to terror. *Annals New York Acad. Sci.*, 1980, **347**, 129.

[15] Ochberg, F. M. The victim of terrorism. *The Practitioner*, 1978, **220**, 293. South Moluccan terrorism in the Netherlands surfaced in the period 1970 to 1978. The island of South Molucca was a colony of the Dutch East Indies and its population was extensively employed in the Dutch colonial army. On decolonisation in 1951, some 4000 South Moluccan soldiers and their families were resettled in the Netherlands, largely against their will. As a community, the South Moluccans, in the main, failed to integrate into Dutch life and their nationalist aspiration increasingly took the form of acts of violence, initially against Indonesian targets and later more indiscriminately. Their most notorious exploit was the hijacking of the train in 1975 but, in all, some six major terrorist incidents can be identified with South Moluccan groups, including a further train hijacking in 1977 and the occupation of a school, occupation of the administrative centre of the province of Drente in 1978, and others.

[16] Cohen, E. A. *Human Behaviour in the Concentration Camp*. Jonathan Cape, London, 1954.

[17] Hillman, R. G. The psychopathology of being held hostage. *Amer. J. Psychiat.*, 1981, **138**, 1193.

[18] Harkis, B. A. The psychopathology of the hostage experience—a review. *Med. Sci. Law.*, 1986, **26**, 48. See also Hatcher, C. A conceptual framework in victimology: The adult and child hostage experience. In Wilkinson, P. and Stewart, A. M. *Contemporary Research on Terrorism*. Aberdeen University Press, Aberdeen, 1987.

[19] Selye, H. *The Stress of Life*. McGraw-Hill, New York, 1956.

[20] Strentz, T. Stockholm syndrome—Law enforcement policy and ego defenses of the hostage. *Annals New York Acad. Sci.*, 1980, **347**, 137. See also McKenzie, I. K. Hostage-captor relationships. (*Bulletin of the British Psychological Society*, 1981, **34**, 161), and Miron, M. S. and Goldstein, A. P. *Hostage* (Pergamon Press, Oxford, 1979).

[21] Turner, J. T. Factors influencing the development of the hostage identification syndrome. *Political Psychology*, 1985, **6**, 705.

[22] The Symbianese Liberation Army were a shady group who came to prominence in the USA in 1974 when they kidnapped Pattie Hearst, the daughter of the American newspaper proprietor Randolph Hearst. They were a radical leftist group whose notoriety was confirmed when their kidnap victim joined them in their activities. See Hacker, F. J. *Crusaders, Criminals, Crazies. Terror and Terrorism in our time*. (Norton, New York, 1976) for a discussion of this, and Hearst, P. (with Moscow, A.) *Every Secret Thing*. (Doubleday, New York, 1982).

[23] Hacker, F. J. *Crusaders, Criminals, Crazies. Terror and Terrorism in our time*. Norton, New York, 1976.

[24] Jackson, Sir G. *Surviving the Long Night*. Vanguard, New York, 1954.

[25] Wardlaw, G. Psychology and the resolution of terrorist incidents. *Australian Psychologist*, 1983, **18**, 179.

[26] Janis, I. *Stress and Frustration*. Harcourt Brace Jovanovich, New York, 1971.

[27] Seybolt, P. J. Terror and conformity. *Modern China*, 1986, **12**, 39.

[28] Ming, Wang *Mao's Betrayal*. Foreign Language Publishing House, Moscow, 1979.

[29] Meerloo, A. M. *Total War and the Human Mind*. George Allen and Unwin, London, 1944.

[30] Schmid, A. P. and de Graaf, J. *Violence as Communication*. Sage Publications, London, 1982.

[31] Friedland, N. and Merari, A. The psychological impact of terrorism. *Political Psychology*, 1985, **6**, 591.

[32] Mayhew, P. and Hough, M. *The British Crime Survey: first report*. Home Office Research Study No. 76, HMSO, London, 1983.

[33] Gunter, B. and Wober, M. Television viewing and public perceptions of Hazards to Life. *J. Env. Psychol.*, 1983, **3**, 325.

[34] Schmid, A. P. and de Graaf, J. *Violence as Communication*. Sage Publications, London, 1982. See also Tugwell, M. Terrorism and propaganda: problem and response, and Crelinsten, R. D. Power and meaning: terrorism as a struggle over access to the communication structure. Both in Wilkinson, P. and Steward, A. M. *Contemporary Research on Terrorism*. Aberdeen University Press, Aberdeen, 1987.

[35] Illich Ramirez Sanchez, nicknamed 'Carlos', is one of the most notorious terrorist leaders of modern times. He was reputedly involved in a number of daring violent exploits, including the raid on the OPEC Oil Ministers Conference in Vienna in 1976. Further details of his childhood are given in Chapter 8.

[36] See Moscovici, S. *The Age of the Crowd*. Cambridge University Press, Cambridge, 1985, and Graumann, C. F. and Moscovici, S. *Changing Conceptions of Crowd Mind and Behaviour*. Springer-Verlag, New York, 1986.

[37] Touraine, A. *The Voice and the Eye: An Analysis of Social Movements*. Cambridge University Press, Cambridge, 1981.

[38] Friedland, N. and Merari, A. The psychological impact of terrorism. *Political Psychology*, 1985, **6**, 591.

[39] Quoted in Melman, Y. *The Master Terrorist. The True Story Behind Abu Nidal*. Sidgwick & Jackson, London, 1987.

[40] Hutchinson, M. C. The concept of revolutionary terrorism. *J. of Conflict Resolution*, 1972, **16**, 383.

[41] Kupperman, R. H. and Trent, D. *Terrorism, Threat, Reality, Response*. Hoover Institution, Stamford, 1979.

[42] Friedlander, R. A. *Terrorism and the Law: What Price Safety?* IACP, Gaithersburg, MD, 1980.

[43] Schmid, A. P. *Political Terrorism*. North Holland Publishing Co., Amsterdam, 1983.

[44] Arendt, H. *On Violence*. Harcourt Brace Jovanovich, New York, 1970.

[45] Schmid, A. P. and de Graaf, J. *Violence as Communication*. Sage Publications, London, 1982.

[46] Bandura, A. *Aggression: A Social Learning Analysis*. Prentice-Hall, Englewood Cliffs, NJ, 1973.

[47] van der Dennen, J. M. G. *Problems in the Concepts and Definitions of Aggression, Violence and some related terms*. Polemologisch Instituut, Groningen, 1980. Cited in Schmid, A. P. *Political Terrorism*. North Holland Publishing Co., Amsterdam, 1983.

[48] Dollard, J., Doob, L., Miller, N., Mowrer, O. H. and Sears, R. R. *Frustration and Aggression*. Yale University Press, New Haven, CT, 1939.

[49] Berkowitz, K. The contagion of violence: an S-R mediational analysis of some effects of observed aggression. In Mudd, W. and Page, H. (Eds.) *Nebraska Symposium on Motivation*. Lincoln, NB, 1971.

[50] Adams, D. The role of anger in the consciousness development of peace activists: where physiology and history intersect. *Int. J. Psychophysiol.*, 1986, **4**, 157.

[51] See Berkowitz, K. The contagion of violence: an S-R mediational analysis of some effects of observed aggression. In Mudd, W. and Page, H. (Eds.) *Nebraska Symposium on Motivation* (Lincoln, NB, 1971), and Margolin, J. Psychological perspectives in terrorism. In Alexander, Y. and Finger, S. M. *Terrorism: Interdisciplinary Perspectives*. John Jay Press, New York, 1977.

[52] Skinner, B. F. *Science and Human Behaviour*. Free Press, New York, 1953

[53] Jenkins, B. M. *The Study of Terrorism: Definitional Problems*. Rand Corporation, Santa Monica, 1980.

[54] Scanlon, J. Domestic terrorism and the media: Live coverage of crime. *Canadian Police College Journal*, 1984, **8**, 154.

[55] Skinner, B. F. *Science and Human Behaviour*. Free Press, New York, 1953.

[56] Rapoport, D. C. Fear and trembling: terrorism in three religious traditions. *The American Political Science Review*, 1984, **78**, 658.

[57] Ibid.

Chapter 3. The Nature of Terrorism

[1] Hacker, F. J. *Crusaders, Criminals, Crazies. Terror and Terrorism in our time.* Norton, New York, 1976.

[2] Bettelheim, B. *Surviving the Holocaust.* Fontana Paperbacks, London, 1986.

[3] Bitner, E. *The Functions of the Police in Modern Society.* National Institute for Mental Health, MD, 1970.

[4] An extensive discussion of the history of British policing of industrial disputes, including the 1984 UK Miners Strike can be found in Geary, R. *Policing Industrial Disputes: 1893 to 1985* (Methuen, London, 1985). The quotations that follow are from this reference.

[5] Simpson, J. and Bennett, J. *The Disappeared. Voices from a Secret War.* Robson, London, 1985. See also Buchanan, P. G. The varied faces of domination: state terror, economic policy, and social rupture during the Argentine 'Proceso', 1976–81. *Amer. J. Political Sci.*, 1987, **31**, 336.

[6] Hacker, F. J. *Crusaders, Criminals, Crazies. Terror and Terrorism in our time.* Norton, New York, 1976.

[7] Simpson, J. and Bennett, J. *The Disappeared. Voices from a Secret War.* Robson, London, 1985.

[8] Stohl, M. and Lopez, G. A. Introduction. In Stohl, A. and Lopez, G. A. (Eds.) *The State as Terrorist. The Dynamics of Governmental Violence and Repression.* Greenwood Press, Westport, 1984.

[9] Stohl, M. International dimensions of state terrorism. In Stohl, A. and Lopez, G. A. (Eds.) *The State as Terrorist. The Dynamics of Governmental Violence and Repression.* Greenwood Press, Westport, 1984.

[10] Epstein, D. G. Police, terrorism and the third world. *Police Chief*, 1986, L11, 50. See also Schiller, D. Th. The police response to terrorism: A critical overview. In Wilkinson, P. and Steward, A. M. *Contemporary Research on Terrorism.* Aberdeen University Press, Aberdeen, 1987.

[11] Wilkinson, P. *Terrorism and the Liberal State.* Macmillan, London, 1977.

[12] Kobetz, R. W. and Cooper, H. H. A. *Target Terrorism.* International Association of Chiefs of Police, Gaithersburg, MD, 1978.

[13] The figures quoted here are largely guesses, but are taken from Boyles, W. The financing of terror: terrorism and organized crime. *Contemporary Affairs Briefing*, 1983, **2**, No. 7. See also Adams, J. The financing of terror. In Wilkinson, P. and Stewart, A. M. *Contemporary Research on Terrorism.* Aberdeen University Press, Aberdeen, 1987.

[14] Quoted in *The Sunday Tribune*, Dublin, 28 December, 1986 and 4 January, 1987.

[15] Clark, R. P. *The Basque Insurgents. ETA 1952–1980.* University of Wisconsin Press, Madison, 1984.

[16] Ibid.

[17] *US Department of State. International Terrorism: Hostage Seizures.* Office for Combating Terrorism, 1983.

[18] Clark, R. P. *The Basque Insurgents. ETA 1952–1980.* University of Wisconsin Press, Madison, 1984.

[19] Figures for insurance premiums were given in *The Observer*, 22 March, 1987.

[20] Clark, R. P. *The Basque Insurgents. ETA 1952–1980.* University of Wisconsin Press, Madison, 1984.

[21] Ibid.

[22] Quoted in *The Sunday Tribune*, Dublin, 28 December, 1986 and 4 January, 1987.

[23] Quoted in Halperin, E. *Terrorism in Latin America.* Sage Publications, Beverly Hills, 1976.

[24] Boyles, W. The financing of terror: terrorism and organized crime. *Contemporary Affairs Briefing*, 1983, **2**, No. 7.

[25] Pilon, J. G. The Bulgarian nexus. *The National Interest*, 1986, Spring, 84.

[26] Morrissey, M. and Pease, K. The black criminal justice system in West Belfast. *The Howard Journal*, 1982, **XXI**, 159.

[27] Policing in difficult environments such as this still continues and to a large extent follows normal policing priorities, with obvious provisos about personal safety. For a discussion of this see Taylor, M. An analysis of police occurrence book entries: an element in a psychology of policing. (*The Howard Journal*, 1982, **XXI**, 145).

[28] Comay, M. Political terrorism *Mental Health and Society*, 1976, **3**, 249.

[29] Wardlaw, G. *Political Terrorism.* Cambridge University Press, Cambridge, 1982.

[30] Wilkinson, P. *Political Terrorism.* Macmillan, London, 1974.

[31] Property damage has been a feature of Welsh language protesters and nationalist movements for many years. For further information, see *The Guardian* February 28, 1986.

[32] Morrissey, M. and Pease, K. The black criminal justice system in West Belfast. *The Howard Journal*, 1982, **XXI**, 159.

[33] Skinner, B. F. *Science and Human Behaviour.* Free Press, New York, 1953.

[34] Cronbag, H. F. M. Some psychological observations on *mens rea*. In Muller, D. J., Blackman, D. E. and Chapman, A. J. *Psychology and Law*, Wiley, Chichester, 1984.

[35] Jones, E. E., Kanouse, D. E., Kelley, H. H., Nisbett, R. E., Valins, S. and Weiner, B. (Eds.) *Attribution: Perceiving the Causes of Behaviour*. General Learning Press, Morristown, 1972.

[36] Taylor, M. An analysis of police occurrence book entries: an element in a psychology of policing. *The Howard Journal*, 1982, **XXI**, 145.

[37] Clausewitz, C. von, *On War*. (Trans. Graham, J. J.) Penguin Books, Harmondsworth, 1968.

[38] Tse-Tung, Mao. *Selected Military Writings*. Foreign Language Press, Peking, 1963.

[39] Clausewitz, C. von, *On War*. (Trans. Graham, J. J.) Penguin Books, Harmondsworth, 1968. For a brief discussion of this issue, see Editor's Introduction, p. 53.

[40] Ibid.

[41] Wilkinson, P. The laws of war and terrorism. In Rapoport, D. C. and Alexander, Y. (Eds.) *The Morality of Terrorism: Religious and Secular Justifications*. Pergamon Press, New York, 1982.

[42] Laqueur, W. *Terrorism*. Weidenfeld & Nicolson, London, 1977.

[43] See discussion by Laqueur, W. *Guerrilla*. Weidenfeld & Nicolson, London, 1977.

[44] Baldwin, R. (Ed.) *Kropotkin's Revolutionary Pamphlets*. Vanguard Press, New York, 1927.

[45] Tse-Tung, Mao. *Selected Military Writings*. Foreign Language Press, Peking, 1963.

[46] Debray, R. *Revolution in the Revolutions*. Monthly Review Press, New York, 1967.

[47] Ibid.

[48] A useful account of the context of the present conflict in Northern Ireland, which addresses the issue of the Provisional IRA and guerrilla warfare can be found in Townshend, C. The process of terror in Irish politics. In O'Sullivan, N. (Ed.) *Terrorism, Ideology and Revolution*. (Westview Press, Boulder, Col., 1986). See also Bishop, P. and Maille, E. *The Provisional IRA* (Heinemann, London, 1987).

[49] Schmid, A. P. and de Graaf, J. *Violence as Communication*. Sage Publications, London, 1982.

[50] Schmid, A. P. *Political Terrorism*. North Holland Publishing Co., Amsterdam, 1983.

[51] One of the most systematic and comprehensive discussions of the conceptual and definitional problems of terrorism can be found in Schmid, A. P. *Political Terrorism*. (North Holland Publishing Co., Amsterdam, 1983), from which the following features are derived.

[52] Ibid.

Chapter 4. Terrorism and Mental Illness

[1] Margolin, J. Psychological perspectives in terrorism. In Alexander, Y. and Finger, S. M. *Terrorism: Interdisciplinary Perspectives*. John Jay Press, New York, 1977.

[2] The Irish National Liberation Front (INLA) is one of the nationalist terrorist groups operating in Northern Ireland. It has a markedly leftist orientation, and a reputation for ruthless violence.

[3] Marighella, C. *Urban Guerrilla minimanual*. Pulp Press, Vancouver, 1974.

[4] A review of the conceptual problems in the identification of abnormal behaviour can be seen in Kazdin, A. E. Basic concepts and models of abnormal behaviour. In Kazdin, A. E., Bellack, A. S. and Hersen, M. *New Perspectives in Abnormal Behaviour*. Oxford University Press, Oxford, 1980.

[5] Cronbag, H. F. M. Some psychological observations on *mens rea*. In Muller, D. J., Blackman, D. E. and Chapman, A. J. *Psychology and Law*. Wiley, Chichester, 1984.

[6] Useful discussions of the issues involved can be found in Sofaer, A. D. The US–UK Supplementary Extradition Treaty. *Terrorism*, 1986, **8**, 327, and Sofaer, A. D. *The Political Offense Exception and Terrorism*. US Department of State, Bureau of Public Affairs, Washington. Current Policy No. 762, 1985. See also Sasoli, M. International humanitarian law and terrorism, and Warner, B. W. Extradition law and practice in the crucible of Ulster, Ireland and Great Britain: A metamorphosis? Both in Wilkinson, P. and Steward, A. M. *Contemporary Research on Terrorism*. Aberdeen University Press, Aberdeen, 1987.

[7] *Diagnostic and Statistical Manual of Mental Disorders* (3rd Edition). American Psychiatric Association. Washington, DC 1980.

[8] Cleckley, H. *The mask of sanity*. C. V. Mosby Co., St. Louis, 1964.

[9] Gray, K. C. and Hutchinson, H. C. The psychopathic personality: a survey of Canadian psychiatrist's opinions. *Canadian Psychiatric Assoc. Journal*, 1964, **9**, 452.

[10] For a discussion of this, see Hare, R. D. Criminal psychopaths. In Yuille, J. C. *Police Selection and Training*. Martinus Nijhoff, Dordrecht, 1986.

[11] Lanceley, F. J. The anti-social personality as hostage taker. *J. Pol. Sci. Admin.*, 1981, **9**, 28.

[12] Cooper, H. H. A. Terrorism: the problem of the problem of definition. *Chitty's Law Journal*, 1978, **26**, 91.

[13] An account of Nilsen's trial, including a detailed commentary on the court debate about his mental status, can be found in Masters, B. *Killing for Company*. Johanthan Cape, London, 1985.

[14] *Sunday Tribune*, Dublin, 4 January, 1987.

[15] Taylor, M. Terrorist behaviour. *The Police Journal*, 1985, **LVII**, 195.

[16] Hacker, F. J. *Crusaders, Criminals, Crazies. Terror and Terrorism in our time*. Norton, New York, 1976.

[17] A discussion of the mental health of the Baader-Meinhof group can be found in Rasch, W. Psychological dimensions of political terrorism in the Federal Republic of Germany. (*Int. J. Law and Psychiat.*, 1979, **2**, 79). For a comprehensive analysis of the Baader-Meinhof group and related groups, see also Bundesministerium des Innern (ed.). *Analysen zum Terrorismus*. 4 Vols. (Westdeutscher Verlag). Vol. 1: Fetscher, I. and Rohrmoser, G. *Ideologien und Strategien* (1981), Vol. 2: Jager, H., Schmidtchen, G. and Sullwold, L. *Lebenslaufanalysen* (1981), Vol. 3: Baeyer-Katte, W., Claessens, D., Feger, H. and Neidhardt, F. *Gruppenprozesse*. (1982), Vol. 4/1: Matz, U. and Schnidtchen, G. *Gewalt und Legitimitat*. (1983), Vol. 4/2: Sack, F. and Steinert, H. *Protest und Reaktion*. (1984). A brief critique of these studies is presented in Zimmerman, E. Terrorist violence in West Germany: some reflections on recent literature. (*J. Political and Military Sociol.*, 1986, **14**, 321). See also Aust, S. *The Baader-Meinhof Group*. The Bodley Head, London, 1987, for a useful narrative account of the activities and individuals involved in the Baader-Meinhof Group.

The West German Terrorist groups are quite complex in their structures. The most infamous group is the *Rote Armee Faktion* (Red Army Faction) which had its origins in the student movements of the early 1970s. Initially, it was called the Baader-Meinhof Bande (Group), and was led by Andreas Baader and Gudrun Meinhof. The change of name is worthy of note, especially in that the initials (RAF) would have significance for the German people as Royal Air Force (with echoes of the Second World War); an apparently deliberate ironic choice. Its first major terrorist attack was in May, 1972, when bombs were placed in Frankfurt, Munich, Karlsruhe, Hamburg and Heidelberg. There then followed a series of terrorist attacks and kidnappings which claimed several lives. On the arrest, and subsequent death by suicide of its leadership, the *Rote Armee Faktion* became less active. Since then, however, there have been several waves of activity and the Group is thought to be currently active.

The 2nd June Movement has close associations in origin with the Baader-Meinhof Group, and is now a part of the *Rote Armee Faktion*. It is named after the date when a student was killed by the police in a violent demonstration during a visit by the Shah of Iran. It seems to have concentrated more on kidnappings than bombing attacks.

The Revolutionary Cells (RZ) and its associated women's grouping, Red Zora, differ in structure and targets from the *Rote Armee Faktion*. They live as normal citizens in the community, unlike the *Rote Armee Faktion* who operate underground. The RZ are organised into small independent groups, with little or no relationship between the groups. They address themselves primarily to property, rather than people, and they tend to address issues covering a broad political spectrum, such as nuclear energy, pollution, microelectronics, unemployment, feminist movement, United States Imperialism and NATO. RZ groups have been less effectively penetrated than the *Rote Armee Faktion* and there has been much less police success in arresting members. Their use of explosives prepared by themselves, as opposed to commercially prepared, makes their identification more difficult.

In addition to this formal structure of groups, there also exists in West Germany what has been termed the 'Terrorist Surrounding'. This probably consists of several thousand people who are followers and supporters of one or other of the various groups. Some might be thought of as little more than hangers-on; others, however, appear to be committed terrorists, who do not wish to live within the more formal structure of one of the groups such as the *Rote Armee Faktion*. The activities of this 'Surrounding' ranges from putting up posters and graffiti to bomb attacks and arson.

[18] Ferracuti, F. and Bruno, F. Psychiatric aspects of terrorism in Italy. In Barak-Glantz, I. L. and Huff, C. R. (Ed.) *Aggression in Global Perspective*. Pergamon Press, Elmsford, 1983.

[19] Lyons, H. A. and Harbinson, H. J. A comparison of political and non-political murderers in Northern Ireland, 1974–1984. *Med. Sci. Law*, 1986, **26**, 193.

[20] Ferracuti, F. and Bruno, F. Psychiatric aspects of terrorism in Italy. In Barak-Glantz, I. L. and Huff, C. R. (Ed.) *Aggression in Global Perspective*. Pergamon Press, Elmsford, 1983.

[21] Clark, R. P. *The Basque Insurgents. ETA 1952–1980.* University of Wisconsin Press, Madison, 1984.
[22] Ibid.

Chapter 5. Fanatics

[1] Laqueur, W. *Terrorism.* Weidenfeld and Nicolson, London, 1977.
[2] Milgram, S. The social meaning of fanaticism, *et cetera*, 1977, **34**, 58.
[3] An interesting account of the Flagellant Movement and its social context can be seen in Ziegler, P. *The Black Death.* Penguin Books, Harmondsworth, 1984.
[4] Watzlawick, P. The pathologies of perfectionism, *et cetera*, 1977, **34**, 12.
[5] Wolman, B. B. On saints, fanatics and dictators. *Int. J. Group Tensions*, 1974, **4**, 359.
[6] Perkinson, H. J. Fanaticism: flight from fallibility, *et cetera*, 1977, **34**, 54.
[7] Eckman, B. Fanaticism in sports, *et cetera*, 1977, **34** 64.
[8] Milgram, S. The social meaning of fanaticism, *et cetera*, 1977, **34**, 58.
[9] Ibid.
[10] Baron, R. A. and Byrne, D. *Social Psychology: Understanding Social Interaction.* (Fourth Edition). Allyn & Bacon, Newton, MA, 1983.
[11] Adorno, T., Frenkel-Brunswick, E., Levinson, D. and Sanford, N. *The Authoritarian Personality.* Harper, New York, 1950.
[12] Rapoport, D. C. *Assassinations and Terrorism.* T. H. Best Printing, Toronto, 1971.
[13] McKnight, G. *The Mind of the Terrorist.* Michael Joseph, London, 1974.
[14] Begin, M. *The Revolt—Story of the Irgun.* Schuman, New York, 1951.
[15] Tugwell, M. A. J. Guilt Transfer. In Rapoport, D. C. and Alexander, Y. *The Morality of Terrorism. Religious and Secular Justifications.* Pergamon Press, New York, 1982.
[16] Festinger, L. *A Theory of Cognitive Dissonance.* Row, Peterson, Evanston, Ill., 1957.
[17] Watzlawick, P. The pathologies of perfectionism, *et cetera*, 1977, **34**, 12.
[18] For an account of anarchist political views and philosophies, see Woodcock, G. *Anarchism. A history of Libertarian Ideas and Movements.* Penguin, Harmondsworth, 1977.
[19] Nechayev, S. The catechism of the revolutionist. Translated in Springer, P. B. and Truzzi, M. (Eds.) *Revolutionaries on Revolution.* Goodyear Publishing Co., Pacific Palisades, CA, 1973.
[20] Crosby, K., Rhee, J. and Holland, J. Suicide by fire: a contemporary method of political protest. *International Journal of Social Psychiatry*, 1977, **23**, 60.
[21] *US Dept. of State, Terrorist Bombings.* Office for Combating Terrorism, 1983.
[22] Lewis, B. *The Assassins.* Octagon Books, New York, 1968.
[23] Clausewitz, C. von, *On War.* (Trans. Graham, J. J.) Penguin Books, Harmondsworth, 1968.
[24] Taheri, A. *Holy Terror. The Inside Story of Islamic Terrorism.* Century Hutchinson, London, 1987.
[25] Lewis, B. *The Assassins.* Octagon Books, New York, 1968.
[26] Taheri, A. *Holy Terror. The Inside Story of Islamic Terrorism.* Century Hutchinson, London, 1987.
[27] Ibid.
[28] Morris, I. *The Nobility of Failure: Tragic Heroes in the History of Japan.* Secker & Warburg, London, 1975. For additional information on these aspects of Japanese society, see also Benedict, R. *The Chrysanthemum and the Sword.* (Routledge & Kegan Paul, London, 1972).
[29] Morris, I. *The Nobility of Failure: Tragic Heroes in the History of Japan.* Secker & Warburg, London, 1975.
[30] Fried, R. Background material for the 'International Scientific Conference on Terrorism', West Berlin, 1978. Published in *Terrorism*, 1980, **3**, 219.
[31] Morris, I. *The Nobility of Failure: Tragic Heroes in the History of Japan.* Secker & Warburg, London, 1975.
[32] Ibid.
[33] Rapoport, D. C. Fear and trembling: terrorism in three religious traditions. *The American Political Science Review*, 1984, **78**, 658.
[34] Rapoport, D. C. Messianism and terror. *The Center Magazine*, 1986, Jan/Feb, 30.
[35] Lewis, B. *The Assassins.* Octagon Books, New York, 1968.
[36] Townshend, C. The process of terror in Irish politics. In O'Sullivan, N. *Terrorism, Ideology and Revolution.* (Westview Press, Boulder, CO, 1986), gives a useful introduction to some of the contextual issues of contemporary Northern Ireland. Accounts of the Irish hunger strikes tend to be partial; however, Beresford, D. *Ten Dead Men.* Grafton, London, 1986, gives a reasonably

non-polemical account of the process of the hunger strike, based on letters smuggled by and to the strikers.

[37] Schmid, A. P. and de Graaf, J. *Violence as Communication.* Sage Publications, London, 1982.

Chapter 6. Terrorists

[1] Schmid (in Schmid, A. P. *Political Terrorism.* North Holland Publishing Co., Amsterdam, 1983) reports a survey of principal investigators in this area. His respondents were almost all critical of the state of theoretical and empirical development in the study of terrorism. The secret nature of much work in this area can lead to a false sense of optimism, in the feeling that there are sound investigations, which are not published. His respondents suggested otherwise.

[2] Kellen, K. *Terrorists — What Are They Like? How Some Terrorists Describe their World and Actions.* Rand Corporation, Santa Monica, 1979.

[3] Russell, C. A. and Miller, B. H. Profile of a terrorist. *Terrorism,* 1977, **1**, 17.

[4] Schmidtchen, G. Terroristiche karrieren. In Jager, H., Schmidtchen, G. and Sullwold, L. *Lebenslaufanalysen. Analysen zum Terrorismus 2.* Westdeutscher Verlag, 1981.

[5] Cooper, H. H. A. What is a terrorist: a psychological perspective. *Legal Medical Quarterly,* 1977, **1**, 16.

[6] Halperin, E. *Terrorism in Latin America.* Sage Publications, Beverly Hills, 1976.

[7] Cooper, H. H. A. What is a terrorist: a psychological perspective. *Legal Medical Quarterly,* 1977, **1**, 16.

[8] Jenkins, B. M. *Future Trends in International Terrorism.* Rand Corporation, Santa Monica, paper no. P-7176, 1985.

[9] Cooper, H. H. A. What is a terrorist: a psychological perspective. *Legal Medical Quarterly,* 1977, **1**, 16.

[10] Galvin, D. M. The female terrorist: a socio-psychological perspective. *Behavioural Science and the Law,* 1983, **1**, 19.

[11] Russell, C. A. and Miller, B. H. Profile of a terrorist. *Terrorism,* 1977, **1**, 17.

[12] Galvin, D. M. The female terrorist: a socio-psychological perspective. *Behavioural Science and the Law,* 1983, **1**, 19.

[13] For an introduction to the analysis of interpersonal behaviour, see Argyle, M. *The Psychology of Interpersonal Behaviour.* Penguin, Harmondsworth, 1967.

[14] Hearst, P. (with Moscow, A.) *Every Secret Thing.* Doubleday, New York, 1982.

[15] Russell, C. A. and Miller, B. H. Profile of a Terrorist. *Terrorism,* 1977, **1**, 17.

[16] Weinberg, L. and Eubank, W. L. Italian women terrorists. *Terrorism,* 1987, **9**, 241.

[17] Galvin, D. M. The female terrorist: a socio-psychological perspective. *Behavioural Science and the Law,* 1983, **1**, 19.

[18] Clark, R. P. Patterns in the lives of ETA members. *Terrorism,* 1983, **6**, 423.

[19] McKnight, G. *The Mind of the Terrorist.* Michael Joseph, London, 1974.

[20] Clark, R. P. *The Basque Insurgents. ETA 1952–1980.* University of Wisconsin Press, Madison, 1984.

[21] Ibid.

Chapter 7. The Individual Psychology of the Terrorist

[1] Fields, R. M. Child terror victims and adult terrorists. *J. Psychohistory,* 1979, **7**, 71.

[2] Heskin, K. *Northern Ireland: A Psychological Analysis.* Columbia University Press, New York, 1980.

[3] Raffay, A. von, Hope, a principle of terrorism. *Analytische-Psychologie,* 1980, **11**, 38.

[4] Kent, I. and Nicholls, W. The psychodynamics of terrorism. *Mental Health and Society,* 1977, **4**, 1.

[5] Clark, K. B. Empathy: A neglected topic in psychological research. *American Psychologist,* 1980, **35**, 187.

[6] Giegerich, W. Terrorism as task and responsibility: reflections of a depth-psychologist. *Analytische-Psychologie,* 1979, **10**, 190.

[7] Knutson, J. N. Towards a United States policy on terrorism. *Political Psychology,* 1984, **5**, 287.

[8] Morf, G. *Terror in Quebec: Case Studies of the F.L.Q.* Clarke and Irwin, Toronto, 1970.

[9] Slochower, H. The bomb and terrorism: their linkage. *American-Imago,* 1982, **39**, 269.

[10] Kelman, H. C. Violence without moral restraint: reflections on the dehumanization of victims and victimizers. *J. Social Issues,* 1973, **29**, 25.

[11] Kampf, H. A. On the appeals of extremism to the youth of affluent, democratic societies. *Terrorism*, 1980, **4**, 161.

[12] Hassel, C. V. Terror: the crime of the privileged. *Terrorism*, 1977, **1**, 1.

[13] Watzlawick, P. The pathologies of perfectionism, *et cetera*, 1977, **34**, 12.

[14] Rapoport, D. C. Fear and trembling: terrorism in three religious traditions. *The American Political Science Review*, 1984, **78**, 658.

[15] Lanceley, F. J. The anti-social personality as hostage taker. *J. Pol. Sci. Admin.*, 1981, **9**, 28.

[16] Sullwold, L. Stationen in der Entwicklung von Terroristen: psychologische Aspekte biographischer Daten. In Jager, H., Schmidtchen, G. and Sullwold, L. *Analysen zum Terrorismus* Vol. 2: *Lebenslaufanalysen*. Westdeutscher Verlag, 1981.

[17] US Dept. of State, *Terrorist Bombings*. Office for Combating Terrorism, 1983.

[18] The problem of the 'fallacy of composition' as it applies to some of the German analyses of terrorism and terrorists has been discussed by Zimmermann, E. Review essay. Terrorist violence in West Germany: Some reflections on recent literature. (*J. Pol. Mil. Sociol.*, 1986, **14**, 321).

[19] Fields, R. M. Child terror victims and adult terrorists. *J. Psychohistory*, 1979, **7**, 71.

[20] Hilke, R. and Kaiser, H. J. Terrorism: can psychology offer a solution to this problem? *Psychologische-Rundschau*, 1979, **30**, 88.

[21] Margolin, J. Psychological perspectives in terrorism. In Alexander, Y. and Finger, S. M. Terrorism: Interdisciplinary Perspectives. John Jay Press, New York, 1977.

[22] Kellen, K. *Terrorists — What Are They Like? How Some Terrorists Describe Their World and Actions*. Rand Corporation, Santa Monica, 1979.

[23] Ibid.

[24] Slochower, H. The bomb and terrorism: the linkage. *American-Imago*, 1982, **39**, 269.

[25] Bougereau, J. M. (Trans. P. Silcock). *The German Guerrilla: Terror, Reaction and Resistance*. Cienfuegos Press, Orkney, 1981.

[26] Ibid.

[27] Kellen, K. *Terrorists — What Are They Like? How Some Terrorists Describe Their World and Actions*. Rand Corporation, Santa Monica, 1979.

[28] Ibid.

[29] Ibid.

[30] Miller, B. M. The language component of terrorism strategy: a text-based linguistic case study of contemporary German terrorism. *Unpublished PhD. Thesis*, Georgetown University, 1983. See also Cordes, B. Euroterrorists talk about themselves: A look at the literature. In Wilkinson, P. and Steward, A. M. *Contemporary Research on Terrorism*. Aberdeen University Press, Aberdeen, 1987.

[31] Porter, B. Mind hunters. *Psychology Today*, 1983, April, 1.

[32] Pinizzotto, A. J. Forensic psychology: Criminal personality profiling. *J. Pol. Sci. Admin.*, 1984, **12**, 32.

[33] Reisser, M. Crime — specific psychological consultation. *The Police Chief*, 1982, March, 53.

[34] Pickrel, E. Federal aviation administrations behavioural research program for defense against hijacking. In Kramer, J. J. *The Role of Behavioral Science in Physical Security. Proceedings of the First Annual Symposium, April 29–30, 1976*. National Bureau of Standards, US Dept. Commerce, Washington, DC, 1977.

[35] Heyman, M. N. The psychologist in operational support. *The Police Chief*, 1982, Jan., 124.

[36] Ibid.

[37] Miron, M. S. and Douglas, J. E. Threat analysis — the psycholinguistic approach. *FBI Law Enforcement Bulletin*, 1979, **48**, 5.

[38] Miller, B. M. The language component of terrorism strategy: a text-based linguistic case study of contemporary German terrorism. *Unpublished Ph.D. Thesis*. Georgetown University, 1983.

[39] Steinke, W. The terrorism of left-wingers in the Federal Republic of Germany and the combat against terrorists. *Proceedings of IDENTA-'85; Anti-terrorism, Forensic Science, Psychology in Police Investigations*. Heiliger, Jerusalem, 1985.

[40] Dror, Y. Facing unconventional terrorism. *Proceedings of IDENTA-'85; Anti-terrorism, Forensic Science, Psychology in Police Investigations*. Heiliger and Co., Jerusalem, 1985.

[41] Jenkins, B. M. Defense against terrorism. *Political Science Quarterly*, 1986, **5**, 773.

[42] Lichter, S. R. Young rebels. A psychopolitical study of West German male radical students. *Comparative Politics*, 1979, **12**, 27.

[43] Merckl, P. *Political Violence Under the Swastika.* Princeton, NJ, 1975.

[44] Ibid.

[45] Adorno, T., Frenkel-Brunswick, E., Levinson, D. and Sanford, N. *The Authoritarian Personality.* Harper, New York, 1950.

[46] Lichter, S. R. Young rebels. A psychopolitical study of West German male radical students. *Comparative Politics*, 1979, **12**, 27.

Chapter 8. Processes of Terrorism

[1] Schmid, A. P. *Political Terrorism.* North Holland Publishing Co., Amsterdam, 1983.

[2] Crenshaw, M. The psychology of political terrorism. In Herman, M. G. (Ed.) *Political Psychology.* Jossey-Bass Inc., San Francisco, 1986.

[3] This may be the case for Western youth, but it is less certain whether this is so in other societies.

[4] Bougereau, J. M. (Trans. P. Silcock). *The German Guerrilla: Terror, Reaction and Resistance.* Cienfuegos Press, Orkney, 1981.

[5] Shaw, E. D. Political terrorists: dangers of diagnosis and an alternative to the psychopathology model. *International J. of Law and Psychiatry*, 1986, **8**, 359.

[6] Weinberg, L. and Eubank, W. L. Italian women terrorists. *Terrorism*, 1987, **9**, 241.

[7] *Sunday Tribune*, Dublin, 16 March, 1986.

[8] Jager, H., Schmidtchen, G. and Sullwold, L. *Analysen zum Terrorismus. Vol. 2: Lebenslaufanalysen.* Westdeutscher Verlag, 1981.

[9] Trotsky, L. *Against Individual Terrorism.* Pathfinder Press, New York, 1974.

[10] Ibid.

[11] Bandura, A. and Walters, R. H. *Social Learning and Personality Development.* Holt, Rinehart and Winston, New York, 1963. Imitation of behaviour seems to be learnt if the imitated behaviour is followed by a reward. Relevant to our discussion, most experimental work in this area has been done on the imitation of aggressive behaviour. Modelling, a technique which has emerged out of this work, is a clinical method for teaching new skills through imitation learning (see Bandura, A. *Social Learning Theory.* Prentice-Hall, Englewood Cliffs, 1977). Explanations of this kind successfully account for the behaviour seen in 'identification' without having recourse to concepts like the 'unconscious'; nor do they draw on the more esoteric aspects of psychodynamic theory. Conceptualising this aspect of the development of terrorist behaviour in these terms is probably of more use than using concepts like 'identification'. Verification becomes possible, and reliance on general *post hoc* interpretations can be diminished.

[12] Shaw, E. D. Political terrorists: dangers of diagnosis and an alternative to the psychopathology model. *International J. of Law and Psychiatry*, 1986, **8**, 359.

[13] Ibid.

[14] Merari, A. A classification of terrorist groups. *Terrorism*, 1978, **1**, 331.

[15] Post, J. M. Hostilité conformité, fraternité: The group dynamics of terrorist behaviour. *Int. J. Group Psychother.*, 1986, **36**, 211. See also Post, J. M. Group and organisational dynamics of political terrorism: implications for counterterrorist policy. In Wilkinson, P. and Steward, A. M. *Contemporary Research on Terrorism.* Aberdeen University Press, Aberdeen, 1987.

[16] Bougereau, J. M. (Trans. P. Silcock). *The German Guerrilla: Terror, Reaction and Resistance.* Cienfuegos Press, Orkney, 1981.

[17] Le Bon, G. *The Crowd.* Ernest Benn, London, 1952.

[18] Moscovici, S. *The Age of the Crowd.* Cambridge University Press, Cambridge, 1985.

[19] Deiner, E. Deindividuation: the absence of self-awareness and self-regulation in group members. In Paulus, P. B. (Ed.) *The Psychology of Group Influence.* Erlbaum, Hillsdale, 1980.

[20] Baron, R. A. and Byrne, D. *Social Psychology: Understanding Human Interaction.* Allyn & Bacon, Newton, MA, 1984.

[21] Prentice-Dunn, S. and Rogers, R. W. Deindividuation in aggression. In Geen, R. and Donnerstein, E. (Eds.). *Aggression: Theoretical and Empirical Reviews.* Academic Press, New York, 1983.

[22] Post, J. M. Hostilité, conformité, fraternité: The group dynamics of terrorist behaviour. *Int. J. Group Psychother.*, 1986, **36**, 211.

[23] Ahna, K. de, Weger zum Aussteig. Fordernde und hemmende Bedingungen. In Baeyer-Katte, W. von, Claessens, D., Feger, H. and Neidhardt, F. *Analysen zum Terrorismus Vol 3: Gruppenprozesse.* Westdeutscher Verlag, 1982.

[24] Brockner, J. and Rubin, J. Z. *Entrapment in Escalating Conflicts.* Springer-Verlag, 1985.

[25] Ibid.

[26] Rubin, J. Z. Psychological traps. *Psychology Today*, 1981, March, 52.

[27] Quoted in Post, J. M. Hostilité, conformité, fraternité: The group dynamics of terrorist behaviour. *Int. J. Group Psychother.*, 1986, **36**, 211.

[28] Clark, R. P. *The Basque Insurgents. ETA 1952–1980.* University of Wisconsin Press, Madison, 1984.

[29] Lamm, H. and Myers, D. G. Group-induced polarisation of attitudes and behaviour. In Berkowitz, L. (Ed.) *Advances in Experimental Social Psychology.* Academic Press, New York, 1978.

[30] Wolf, J. B. Organizational and management practices of urban terrorist groups. *Terrorism*, 1978, **1**, 174.

[31] Strentz, T. A terrorist organizational profile: a psychological role model. In Alexander, Y. and Gleason, J. M. *Behavioural and Quantitative Perspectives on Terrorism.* Pergamon Press, New York, 1981.

[32] Bougereau, J. M. (Trans. P. Silcock). *The German Guerrilla: Terror, Reaction and Resistance.* Cienfuegos Press, Orkney, 1981.

[33] Dror, Y. Facing unconventional terrorism. *Proceedings of IDENTA-'85; Anti-terrorism, Forensic Science, Psychology in Police Investigations.* Heiliger and Co., Jerusalem, 1985.

[34] Ibid.

[35] Clausewitz, C. von, *On War* (Trans. Graham, J. J.), Penguin Books, Harmondsworth, 1968.

[36] Ibid.

[37] Marighella, C. *Urban Guerrilla minimanual.* Pulp Press, Vancouver, 1974.

[38] Policing in difficult environments like Northern Ireland retains the typical characteristics of British policing. The range of duties undertaken are remarkably similar to those undertaken in less hostile environments, but these are overlayed by the problem of working in hostile, and occasionally lethal, situations. See Taylor, M. Police service and public satisfaction. (*The Police Journal*, 1986, **LX**, 1), for a brief discussion of this with respect to the UK.

[39] Dror, Y. Facing unconventional terrorism. *Proceedings of IDENTA-'85; Anti-terrorism, Forensic Science, Psychology in Police Investigations.* Heiliger and Co., Jerusalem, 1985.

[40] Wright, F. and Wright, P. Violent groups. *Group*, 1982, **6**, 25.

[41] Steinke, W. The terrorism of left-wingers in the Federal Republic of Germany and the combat against terrorists. *Proceedings of IDENTA-'85; Anti-terrorism, Forensic Science, Psychology in Police Investigations.* Heiliger, Jerusalem, 1985.

Chapter 9. Terrorist Behaviour

[1] Margolin, J. Psychological perspectives in terrorism. In Alexander, Y. and Finger, S. M. *Terrorism: Interdisciplinary Perspectives.* John Jay Press, New York, 1977.

[2] Merari, A. A classification of terrorist groups. *Terrorism*, 1978, **1**, 331.

[3] Kaplan, M. A. The role of forensic science in criminal investigation. *Proceedings of IDENTA-'85; Anti-terrorism, Forensic Science, Psychology in Police Investigations.* Heiliger and Co., Jerusalem, 1985.

[4] Merari, A. A classification of terrorist groups. *Terrorism*, 1978, **1**, 331.

[5] Wardlaw, G. Psychology and the resolution of terrorist incidents. *Australian Psychologist*, 1983, **18**, 179.

[6] Eysenck, H. *Crime and Personality.* Paladin, London, 1970.

[7] Brody, S. *The effectiveness of sentencing.* Home Office Research Study, No. 35, HMSO, London, 1976.

[8] Martinson, R. M. What works? Questions and answers about prison reform. *Public Interest*, 1974, **35**, 22.

[9] Hough, M., Clarke, R. V. G. and Mayhew, P. *Designing out crime.* HMSO, London, 1980.

[10] Bennet, T. and Wright, R. *Burglars on Burglary. Prevention and the Offence.* Gower, Aldershot, 1984.

[11] Sykes, R. E. and Brent, E. E. *Policing, a Social Behaviourist Perspective.* Rutgers University Press, Newark, 1984.

[12] Simon, H. A. Rationality as a process and product of thought. *American Economic Review*, 1978, **8**, 1.

[13] Cornish, D. B. and Clarke, R. V. G. *The Reasoning Criminal. Rational Choice Perspectives on Offending.* Springer-Verlag, New York, 1986.

[14] Becker, G. S. Crime and punishment: An economic approach. *J. Political Economy*, 1968, **78**, 169. See also Heineke, J. M. *Economic Models of Criminal Behaviour.* North Holland, Amsterdam, 1978.

[15] Cornish, D. B. and Clarke, R. V. G. *The Reasoning Criminal. Rational Choice Perspectives on Offending.* Springer-Verlag, New York, 1986.

[16] The behavioural approach proposed here is characterised by an emphasis on the relationship between the relevant consequences of behaviour and events associated with those consequences. The important consequence to behaviour is reward, or *reinforcement*. Behaviour which is followed by reinforcement tends to have an increased probability of occurrence. Many things can act as reinforcers to us—social approval, gaining status, financial gain, food, and so forth. Specific reinforcers are mainly personal but there are broad classes of reinforcers (like those mentioned earlier) which are largely universal.

Events associated with behaviour can be thought of as stimuli. Some stimuli set the occasion for responding (discriminative stimuli)—that is to say, when the stimulus occurs, the appropriate behaviour follows if that behaviour has in the past been reinforced. When this occurs, the behaviour is said to be 'under the control of the stimulus'.

Behavioural interpretations offer a very powerful way of explaining why behaviour occurs, and predicting when particular behaviours will occur. From this point of view, explanations of behaviour are expressed in terms of the environmental features associated with the behaviour. There is no need to have recourse to concepts like 'unconscious processes', for example. Interpreting terrorism in this way offers the opportunity for empirical analysis. Discussions of terrorism using this approach have been conspicuously absent in the available public terrorist literature.

[17] Nee, C. and Taylor, M. Residential burglary in the Republic of Ireland: A situational perspective. *The Howard Journal*, 1988, *in press*.

[18] Skinner, B. F. *Science and Human Behaviour*. Free Press, New York, 1953.

[19] Wardlaw, G. Psychology and the resolution of terrorist incidents. *Australian Psychologist*, 1983, **18**, 179.

[20] Karber, P. A. and Mengel, R. W. A behavioural analysis of the adversary threat to the commercial nuclear industry—A conceptual framework for realistically assessing threats. In Kramer, J. J. *The role of behavioral science in physical security. Proceedings of the second annual symposium, March 23–24, 1977.* National Bureau of Standards, US Dept. Commerce, Washington, DC, 1978.

[21] Sandler, T. *et al.* Economic methods and the sudy of terrorism. In Wilkinson, P. and Stewart, A. M. *Contemporary Research on Terrorism.* Aberdeen University Press, Aberdeen, 1987. See also Atkinson, S. E., Sandler, T. and Tschirhart, J. Terrorism in a bargaining framework. *J. Law and Economics*, 1987, **30**, 1.

[22] Schmid, A. P. *Political Terrorism*. North Holland Publishing Co., Amsterdam, 1983.

[23] Lyons, H. A. and Harbinson, H. J. A comparison of political and non-political murderers in Northern Ireland, 1974–1984. *Med. Sci. Law*, 1986, **26**, 193.

[24] Pockrass, R. M. Terroristic murder in Northern Ireland: Who is killed and why? *Terrorism*, 1987, **9**, 341.

[25] Clark, R. P. *The Basque Insurgents. ETA 1952–1980.* University of Wisconsin Press, Madison, 1984.

[26] Bennet, T. and Wright, R. *Burglars on Burglary. Prevention and the Offence.* Gower, Aldershot, 1984.

[27] Simmond, J. *Poems 1956–1986.* The Gallery Press, Dublin, 1986.

Index